SLOW FIRES

SLOW FIRES

MASTERING NEW WAYS TO BRAISE, ROAST, AND GRILL

JUSTIN SMILLIE

WITH KITTY GREENWALD

PHOTOGRAPHS BY ED ANDERSON

CLARKSON POTTER/PUBLISHERS
NEW YORK

Library of Congress Cataloging-in-
Publication Data
Smillie, Justin.
    Slow fires : mastering new ways to braise,
roast, and grill / Justing Smillie, Chef of
Upland with Kitty Greenwald ; photographs
by Ed Anderson. —First Edition.
            pages cm
    Includes index.
    1. Roasting (Cooking) I. Greenwald, Kitty,
1978- II. Anderson, Ed (Photographer) III.
Title.
    TX690.S65 2015
    641.7'1—dc23
            2015020663

ISBN 978-0-8041-8623-0
eISBN 978-0-8041-8624-7

Printed in China

Cover photograph and design
by Ed Anderson
Endpaper illustration by Wayne Pate/
Illustration Division

10 9 8 7 6 5 4 3 2 1

First Edition

This book is dedicated to my wife, Megumi. Without her unending support, I never could have become the cook I am today. And to my sons, Colin and Oliver, who waited for playtime so patiently. You all are my beginning and my end. I look forward to our adventures and all the meals yet to be shared.

—Justin

For Mom and, therefore,
for beauty. Com saudades.
—Kitty

CONTENTS

GRILLING

FOUNDATIONS AND FINISHES

INTRODUCTION

When I'm standing over a cutting board with a stockpot sputtering behind me, a roast in the oven, shallots mellowing in vinegar off to the side, I'm in my element. Whether I'm at home or at my restaurant, Upland, in New York City, I'm a chef who loves to *cook*. While that seems like an obvious thing to say, what I mean is that I love putting my hands on my food, feeling the salt between my fingers and knowing how those crystals will transform the ingredients before me. It's seeing how their colors change as they sear, noticing how the aromas have developed when I walk by the oven an hour later, feeling how the heat of the grill softens as the coals crackle and ash over, whiter and whiter.

Cooking is all about using your senses. It's about understanding transformations and it's about understanding heat—how it works and mutates, from the wet to the dry; from a rolling boil to a gentle simmer; from a crust-forming roast to a smothering steam bath in the oven; from the hard, charring sear of the grill to a low, soft smoke.

Coming up as a young cook, I learned a lot from my colleagues, chefs, and mentors. Often, they would insist their way with a particular step would be the *right* way: You only sear on high heat, you never salt meat except just before you cook it. But as I grew, from my first kitchen job as a crab boil cook, to a brief stint at culinary school, to some of the finest kitchens in New York City—Mercer Kitchen, Washington Park, Barbuto, il Buco Alimentari e Vineria—I developed an Italianesque style that is both rustic and detailed, one that follows the rules . . . until it's time to break them.

Take, for example, the dish that has become my signature: a beef short rib coated in peppercorns. I'll say more about it in the roasting chapter, but I'm guessing it's developed a following in part because of its springy, juicy bite and crisp exterior, a result I was only able to achieve by steam-roasting the ribs before setting the crust in a hot pan. That is, by ignoring the standard process of flash-searing meat and then finishing it in the oven, and imagining a better way.

A lot of love goes into those ribs—into all of my dishes—and this book is about developing an understanding of the traditional methods of braising, roasting, and grilling . . . and then expanding on them. Curiosity, deference to tradition, and a little bit of a rebellious streak made me an intuitive, confident cook, and that's how I want to help my cooks—and readers—think for themselves. Like all restaurants, Upland is always evolving, but the basic principles found in this collection of recipes inform what we do there.

This cookbook is dedicated to delicious eating, slowly built flavor, and balanced dishes. The recipes are generous, easily shared, and taste best in good company. My hope is that you derive as much pleasure from eating them as you do from cooking them, as there is so much enjoyment to be found in both.

MEALS TO MASTER BRAISING, ROASTING, AND GRILLING

The recipes that make up this cookbook are grouped into fifty-two meals. They are meals you plan for, anticipate, and, for the most part, tuck into on a weekend, when you have the luxury of time. When you can lose yourself in the small steps that mark a dish's evolution: the olive pitting, the spice toasting, the salt rubbing. That's why these recipes are thorough and packed with sensory cues. Responding to the smells, sights, and textures of a dish is how I learned to cook, and that's what excites me.

Taken together, this year's worth of feasting also teaches you about the different techniques and approaches that make up the majority of my repertoire. There's a methodology for how a braise is built, how a roast is seasoned, and even how a grill is lit, and, to make exceptional meals, you should understand these principles.

We begin with the braising chapter because it is a more forgiving technique—there's no rapidly closing window to hit a perfect medium rare—that is delightfully broad and expansive. Then we move on to roasting, which involves mostly dry cooking in the oven or on the stovetop. Finally, we end by grilling over a live fire, which is the driest and most rustic approach.

Each chapter starts with a detailed explanation of the basic technique, then delves deeper into the minutiae, breaking rules and exploring ways to get at a broad range of results. The recipes in each chapter start as by-the-book as possible, and then evolve to alter or build on what comes before.

But, of course, dabble in the fifty-two meals as you like, in the order you'd like, or make just a main dish from one meal and pair it with a salad or a sauce from another. These recipes are meant to stand alone and function as part of a larger spread, and the most important sensibility is your own.

PLANNING THE MEALS

There is no getting around the fact that many of these meals take more time than the average because they taste far better than the average. (To be fair, more than a handful of them can be made on a weeknight.) Though I realize time is a luxury, building big flavor often depends on it.

But don't be nervous. A lot of the time called for is resting time, time for the seasonings to work their way into a cut of meat, or time for surfaces to dry out in the refrigerator to help ensure a good crust. The challenge is just a little bit of planning, with light work dispersed over a couple of days.

To help these meals work into your schedule, a how-to-plan box accompanies every feast. This is your road map, designed to help you cook confidently. While working in a restaurant is prominently marked by stress, I always come back to the joy I find in cooking, and I hope these meals provide you with that joy—the big, generous, messy kind—both in the kitchen and at the table.

SALT, OIL, AND A FEW ESSENTIALS

Much of my training and background as a cook is Italian and French, but as a chef in a global city, my tastes range far and wide, and I often bring spices from Tunisia or flavors from Japan into my cooking. That said, most of the dishes in this collection don't require too many unusual ingredients, and a basic pantry stocked with good salts, oils, acids, and a couple of extras should suit you just fine. And I'd love to say a few things about each of these.

SALTS

Many years ago, I saw my mentor Jonathan Waxman cure a pork chop for three days before cooking it and my fascination with brining began. That chop's prolonged nap in salt gave it a pronounced nutty-sweet flavor and juiciness that took me completely by surprise. It tasted of itself but better and bolder.

Now, I like to say 90 percent of my job happens before turning on the stove. That 90 percent is what I call pre-cooking, which almost always involves wet- or dry-brining. While most of my brines include different flavor components, salt is the key one.

Kosher salt has a flakier, larger granule than common table salt, and is popular with chefs because of its coarse texture; you can gauge how much is getting sprinkled onto a dish by feel. If you can have only one salt in your pantry, this should be it.

While kosher salt is no saltier than table salt pound for pound, its large crystal structure means it packs into a cup or spoon differently, which means 1 cup or 1 teaspoon of kosher salt will make your food less salty than the same measurement of table salt. Complicating matters is the fact that there is a difference between brands of kosher salt, too.

I cook with Diamond Crystal Kosher Salt. Diamond Crystal is flakier than Morton's Kosher Salt, the other

common brand, and is therefore less salty cup for cup. I used Diamond Crystal to test all of the recipes in this book. If you are using Morton's, simply reduce the kosher salt measurement in the recipe by about one-third. Or, as I always suggest, salt, taste, and salt some more.

I tend to season vegetables and salads with fine sea salt. It's a bit more expensive, but the mineral quality and nuance it imparts is worth it.

If I am seasoning proteins with sea salt instead of kosher, I'll usually use coarse sea salt. When you bite into anything seasoned with coarse sea salt, you bite into the granule itself, and, as with salted pretzels, that salty burst becomes part of the experience. Since coarse salt is more likely to fall off your food, reapplying it may be necessary.

Like many chefs, the finishing salt I can't live without is flaky sea salt and the most common variety is Maldon. Its shape reminds me of a snowflake, and the way it snaps adds textural intrigue and bursts of delicate salinity.

OILS

I almost exclusively cook with olive oil and most of the time, the ones in my pantry are extra-virgin. I have had great olive oils from small producers that do not bear the "extra virgin" label, though, so I prefer to keep the specification loose in these recipes. But in general, you want an oil with flavor and character, be it buttery or peppery or grassy.

Buy your olive oil from a reliable store that has a good selection of oils to choose from. There should be no sediment on the bottom of the bottle. And while olive oils come in a range of shades, they should be neither milky nor foggy. On the spoon, a sample should slink about slowly.

Oils are not like wines and do not improve with age, so skip over a bottle if its harvest date is years past. Buy it in small quantities and store it in a cool, dark place.

And, while you don't necessarily need a finishing olive oil, I highly recommend having one on hand. These, typically pricier and with a robust character, should be drizzled on dishes after they've been cooked as a punchy condiment. If you heat a finishing olive oil, all of its nuanced luxury goes out the window.

VINEGARS

I love a lot of acid in my food. The longer something cooks, the denser its flavor becomes, and a spark of tartness wakes things up. So I keep an endless supply of lemons on hand as well as many vinegars. Adding acid is nearly as important as adding salt and, when finishing a dish and giving it form and balance, I frequently season to taste with both.

I often work with soft vinegars, ones I find palatable sipped straight. The mildest in my collection are rice wine vinegar and agrodolce vinegar (*agrodolce* is the Italian term for sweet and sour). I use these subtly sweet options to politely temper richness without leaving a harsh mark. In general, soft vinegars work well on either sweet or delicate ingredients.

A touch more acidic are the mid-range vinegars: the chardonnay, champagne, sherry, and apple cider options.

For a headier jolt, I opt for a red or white wine vinegar. These cut through fatty and robust dishes with gumption. If you only keep these on hand, go ahead and temper them with a little water and use this in place of milder vinegars called for in recipes.

CAPERS AND ANCHOVIES

Two ingredients I reach for often to bring punchy salinity and depth are capers and anchovies.

A good caper tastes floral, musky, and salty; its texture should be snappy. I have found that salt-packed capers retain their natural flavor and texture better than brined ones. That said, while all capers should be rinsed before using, the salt-packed variety requires a bit more handling (see page 154). In all cases, rinse and dry your capers before using them.

As for anchovies, which I use in a host of ways, these gorgeous fillets are pure salty umami magic. Even people who think they don't like anchovies often like anchovies when they are good quality and used smartly to lend background flavor and sexy depth.

If you buy anchovies whole and packed in salt, rinse them, then peel the meaty fillets off the bones before using. Ones packed in oil are typically ready to use. Whichever you use, your anchovies ought to be plump, firm, and good-tasting when sampled raw (or post-rinse if they're packed in salt). Good anchovies may surprise you with their price, but they are well worth it.

Since I'm crazy for anchovies, I also keep on hand a bottle of colatura, the ancient Roman seasoning that is basically anchovy essence. It's delicious but can be hard to find. If you are looking for a substitute, high-quality Asian fish sauce is fine. My preferred brand is Red Boat Fish Sauce.

SPICES

Good spices can transform a dish. Buy your spices whole, in small batches, and from a purveyor with high turnover. Fresh, whole spices are much more intensely aromatic.

I always toast my spices before using them too; this activates their oils and opens up their perfume. Here's how: Set a small pan over medium heat. Add the spices so they fit comfortably in a single layer. Then, while shaking, toast your spices until their color deepens and their scent blooms. Pay attention throughout this process; spices go from ideal to burnt in a snap.

To grind your spices, a mortar and pestle, a spice grinder, or a clean coffee bean grinder all work well.

CITRUS AND HERBS

With both herbs and citrus zest, you also want to activate their oils so they are at their most pungent when incorporated into your dish. To do so, either press down on the herbs with the broad side of a knife or lightly crush them in the palm of your hands. If you have doubts about this little extra step, take a whiff of the ingredient before and after this exercise.

I use citrus juice as much or more often than vinegars. I like its fresh acidity and recommend you use it to taste when adding it to a dish, even if an amount is specified in the recipe. All lemons are not created equal, so keep that in mind when squeezing.

BRAISING

Braised Snapper with Gremolata
and Bean Ragu (page 65)

WHEN I WAS TWENTY-SIX, I JOINED JONATHAN WAXMAN'S OPENING TEAM AT Barbuto, an Italian restaurant tucked away on the fringes of the West Village. What followed was formative: With Jonathan, I grew as a chef and was given the freedom to explore the nuances of rustic, Mediterranean cooking. That was also when I found my family in the restaurant industry, which is sprawling and animalistic in New York.

During those years, I braised more often than any other technique. Partly, this was because I was mesmerized by the transformation that happens, slowly, when a main ingredient cooks down in liquid to yield a lush, sauce-bound result, one that far exceeds the sum of its parts. But there was also something less technical and geeky to my fascination. It had to do with how I felt at Barbuto, which was completely at ease, and how those braises turned our kitchen into a home.

Barbuto is steely: It occupies a former garage space; the floors are made of poured cement, and the walls are garage doors that lift up and open in the summertime. But the kitchen, in the back, has a warmer feel. That's where the coal- and wood-burning oven lives. Whenever I braised in that far corner, I'd watch the wear from the night before melt from my colleagues' faces. Shoulders would slacken and expressions would soften as a sauce burbled and transformed an imposing cut, perfuming our dining room. I tended to those braises with meticulous care.

Once the meat was springy and tender and the sauce dribbled off the spoon, perfectly viscous, I'd remove my braise from the oven and set it on the counter to rest. Inevitably, I'd get dragged away to see to some other detail. Always, always, always, when I returned, there would be crumbs floating in the sauce—evidence that someone (or a few someones) had snuck in with a wad of bread and soaked up a taste. Or worse, there would be a bite missing from the glistening edge of the meat itself. I wouldn't be happy about it. No one ever fessed up.

But, now that I'm not getting ready for service, I understand. A great braise is hard to resist and I love the familial feeling it invites. And, to be honest, I liked the fact that people who knew better still couldn't help but sample a taste.

You may know the "basic" braise as a brown-submerge-and-simmer affair, but to my mind, the technique encompasses much more than that. In the following meals, we'll explore those variations, and the truth is, the strength of each will reveal itself during the cooking process. If the braise transforms your home and encourages all sorts of irrepressible behavior, then you've got something irresistible on your hands.

BRAISING: TECHNIQUE AND DETAIL

My definition of a braise is a broad one—simply put, it's a dish that centers on two basic parts: a "meat" (or fish or vegetable) and a cooking liquid. Anything made with these two elements counts, and so in this chapter we explore soups, stews, a saucy casserole, and confits as well as more classic notions of braising. What I'd like to do is to show you how my mind thinks of braising—how the interactions of ingredients, heat, moisture, and time result in surprisingly diverse, delicious results.

THE MAIN INGREDIENT

Braising is the go-to technique for tougher, fibrous cuts. But more versatile ingredients, such as chicken legs or even humble leeks, also benefit from the flavor and moisture that the technique affords. Almost anything can be braised; it's just a question of how.

Delicate ingredients, as a rule, are braised for less time and often in less liquid, so their structural integrity—an important factor to keep in mind—remains intact. In the Braised Snapper with Gremolata and Bean Ragu (page 65), for example, the fish comes out juicy with only a slick of delicious gravy; the small amount of liquid cooks the fish and reduces quickly. Similarly, the Leeks Braised with Oranges (page 86) cook down in just a touch of orange juice so their layers maintain their bite. Unless you are making a braise that's more about the liquid than the ingredients, these more delicate products do best when cooked for less time, in a controlled amount of well-seasoned liquid. This principle is at the heart of shallow braising.

Bigger cuts with more connective tissue require the opposite—a deep braise, in which food cooks in a generous amount of liquid until it becomes supple. A deep braise simmers for an extended period, dissolving the gelatin and harmonizing with the flavor of the meat, emerging much altered in the end.

None of this is earth-shattering; it may well feel intuitive. But I hope the recipes in this chapter afford a richer understanding of these principles, and ultimately help you to create braises of your own.

THE COOKING LIQUID

Early on in my career, I realized how much more finely honed the flavor of a braise became when a meat was matched with the right liquid. Sometimes that means using something meaty (lamb stock, cod stock, chicken stock), lean (dashi, infusions, wine and vinegar), vegetal or fruity (corn milk, tomato water and orange juice). I also like to use fattier liquids (oils, butters, animal fats and dairy). Through the meals in this chapter, you'll see how those pairings of liquids and ingredients work—sometimes a rich liquid bolsters an ingredient; sometimes a light one offsets it—but never be afraid of experimenting. A braising liquid can come from anywhere, and there are a few go-tos that are always worth keeping in mind, and on hand.

At my house, we always have *kombu* (Japanese dried kelp) and bonito flakes in the pantry. My wife is Japanese and we use them often to whip up a quick dashi, the staple

Japanese stock famous for its lean, mineral, smoky flavor and its savory umami. It's a great crutch, better than anything premade for sure and it takes almost no time to pull together. If you are on the fence about making one of the more involved broths in this chapter, I encourage you to just make dashi instead (page 286).

In a pinch, water can also make for a fine braising liquid. It's bare-bones and brings in no extra flavor, but it yields the most "pure" tasting end result. If you toss in some garlic cloves, thyme, and/or a bay leaf, you'll solve the flavor problem. In fact, you will actually have something similar to *aïgo boulido*, a Provençal staple that is essentially just boiled garlic. It's a delicious broth, rustic and earthy. Equally fast and scrappy is the Parmesan-Pecorino broth (page 290). This Italian stroke of genius is made by simmering tired old cheese scraps in salted water until the liquid turns tasty, round, salty, and nutty. It's especially wonderful with braised vegetables and soups.

If you decide to opt for a store-bought chicken or vegetable broth, these recipes will work fine with those too—though they might not taste quite as unique. Often these premade broths are high in sodium and they need to be tasted and tempered with a few splashes of water beforehand. Taking this cautionary step prevents braises from getting too salty as they cook down and concentrate. (I usually recommend buying low-sodium versions when available.)

THE BASIC TECHNIQUE

Over time, I have developed a standard braising technique that takes cues from the classical approach, in which flavor is built, as master chef Paul Bertolli said, from the bottom up. My tendency is to lavish extra care in certain places along the way. This is what that path looks like:

PHASE 1: BUILDING FLAVOR

First, wet- or dry-brine the meat a few hours, or days, ahead of time to guarantee that the cut is seasoned all the way through. Once brined, the meat then dries, uncovered, in the refrigerator to set up the exterior for browning, as surface moisture—the enemy of caramelization—evaporates. Don't worry; it doesn't actually dry out the meat because the salt from the brining step locks in its internal moisture.

Browning is the next step, and this is where many home cooks often err. It's important to have patience and to push the envelope when browning. Often, the color that you want to achieve is a deep, caramelized brown, such that you start to worry about burning your meat a little. This is the key to rich depth, and it takes time. Think of it more as building a crust rather than a quick sear.

Once your meat is browned, remove it from the pan and chase the tasty morsels stuck to the pot's surface by stirring in minced aromatic vegetables, like an Italian *soffritto* or French *mirepoix*. The moisture the vegetables release allows you to scrape up all that meaty *fond* and collect it, and of course they provide their own flavor and sweetness to layer and balance the braise.

Again, patience is key: Give the vegetables time to gently cook down into a bodiless shmoo. You want all their water to evaporate, their cells to break down, and their flavors to concentrate. Then layer in the other ingredients and flavors, such as tomato paste or anchovies. After each addition, gently sauté and continue to distill the essence of each addition slowly and methodically. When deglazing with wine or vinegar, do the same and cook it nearly dry before moving on. This, you see, is what Bertolli meant by bottom-up cooking.

PHASE 2: MEAT AND LIQUID MEET

Up until now, you have been building a base. Now it's time to return the browned meat to the pot, swoosh it around in the tasty vegetable matter, and pour in the liquid to get the braise going. Before slipping the whole dish into the oven, if that's its destiny, I like to bring it to a simmer on the stovetop to make sure the dish gets off to a running start.

Though the rest is less active, don't slack off. Keep an eye on both the meat and sauce as your braise gently evolves. Feed it more or less heat, and maybe some extra liquid too. Stir the braise, turn the pot, jostle the ingredients, and baste your meat. I'm an active cook throughout, and to be in touch with your dish as it changes affords you control over the end result. Sometimes ovens run hot or cold, sometimes the liquid evaporates too quickly, sometimes a cut juts out of the liquid a little too much, sometimes it cooks a little faster than expected and if you are plugged into what's happening, you can adjust. As you reach the finish line, check in with your braise with increasing frequency to guarantee even, proper cooking.

Every cut has its textural sweet spot, where the meat flakes off the bone but still has integrity, a little bit of chew. Just as barbecue aficionados say that "falling off the bone" meat is actually overcooked, I find the same applies to braises. When cooked too far, the meat shreds and loses all tension, and there is no going back once that happens. Despite what you might have heard, the term "fork-tender" should *not* apply to a braise. I find fork-tender bites mostly structure-less, homogenous, and boring. The state I prefer is a bouncier one, where the meat yields, but still has enough body to keep it interesting.

PHASE 3: RESTING AND FINISHING

Once your braise is properly cooked, let it rest in the liquid so its juices settle. We often afford roasts a resting period, and braises deserve the same consideration. Let the meat relax a bit so the symbiosis between it and the sauce continues. Also, remember, braises are often better the next day, so if you need to make a dish in advance, these are ideal.

As the meat rests, if the sauce is rich, fat will rise to the surface. Before reheating, skim off this layer. Then, before serving, reheat and brighten the dish with herbs or another flourish to play off the big, mellow flavors you have just spent so much time developing.

GOING ROGUE

The last word I want to say about braising is that every rule is meant to be broken. In the following recipes, nearly every one of these steps gets altered, bent, or ignored to get a specific result. In the case of the Zuppa di Pesce (page 88), for example, I don't brown anything, so all the flavors stay light and soft. In the Lamb Stewed with Almonds and Tunisian Spices (page 41), I overcook the meat intentionally so it shreds a bit and releases all its flavor into the sauce. (Springy pearled couscous provides the textural interest in that dish.) In short, deciding when to deviate from the above "rules" is as important as understanding them.

HOW THIS CHAPTER IS ORGANIZED

The first half of this chapter more or less follows the preceding detailed procedure, but I begin fiddling with techniques as the chapter progresses. In the second half of the chapter, I broaden the "braising" definition. I start playing with the textures and appearance a braised dish can have. As the chapter evolves, so too will your understanding of what a braise is and what it can be. I hope you enjoy the ride.

1

RED WINE-BRAISED OXTAILS
WITH MARINATED SAVOY CABBAGE AND FLATBREADS

SERVES 4 TO 6

I can think of no better example than oxtails or shanks to demonstrate the virtues of traditional slow braising. Inexpensive, with tons of connective tissue, these cuts must be braised to reveal their beautiful character.

Here, burnt-onion dashi is the primary liquid. It's mineral and light, a balance to the red wine, and the collagen-rich cut will make it viscous and lush.

Lavish time and attention on each step of this recipe and you will get a delicious tutorial on the basics of braising. Really brown the meat; thoroughly melt the vegetables; scrape up all the fond as you go. When you add the wine and vinegar, let it steam, sizzle, and simmer off, so it just streaks the pan's base and cooks into the soffritto. With each step you are building baseline flavor and understanding of the technique.

As the braise simmers, baste the meat and turn the pan until the oxtails hit their tender sweet spot. Then take a deep breath. That scent is part of the reward.

A quick note if you are buying oxtails: Ask your butcher to cut pieces from the tail's center. You want plump cuts, or this rags-to-riches transformation won't impress.

Zest of 1 lemon, removed in strips with a vegetable peeler

15 fresh thyme sprigs

1 gallon water

1 tablespoon Aleppo pepper (optional)

1 cup kosher salt, plus more

¼ cup (packed) light brown sugar

2 tablespoons black peppercorns, toasted and freshly cracked, plus more

1 tablespoon coriander seeds, toasted

1 tablespoon mustard seeds, toasted

1 whole head of garlic, halved crosswise

8 2-inch-high oxtails, short ribs, or beef shanks (about 6 pounds total)

Olive oil, as needed

4 medium onions, diced fine

4 celery stalks, diced fine

2 medium carrots, diced fine

12 garlic cloves, finely grated

2 tablespoons tomato paste

5 salt-packed anchovies, rinsed and chopped

2 tablespoons finely chopped fresh oregano leaves

2 tablespoons pimentón (smoked paprika)

½ cup red wine vinegar

¼ cup agave or honey

1 cup red wine

4 cups Burnt-Onion Dashi (page 287) or Chicken Broth (page 288)

Gremolata (page 301), for serving (optional)

BRINE AND DRY THE OXTAILS

Press the lemon zest and the thyme with the broad side of a chef's knife to release their essential oils. Pour the water into a deep container and stir in the Aleppo pepper, if using, salt, and brown sugar. Once the salt dissolves, stir in the toasted peppercorns, coriander and mustard seeds, garlic, thyme, and lemon zest. Submerge the oxtails in the brine and cover the container. Refrigerate the meat for 24 hours.

Lift the oxtails out of the brine and place them on a cooling rack set over a rimmed baking sheet. Pat the meat dry and discard the brine.

Return the oxtails to the refrigerator and let the meat rest, uncovered, until it feels dry and tacky, about 12 hours.

(recipe continues)

MAKE THE BRAISE

Aggressively season the oxtails with freshly cracked pepper.

Set a lidded large Dutch oven over medium heat and swirl in enough olive oil to generously slick the bottom. When the oil turns shimmering-hot, add as many oxtails as will fit comfortably. Brown the meat at a steady, controlled sizzle. Once the oxtails release from the pot and turn a rich golden brown, sear the reverse sides. After both flat sides brown, turn the oxtails onto their sides and brown their edges. Set the browned meat on a platter and repeat with the remaining oxtails. Give each batch 15 to 20 minutes to thoroughly brown.

If the fond gets too dark while searing, remove the meat from the pot and deglaze the fond with a splash of water. Scrape up all the meaty bits and pour the drippings into a small bowl. Set the bowl of drippings aside, wipe out the pot, reheat, slick with oil, and continue browning the next batch.

Once the oxtails are browned, preheat the oven to 325°F. Pour off the fat (or add some oil) until you have 2 tablespoons of fat in the pot. Set the pot back over medium-low heat and stir in the onions, celery, carrots, and garlic. Make sure to scrape up the fond while sautéing the soffritto. Gently sweat the vegetables, stirring often, for 15 minutes, or until they collapse and soften. Season lightly with salt.

Stir in the tomato paste and anchovies. Sauté the mixture for 5 minutes, or until the anchovies melt into the vegetables. Add the oregano and pimentón and sauté 1 minute more, or until their perfume blooms. There should be no liquid in the pot at this point, but the vegetables should be meltingly soft and juicy enough to streak the pan's base.

Pour in the vinegar, agave or honey, and wine. Increase the heat to medium and gently simmer the liquid for 10 minutes, or until it evaporates. Increase the heat to high and stir in the burnt-onion dashi and any reserved drippings, if you deglazed while browning. Bring everything to a rolling boil.

Remove the pan from the heat and carefully nestle the browned oxtails into the pot, shingling them so the meat overlaps and lies evenly. Set the pot back over medium-high heat and simmer the braising liquid for 5 minutes. There should be enough liquid to keep the oxtails two-thirds submerged. If necessary, add more stock or water.

Turn off the heat and cover the pot. Transfer the oxtails to the oven and gently braise them for 3 hours, or until the meat shrinks, pulls away from the bone, and, when prodded in its thickest portion, gives but does not collapse. The meat should feel tender but bouncy. Every 30 minutes throughout the braising process, uncover the pot, baste the meat, re-cover, and rotate the pot 90 degrees.

Once they are perfectly cooked, remove the oxtails from the oven and season with salt and pepper to taste. Let them rest at room temperature for 1 hour. If not serving the oxtails on the same day, cool the pot in a sink of ice water, then cover and refrigerate. Properly stored, these keep for up to 4 days.

FINISH AND SERVE

Skim the congealed fat off the surface. Set the braise back over medium heat and rewarm at a steady simmer until heated through to the bone, 15 to 20 minutes.

To serve, scoop the oxtails and sauce onto a large, warm serving platter. Serve with Marinated Savoy Cabbage and Remina's Piadini (recipes follow) alongside. Gremolata (page 301) also does well here.

MARINATED SAVOY CABBAGE

SERVES 4 TO 6

This cabbage slaw perfectly offsets the richness of the braised oxtails. Once the leaves are rubbed in an acidic vinaigrette made with colatura (an ancient Italian version of fish sauce), vinegar, and lemon juice, their snappy bite softens slightly, and the leaves' sweetness steps forward.

2 quarts water

½ cup kosher salt

2 cups ice

1 small head of Savoy cabbage, leaves separated and rinsed

2 tablespoons chardonnay vinegar or apple cider vinegar

1 tablespoon colatura or high-quality fish sauce, such as Red Boat

2 tablespoons lemon juice (from about 1 lemon)

1 teaspoon finely grated lemon zest (from about 1 lemon)

1½ tablespoons olive oil

2 tablespoons sliced fresh flat-leaf parsley leaves

1 tablespoon finely sliced fresh chives

Fine sea salt and freshly cracked black peppercorns

BRINE THE CABBAGE

In a large container, combine the water, kosher salt, and ice.

Place the cabbage leaves in the ice bath and refrigerate the container. Brine the cabbage for 1 hour, or until the leaves crisp.

PREPARE THE LEAVES AND SERVE

Drain the cabbage. Tear the leaves into rough 2-inch pieces. Working in batches, use a salad spinner to dry the leaves. Transfer the cabbage to a large salad bowl.

In a small bowl, mix the vinegar, colatura, and lemon juice and zest. Whisk in the olive oil.

Using your hands, rub the cabbage with enough dressing to liberally coat the leaves. Let the slaw rest for 10 minutes, or until the cabbage softens a bit. Just before serving, toss in the parsley and chives. Season the slaw with sea salt and pepper to taste, if necessary. Serve.

HOW TO PLAN THIS MEAL:

2 days before: Brine oxtails.

1 day before: Dry oxtails and make burnt-onion dashi.

6 hours before: Sear oxtails and prepare braise.

3 hours before: Make piadini dough.

90 minutes before: Brine cabbage.

30 minutes before: Dry cabbage and make dressing.

20 minutes before: Rewarm oxtails and cook piadini.

10 minutes before: Dress cabbage.

REMINA'S PIADINI

MAKES EIGHT 6-INCH FLATBREADS

My career as a chef reached a new level while I was at the Italophile Il Buco Alimentari, in New York's NoHo. One year, Donna Lennard, the owner, took me to the motherland for research. One of the most profound experiences happened in Emilia Romagna, at the home of a skilled cheese maker, Renato Brancaleoni.

Renato and his wife, Remina, invited us for dinner and served a simple braised beef with just-griddled flatbreads, piadini, alongside. Renato set out a beautiful cow's and sheep's milk cheese, and everything tasted too good to be believed. Before we sat down, Remina nonchalantly finished cooking these piadini at her stovetop.

She gauged the temperature of the terra-cotta cooking plate by splattering water onto it, flipped the piadini at the exact right moment, and used her hands to remove the bread once crisped. Watching a cook make a dish she has made for half a century is a sight indeed.

When making these, keep the dough as cold as possible until it hits the griddle.

---

4 cups all-purpose flour, plus more for dusting

1 tablespoon baking powder

2 teaspoons kosher salt

½ cup vegetable shortening or lard, chilled

1¼ cups ice-cold water

Olive oil, for brushing

MAKE THE DOUGH

Sift the flour, baking powder, and salt into a large mixing bowl. Cut the chilled shortening into $1/4$-inch bits and, using your fingers, rub it into the flour until only pea-sized lumps remain. Make a well in the center of the flour mixture and add the water. Stir with a fork to form a loose, shaggy dough.

Turn the dough onto a lightly floured surface and knead it for about 8 minutes, or until the dough is smooth and elastic. Set a 12-inch square of plastic wrap on a work surface and brush it with oil. Turn the dough out onto the oiled sheet. Lift up the edges and tightly wrap the dough in the plastic. Refrigerate for 1 hour, or until well chilled. The dough can be made 1 to 2 days in advance and stored, wrapped in plastic, in the refrigerator.

MAKE THE PIADINI

Turn the chilled dough out onto a work surface and remove the plastic wrap. Cut it into 8 pieces and, with the palm of your hand, gently roll each portion into a smooth ball. Set the balls aside and loosely cover with plastic wrap.

Lightly dust a work surface and rolling pin with flour. Roll each ball into a disk 6 inches in diameter and $1/8$ inch thick.

Heat a cast-iron pan or heavy griddle over medium-high heat until drops of water bounce on the hot surface once or twice before evaporating. Lay a disk or two on the hot pan; the dough should gently sizzle immediately. Griddle the bread for 1 minute per side, or until it turns golden and blisters in spots. Transfer the cooked flatbread to a warm platter and cover with a dry kitchen towel. Repeat with the remaining dough. Serve warm.

2

PORK SHANKS WITH LATE-SEASON TOMATOES AND POLENTA

SERVES 6

I make these braised pork shanks, which are cloaked in a vibrant tomato sauce and served over a bed of soft polenta, from the end of summer through mid-fall, when tomatoes are big and sweet and bursting with juice. Here, ripe tomatoes are grated to a pulp, or a passata, before being added in two installments: The first serves as part of the cooking liquid, melding with the meat and sauce; the second, at the end, lends the dish sun-drenched flavor and needed acidity.

Built in much the same way as the oxtails in the preceding meal, these shanks also extol the virtues of a classic braise. But, unlike the oxtails, this dish simmers stovetop to facilitate easy basting, which you should do often, and allows you to keep an eye on the braising liquid. Because the sauce is thick, you need to make sure it doesn't scorch as it reduces.

You may be surprised that tomato stems or leaves are called for here. The way they enhance the sauce's tomato flavor is unparalleled. But they're optional, and if adding them makes you nervous, skip them. (They have trace amounts of toxins, as do peach pits or apple seeds.) If you can't get your hands on tomato leaves but want a similar effect, vines from tomato bunches or just the stem ends from tomatoes do the trick.

---

1 tablespoon finely grated orange zest (from 1 orange)

3 tablespoons chopped fresh rosemary leaves

12 garlic cloves, finely grated

2 tablespoons black peppercorns, toasted and roughly crushed, plus more for seasoning

¼ cup kosher salt, plus more for seasoning

6 3-inch-thick skinless pork shanks (about 8 pounds total)

2¾ pounds ripe tomatoes, halved equatorially

2 jalapeño peppers

6 garlic cloves

Olive oil, as needed

1 tablespoon butter

1½ medium red onions, finely chopped

2 celery stalks, finely chopped

2 medium carrots, finely chopped

1 tablespoon tomato paste

2 fresh bay leaves

3 fresh thyme sprigs

1½ tablespoons chardonnay or apple cider vinegar

6 tomato leaves or a handful of tomato stems (optional)

6 cups Burnt-Onion Dashi (page 287) or Chicken Broth (page 288), warm

DRY-BRINE THE SHANKS

Place the orange zest, rosemary, grated garlic, and peppercorns in a medium bowl. Stir in the kosher salt until well combined.

Set the pork shanks in a large roasting pan. Rub the salt mixture into the meat, packing it all over the shanks and into the crevices. Transfer to the refrigerator, and dry-brine for 24 hours.

Remove the shanks from the refrigerator and rinse off the salt. Pat the meat dry and arrange the shanks on a baking rack set over a rimmed baking sheet. Return the shanks to the refrigerator and let rest, uncovered, for 12 to 24 hours, or until they feel dry and tacky.

(recipe continues)

MAKE THE PASSATA

Set a box grater inside a large bowl. On the small teeth of the grater, rub the tomatoes' cut sides until nothing but their skins remains. Discard the skins. Transfer 2 cups of the grated pulp to a small bowl and set aside. There should be about 2$\frac{1}{2}$ cups of pulp remaining in the large bowl.

Finely grate the jalapeños, stopping at the stems, and 3 of the garlic cloves. Stir their pulp and 2 tablespoons olive oil into the large bowl with the tomato pulp. Cover and refrigerate the tomato-jalapeño pulp, or passata, until ready to use. The passata holds for 1 day in the refrigerator.

BUILD THE BRAISE

Cut a piece of parchment paper to just fit inside a large Dutch oven. Set the Dutch oven over medium-high heat and coat the pot with olive oil. Once the oil is shimmering-hot, place as many shanks as will fit comfortably in the pot, laying them on their sides. Lower the heat to medium and brown the shanks at a steady, controlled sizzle until they easily release from the pot and turn a deep golden brown. Rotate the shanks, searing all sides in this fashion. Once the meat is evenly browned all around, transfer to a platter and brown the remaining shanks. Cook each batch at least 15 minutes to thoroughly sear.

Meanwhile, if the fond gets too dark, remove the meat and deglaze the pot with splashes of water; pour the drippings into a small bowl and set

aside. Wipe out the pot, reheat, re-oil, and continue browning the shanks until all are done. Set all the browned shanks aside.

Pour off the fat from the pot while keeping the fond in place. Set the pot back over medium heat and swirl in 1 tablespoon oil and the butter. Once the butter melts, stir in the onions, celery, and carrots. Pound the remaining 3 garlic cloves into a rough pulp and stir into the pot, making sure to scrape up all the fond stuck to the base. Reduce the heat to medium-low and gently sauté the soffritto for 15 minutes, or until the vegetables soften but do not color. Stir in the tomato paste and cook for 3 minutes, or until the paste cooks into the vegetables.

Increase the heat to medium and stir the bay leaves, thyme, vinegar, unseasoned tomato pulp, and tomato leaves or stems (if using) into the pot. Scrape up all the fond to combine with the pulp. Bring the liquid to a simmer and cook it down for 5 minutes, or until half of it evaporates.

Return the shanks to the pot, arranging them so their bones stick straight up. Spoon the vegetable matter all over the shanks and increase the heat to medium-high. Pour the burnt-onion dashi or chicken broth into the pot so the shanks are three-quarters submerged.

Bring the liquid to just below a boil and reduce the heat to medium-low, maintaining a gentle but steady simmer.

Cover with the parchment and braise the shanks for 2 to 2$\frac{1}{2}$ hours. Every 20 minutes, baste and flip the meat and turn the pot 90 degrees. As the sauce simmers down and thickens toward the end of cooking, pay extra attention and stir it often to avoid scorching the bottom.

You're done when the liquid reduces to a thick tomato sauce, and the shank meat gives easily, but does not fall apart when prodded at its thickest part. Taste and season with salt and pepper as needed.

Let the shanks cool in the braising liquid for 1 hour, then set the pot in a sink filled with ice water to cool to room temperature. Cover and refrigerate the braise for 6 hours or for up to 3 days.

FINISH AND SERVE

Remove the braise from the refrigerator and skim off any congealed fat from its surface. Gently rewarm the dish over medium heat, stirring occasionally to prevent scorching. After about 30 minutes, once the shanks warm through, stir in the reserved tomato-jalapeño passata. Continue simmering the braise, while constantly basting the meat, until the sauce tightens and coats the shanks.

To serve, distribute the polenta (recipe follows) among 6 plates and nestle 1 hot shank on each serving. Spoon additional pan sauce over the meat and serve immediately.

OLD-WORLD POLENTA

SERVES 6 TO 8

Made the old-fashioned way, this polenta serves two roles: Its mellow flavor grounds the meal, lending it a sweet earthiness, while its body absorbs all the runoff juices from the shanks and sauce.

You don't need to constantly stir the polenta, but you *do* need to stand guard and stir it often enough to ensure it doesn't stick to the pot. Cooking times for polenta can vary, depending on a host of factors, so bear that in mind and give yourself some time here. Polenta has the advantage of retaining heat incredibly well, so if need be, make this in advance.

Fine sea salt

1½ cups medium-grain polenta, preferably fresh milled

1½ cups freshly grated Parmesan

Pour 7 cups water into a large heavy saucepan and season with salt until it tastes lightly salted.

Bring the water to a rolling boil over high heat, then reduce the heat to medium-low to maintain a gentle simmer. Slowly pour in the polenta, whisking all the while.

Gently simmer the polenta for 1 to 1½ hours, or until the grains tenderize. While it cooks, stir the polenta often with a wooden spoon and scrape down the sides so the grains don't scorch. Add water as needed to loosen. Once properly cooked, the polenta should be so thick it slowly oozes across a plate. At this point, the polenta can be held for up to 2 hours at room temperature, covered.

Just before serving, stir the Parmesan into the polenta and season with salt to taste. Be careful when tasting it, as bubbling polenta is scorching hot. If rewarming the polenta, loosen it with a few splashes of water if needed and simmer over medium-low heat, stirring, until lump free. Remove from heat and serve.

HOW TO PLAN THIS MEAL:

3 days before: Dry-brine shanks.

2 days before: Rinse and dry shanks. Make burnt-onion dashi or chicken broth.

1 day before: Braise shanks.

2 hours before: Make polenta.

30 minutes before: Rewarm shanks.

3

PAPPARDELLE WITH YEAR-ROUND SUGO

SERVES 4 TO 6

Sugos are Italian meat sauces often made with braised bone-in meat, hand-torn and reintroduced, plump and supple, back into the lush sauce. Way more interesting than your standard ragu, which calls for ground meat, a sugo has a mix of inviting, soft textures. This one, made with a rich chicken broth, is meaty and balanced with sweetly caramelized vegetables.

With lean, muscular cuts like these slightly gamy rabbit legs, it's easy to know when you've cooked the meat perfectly because it shrinks and puffs on the bone; at that moment, it's bouncy, juicy, and just the tiniest bit tense. If you look closely enough, you'll spot natural seams in the meat; follow those lines when pulling off smooth, tender bites.

Tossed with pappardelle, this sugo is a home-run meal that's versatile year-round. In the winter, I like to add more meat and in the summer I scale back on the meat a bit and add some fresh vegetables, like peppery arugula, at the last minute. In the spring, favas are a go-to and in the early fall it's fresh tomatoes. If rabbit makes you squeamish, or if it's hard to find, chicken legs may be used instead.

1 tablespoon black peppercorns, toasted and freshly cracked, plus more

1 tablespoon fennel seeds, toasted and freshly cracked

1 tablespoon coriander seeds, toasted and freshly cracked

¼ cup kosher salt, plus more

1 teaspoon finely grated lemon zest (from 1 lemon)

2 teaspoons finely grated orange zest (from 1 orange)

2 tablespoons roughly chopped fresh oregano leaves

2 pounds skinless rabbit hind legs (about 4 legs) or chicken legs

¼ cup dried porcini mushrooms

½ teaspoon sugar

Olive oil, as needed

½ cup very finely diced red onion

¼ cup very finely diced fennel

3 tablespoons fennel fronds, roughly sliced

½ cup finely diced carrot

¼ cup very finely diced celery

4 garlic cloves, finely grated

1 tablespoon tomato paste

2 tablespoons champagne vinegar

3 cups Chicken Broth (page 288), plus more as needed

1 pound Fresh Pappardelle (recipe follows)

1½ tablespoons butter

3 tablespoons finely sliced fresh flat-leaf parsley leaves

DRY-BRINE THE RABBIT LEGS

In a small bowl, mix the cracked pepper, fennel and coriander seeds, kosher salt, lemon and orange zest, and oregano until well combined.

Lay the rabbit legs on a rimmed baking sheet and thoroughly rub the meat with the salt mixture. Arrange the legs in a single layer and transfer to the refrigerator. Dry-brine the rabbit, uncovered, for 24 hours.

Rinse the legs under cold water, washing off all the salt rub. Blot them dry with paper towels and transfer to a cooling rack set over the baking sheet. Refrigerate the legs, uncovered, for 6 to 12 hours, or until the meat feels dry and tacky.

(recipe continues)

SOAK THE PORCINIS

Meanwhile, place the dried porcinis and sugar in a small bowl. Cover with 1 cup warm water and let soak for 1 hour, or until they plump and tenderize. Lift the mushrooms out of the water and transfer to a fine-mesh sieve. Hold the sieve over the bowl with the soaking liquid and press down on the mushrooms to capture their juices below. Set the bowl aside and finely chop the rehydrated porcinis.

BUILD THE BRAISE

Preheat the oven to 300°F. Set a large Dutch oven over medium-high heat and swirl 2 tablespoons olive oil into the pot. Once the oil is shimmering-hot, lay in 2 of the legs, working in batches to avoid overcrowding. Brown the legs for 4 minutes on each side, or until they easily release from the pot and turn a deep, golden brown. Transfer the browned legs to a platter. Repeat with the remaining legs, adding more oil if necessary.

Pour off all the fat from the pot, making sure to leave the fond in place. Set the pot back over medium-low heat and swirl in 3 tablespoons olive oil. When the oil is hot, stir in the onion, diced fennel and fennel fronds, carrot, celery, and garlic. Sauté the vegetables, taking care to stir and scrape up all the fond, for 15 minutes, or until the soffritto collapses and softens. Increase the heat to medium and stir in the tomato paste. Sauté the soffritto for 3 to 5 minutes more, or until the paste darkens. Stir in the chopped porcinis and sauté for 4 minutes, or until aromatic.

Pour in the vinegar and reserved porcini water. (If any grit has gathered in the porcini water, pass it through a cheesecloth-lined strainer before using.) Simmer the liquid for 10 minutes, or until it mostly evaporates.

Return the browned legs to the pot, arranging them in a single layer so their meatiest side faces up. Smear the soft vegetables all over the meat and increase the heat to medium-high. Pour in enough chicken broth so two-thirds of the legs are submerged. Bring the liquid up to a simmer, then cover the pot and transfer it to the oven.

Gently braise the legs for 1½ hours, or until the legs' thickest portions are tender but a little bouncy when prodded. Every 20 minutes, uncover the pot, baste the legs, re-cover the pot, and rotate it 90 degrees. When the meat is perfectly cooked, remove the pot from the oven, uncover, and let the legs cool in their braising liquid until they are cool enough to handle, at least 1 hour. (For faster cooling, set your pot in a sink filled with ice water.)

PULL THE MEAT

Working with one leg at a time over a medium bowl, pick the meat off the bone: Hold a leg at its joint with one hand. With your other hand, gently pull the meat along its natural seams; it should flake off in bite-size pieces. When breaking larger pieces into smaller bites, avoid shredding. Instead, pull off smooth, plump bites. Repeat with the remaining legs. Set the picked meat aside and discard the bones.

Stir the picked meat back into the pot. The meat should be just barely submerged. If there's too much liquid, you can gently reduce it when reheating the sauce, just before combining it with the pasta. Stir the sugo and season to taste with salt and pepper. Cover, refrigerate, and let rest for at least 6 hours. At this point, the sugo will hold for 2 to 3 days in the refrigerator.

REWARM THE SUGO AND COOK THE PAPPARDELLE

Remove the sugo from the refrigerator and bring it up to a gentle simmer over medium heat.

Meanwhile, bring a large pot filled with well-salted water to a rolling boil over high heat. Just before dropping in the pasta, taste the water to make sure it is pleasantly salty. Drop in the pappardelle and boil for 2 minutes, or until it whitens but is not yet al dente. As the pasta cooks, raise the heat under the sugo to medium-high.

Scoop out a cup of the pasta water and reserve. Quickly drain the pasta and add it to the simmering sugo. Gently toss the noodles in the sugo for 1 to 2 minutes, or until the pasta is just al dente. If the dish looks too dry, meaning the noodles do not glisten, add small splashes of the reserved pasta water. When the noodles are al dente, remove the pot from the heat and stir in the butter, 1 tablespoon olive oil, and the parsley. Serve immediately.

FRESH PAPPARDELLE

MAKES ABOUT 1 POUND PASTA

Fresh pastas are richer and more complex than dry pastas, but you have to be extra careful not to overcook them, since they cook very quickly. Err on the side of caution and undercook these eggy ribbons a hair. They can finish cooking with the sugo, along with an extra splash of pasta water if need be.

Made with a mixture of low-protein Italian 00 flour (available online and at specialty stores) and semolina, this pasta dough is both supple and sturdy.

---

2 cups 00 or all-purpose flour, plus more for dusting

½ cup semolina flour

¼ teaspoon kosher salt

3 large eggs

2 to 3 tablespoons cold water

SPECIAL EQUIPMENT

Pasta machine

MAKE THE DOUGH

In a medium bowl, whisk together the 00 flour, semolina, and salt. Dump the dry mixture out onto a clean work surface, forming a mound, and punch a 3-inch-wide well in the center. In a small bowl, beat the eggs and water until well combined. Pour the egg mixture into the center of the well.

With a fork, whisk the eggs while slowly scraping in the flour from the well's sidewalls. Take time—a full minute—to slowly and thoroughly whisk the dry into the wet ingredients, until a shaggy dough forms.

With the base of your palm, knead the dough, working it back and forth until a smooth, slightly marbled, damp mass comes together. Form the dough into a ball and wrap it in plastic. Refrigerate the dough, ideally for at least 12 hours, or until it holds a thumb imprint for 10 seconds after you press it.

ROLL THE DOUGH

Remove the dough from the refrigerator and let it come up to room temperature, about 45 minutes. Cut the dough into 6 equal pieces and cover them with a lightly dampened kitchen towel.

Lightly dust a clean work surface with 00 flour. Place 1 piece of dough on the floured work surface and lightly dust it as well.

Turn on your pasta machine, if it is automatic. Set the machine's rollers to the thickest setting on the dial, so they are about ¼ inch apart. On most machines, the largest setting is #1. Pass the dough through the machine. Now, turn the dial one setting thinner (#2) and pass the pasta through the machine once more. Keep the machine on without changing the settings.

Lay the pasta sheet back down on the floured surface and lightly redust it with flour. Fold a third of the stretched pasta dough back over itself. Then fold the sheet's other end back over the center portion as well. The idea is to fold the dough into thirds and create straight edges.

Pass the folded dough through the rollers once more at the #2 setting. Turn the dial to #3 and pass the pasta sheet through this thinner setting once.

Refold your pasta sheet into thirds as detailed above, making sure that the folded pasta is not wider than the roller.

Pass the folded pasta through setting #3. Turn the dial down to #4 and pass the pasta through this thinner setting. Turn the dial to #5 and put the pasta sheet through this thinnest setting for a final pass. This should yield a pasta sheet about as thick as construction paper.

When done, the stretched pasta sheet should feel a bit damp and have the rough texture of a cat's tongue. Those tiny ridges help the sauce to adhere to the noodle.

CUT AND STORE THE PAPPARDELLE

Lay the long pasta sheet out flat on the work surface. Working from one end to the other, cut crosswise through the sheet at 6-inch intervals. You should end up with approximately six 6-inch pasta sheets.

Line a large baking sheet with parchment paper and lightly dust it with flour.

Roll one of the pasta sheets into a long tube. Slice the tube crosswise at $1\frac{1}{2}$-inch intervals. Unfurl the roll and scatter the noodles, which should be approximately $6 \times 1\frac{1}{2}$ inches, onto the baking sheet. Repeat with the remaining pasta sheets.

Repeat the entire pasta rolling process with the remaining balls of pasta dough. The pappardelle will hold at room temperature for about 3 hours. Afterward, the cut pasta will keep in the freezer, in an airtight container, for 3 days.

HOW TO PLAN THIS MEAL:

2–3 days before: Dry-brine rabbit legs. Make chicken broth.

36 hours before: Rinse and dry rabbit legs.

12–24 hours before: Braise rabbit legs. Pull meat and let sugo rest. Make pappardelle dough.

3 hours before: Roll and cut pappardelle. (Pasta can also be cut up to 3 days before and frozen.)

30 minutes before: Gently rewarm sugo.

10 minutes before: Boil pappardelle. Toss noodles with sauce and dress dish.

4

LAMB STEWED WITH ALMONDS AND TUNISIAN SPICES

SERVES 6 TO 8

As I've insisted over and over, one of the central tenets of my braising technique is that you must *not* overcook a braise. Well, every rule has its exceptions. In this recipe, we stew lamb shoulder until it turns fork-tender. That's right, fork-tender: my dreaded phrase. But in this case, it's not until the diced lamb can practically collapse when pressed that this dish is good to go. This stew should feel round, soft, and buttery, providing the spices and almonds with a gamey, warm backdrop against which to bloom.

You needn't let it rest in the braising juices at the end. Since this preparation is technically overcooked, the liquid has seeped through the meat. One more unusual thing about this procedure: The lamb does not thoroughly brown. Instead, we just lightly sear the meat. Doing so ensures that the spices are the star, rather than browned meat flavor. A bed of nutty, chewy Sardinian couscous rounds out the meal and soaks up the stew's gorgeous, aromatic sauce.

---

2 tablespoons kosher salt

4 pounds boneless lamb shoulder, cut into 1-inch cubes

1 cup Marcona almonds, plus more for garnish

Fine sea salt

2 tablespoons coriander seeds

1 tablespoon cumin seeds

1 tablespoon whole black peppercorns, plus cracked pepper to season

1 teaspoon cayenne

1 teaspoon paprika

1 cinnamon stick

Olive oil, as needed

2 medium red onions, finely diced

1 carrot, finely diced

2 medium celery stalks, finely diced

1 fresh bay leaf

5 fresh thyme sprigs

6 plump garlic cloves, finely grated

1 2-inch piece of ginger, peeled and finely grated

1 tablespoon tomato paste

1 quart Roasted Lamb Broth (page 291), Chicken Broth (page 288), or water

3 tablespoons finely sliced fresh flat-leaf parsley leaves

2 tablespoons finely sliced fresh cilantro leaves

1 tablespoon finely sliced fresh chives

DRY-BRINE THE LAMB

In a large bowl, rub the kosher salt into the cubed lamb. Cover the bowl and refrigerate for 24 hours.

One hour before cooking, remove the lamb from the refrigerator and thoroughly pat the meat dry.

PREPARE THE SPICES AND ALMONDS

Using a mortar and pestle or a food processor, smash or pulse the almonds and a pinch of sea salt together until a crumb forms, somewhere between sand and whole peppercorns. Set the almonds aside.

To make the spice mixture, heat a medium, heavy sauté pan over low heat until hot. Add the coriander, cumin, black peppercorns, and cayenne and toast the spices until aromatic, about 1 minute. Add the paprika and

cinnamon stick and toast, stirring, until their scent blooms, about 30 seconds more. Turn off the heat. Remove the cinnamon stick and set it aside.

Transfer the toasted spices to a spice or coffee grinder and pulse until finely ground. Set the spice mix aside.

BRAISE THE LAMB

Set a large terra-cotta pot, tajine, or Dutch oven over medium-low heat. Swirl in 2 tablespoons olive oil. When the oil shimmers, add a quarter of the cubed lamb. Gently sear the meat on all sides for 7 to 8 minutes, or until just lightly browned all over. Transfer to a platter, pour any juices into a small bowl, and repeat with the remaining lamb, adding olive oil as needed to maintain a thin coating in the pan.

Increase the heat to medium and add 2 tablespoons olive oil to the pan. Stir in the onions, carrot, celery, bay leaf, and thyme, taking care to scrape up all the fond. Sauté the soffritto for 20 minutes, or until it caramelizes thoroughly.

Stir in the garlic, ginger, and tomato paste. Sauté until the tomato paste darkens, about 3 minutes. Stir in the cinnamon stick and reserved spice mix and cook for 3 minutes, or until the spices and vegetables are thoroughly combined and aromatic. Return the lamb and any reserved drippings to the pot. Roll the lamb around in the vegetables.

Pour in the lamb broth; about three-quarters of the meat should be submerged. Bring the broth to a gentle simmer, then reduce the heat to medium-low. Cover the pot and gently braise the lamb for 1½ to 2 hours, or until the lamb pieces are nearly fall-apart tender and give completely when pressed. Every 30 minutes, lift the lid, stir, adjust the heat to maintain a very gentle, lazy bubble, rotate the pot 90 degrees, and re-cover. Once the lamb is done, taste and season the stew with extra sea salt and pepper if necessary, bearing in mind that the almonds, which will be added next, are also salted. (At this point, you may cool the braise—ideally by setting the pot in a sink full of ice water—and refrigerate for up to 3 days.)

FINISH AND SERVE

To reheat the stew, set the pot over medium heat. Once the liquid begins to simmer, add the Marcona almonds. Simmer the stew for 7 minutes, or until the sauce thickens. The bigger bits of almonds will lend crunch to the sauce while the pulverized bits will lend body.

To serve, remove the stew from the heat and stir in the parsley, cilantro, and chives. Top with extra almonds and generously drizzle with olive oil. Serve warm or room-temperature with Sardinian Couscous (recipe follows) alongside. Remina's Piadini (page 29) also go well with this meal.

SARDINIAN COUSCOUS

I love the starchy spring of Sardinian couscous (often called fregola), the pasta-like pearls that are made with semolina flour, then toasted and dried. They taste nuttier than their smaller couscous cousins. When paired with this braised lamb, the pellets soak up the almond-enriched juices wonderfully. The lemon zest and parsley that season this mixture complement the main dish's spices.

Kosher salt

2 cups Sardinian couscous

Olive oil

2 teaspoons finely grated lemon zest (from 2 lemons)

¼ cup lemon juice (from 2 lemons)

Freshly cracked black peppercorns

½ cup finely sliced fresh flat-leaf parsley leaves

Fill a medium pot with water and bring to a boil over high heat. Add enough salt so the water tastes of the ocean.

Pour in the couscous and boil for 8 minutes, or until al dente. Strain the couscous, toss dry, and transfer to a large bowl.

Dress the couscous with the olive oil, lemon zest and juice, and salt and pepper to taste. Fold in the parsley. Serve hot or at room temperature.

HOW TO PLAN THIS MEAL:

1 day before: Dry-brine lamb.

3 hours before: Prepare spices and almonds. Braise lamb. (Braise may also be made up to 3 days before.)

30 minutes before: Make couscous. Finish stew with almonds.

5

BRAISED LAMB SHOULDER WITH ONION-ANCHOVY JAM

SERVES 6 TO 8

I grew up eating my grandmother's pot roasts on Sundays and I loved that tradition. As a chef, I've often found myself re-creating elements of this weekly ritual. And so it is with this slow-braised lamb shoulder, which gets a sweet-salty-savory onion and anchovy coating, nodding to one of Italy's most clever pairings. While at first glance this meal bears little resemblance to my grandmother's cooking (she was Irish American and not really hip to the onion-and-anchovy thing), at the heart of this braise you'll find the same meaty, minerally pot-roast essence I fell for as a kid.

The basic braising practice outlined in preceding recipes is more or less followed in this preparation, with the onion-anchovy jam serving as the soffritto. As the shoulder braises, its outside turns soft and salty-sweet while its inside remains more taut and tasting more purely of lamb. Once sliced, fanned out, and doused in the reduced caramelized onion pan sauce, everything comes together like an unfussy Sunday supper ought to. But better.

3 to 4 pounds boneless lamb shoulder, preferably with a thick fat cap

2 tablespoons kosher salt, plus more

3 tablespoons whole black peppercorns, toasted and lightly crushed

Olive oil, as needed

3 medium red onions, sliced very thin

10 garlic cloves, smashed or finely grated to a paste

2 tablespoons tomato paste

2 tablespoons Dijon mustard

¼ cup Anchovy Paste (page 300)

2 tablespoons finely chopped fresh rosemary leaves

1 tablespoon pimentón (smoked paprika)

½ cup red wine vinegar

1 cup fruity red wine

1 tablespoon agave or honey

1 quart Roasted Lamb Broth (page 291) or Chicken Broth (page 288)

SCORE, TIE, AND DRY-BRINE THE LAMB

If your lamb shoulder does not come with a thick fat cap, skip this scoring step. Place the lamb on a clean work surface so its fat side faces up. Hold a razor blade or very sharp paring knife at a 45-degree angle over one of the fat cap's top corners. Score the fat on a diagonal, running the blade from the top corner down and across. When scoring, make sure not to cut through into the meat; each incision should just barely cut into the fat, about ⅛ inch deep. Continue scoring the fat in this fashion, spacing incisions ¼ inch apart. Stop scoring the cap when the fat begins to taper off. Now, working in the opposite direction, repeat the scoring so a tight diamond pattern forms across the fat cap.

Season the lamb on all sides with 2 tablespoons of salt and the pepper. Tie the lamb up with butcher's twine, using a standard butcher's loop spaced at 1-inch intervals. The tied shoulder should form a uniform cylinder.

Place the shoulder on a cooling rack set over a rimmed baking sheet. Dry-brine the shoulder, uncovered, in the refrigerator for 12 to 24 hours.

BUILD THE BRAISE

Remove the lamb from the refrigerator. Set a large Dutch oven over medium-high heat and swirl in 2 tablespoons olive oil (¼ cup if your shoulder does not have a fat cap). When the oil is shimmering-hot, lay in the lamb, fat side down if that applies.

Sear the fat cap, lowering the heat if necessary to prevent scorching, for 10 minutes, or until it crisps and browns deeply. Then rotate, lightly searing all sides of the shoulder until they easily release from the pot and are a light golden brown. Transfer the lamb back to the cooling rack and set it aside. Pour off all but 2 tablespoons of fat from the pot, making sure to keep the fond in place.

Set the pot back over medium-low heat and stir in the onions, scraping up all of the fond on the bottom. Gently stew the onions for 45 minutes, or until they collapse and caramelize richly. Stir frequently so they color evenly; the longer you take in the step and the more you stir, the more profound the flavor will be.

Preheat the oven to 325°F.

Stir in the garlic and cook for 10 minutes, or until its aroma blooms and softens.

Stir in the tomato paste and mustard and sauté for 2 minutes, or until the paste cooks into the onions. Add the anchovy paste, rosemary, and pimentón. Raise the heat to medium-high. Pour in the vinegar, wine, and agave. Simmer for 15 minutes, or until the liquid turns syrupy and the onions are spreadably soft. Season with salt to taste.

Return the lamb shoulder to the pot with its fat cap facing up. Spoon and smear the onion jam all over the lamb and pour in enough lamb broth to cover two-thirds of the shoulder. Bring the broth up to a simmer, then reduce the heat to a lazy bubble.

Cover the pot and transfer to the center rack of the oven. Braise the lamb for 1¹/₂ hours, or until its center is easily pierced with a knife or cake tester, but the meat is still bouncy when prodded. Every 30 minutes, baste the lamb, re-cover, and rotate the pot 90 degrees.

FINISH AND SERVE

Remove the pot from the oven and thoroughly baste the lamb shoulder with the juices and caramelized onions. Season with salt to taste. Re-cover and let the lamb rest for 30 minutes, or until the internal juices settle. (At this stage, you may cool it—ideally by placing the pot in a sink filled with ice water—and refrigerate it overnight. Rewarm it over a gentle, medium-low flame.)

To serve, transfer the lamb to a cutting board and cut away the twine. Slice the meat into thick slices and arrange them on a warm platter. Spoon the onion-anchovy pan sauce on top and serve with the Black-Eyed Peas with Butter Lettuce and Warm Butter Dressing (recipe follows) alongside or directly on top.

BLACK-EYED PEAS WITH BUTTER LETTUCE AND WARM BUTTER DRESSING

SERVES 6

I like salads to undulate across platters as this one does. The black-eyed peas, bathed in a warm butter dressing, are spooned all over the crisp, cool leaves just before serving, nestling into their pockets. Served alongside the braised lamb shoulder, this salad provides more than just a fresh bite. Truth be told, it's so unexpectedly good it may just steal the show.

If you can't find fresh black-eyed peas, which appear in the summer, swap in edamame, available year-round in the frozen foods section. I don't call for dried peas because I don't want their creaminess to detract from the dish's freshness.

Kosher salt

2 cups fresh shelled black-eyed peas or frozen edamame, thawed

6 tablespoons butter, chilled

½ teaspoon lemon zest (from ½ lemon)

Flaky sea salt and freshly cracked black peppercorns

2 medium heads of butter lettuce, leaves separated

½ lemon

1 tablespoon thinly sliced fresh chives

½ cup whole fresh flat-leaf parsley leaves

BLANCH THE PEAS

Fill a medium pot with water and bring it to a boil over high heat. Add enough kosher salt so the water tastes of the ocean. Set up an ice-water bath beside the stove.

Blanch the shelled peas for 2 minutes, or until tender. If using edamame, blanch them for 30 seconds, or until they just turn bright green. Drain the peas and quickly transfer them to the ice bath. Once completely chilled, remove the peas from the bath, toss dry, and set aside.

PREPARE THE SALAD

Set a small heavy pot over medium-low heat. Add 2 tablespoons water; when it steams, whisk in the butter. Once the butter binds with the water to form an emulsion, stir in the blanched peas. Cook, stirring, for 1 minute, or until the peas are coated in the butter sauce and warmed through. Be sure to keep stirring throughout so that the

butter stays emulsified, and do not let the sauce boil. Stir in the lemon zest, season with flaky salt and pepper, and continue cooking for 30 seconds, or until aromatic.

Just before serving, arrange the lettuce leaves on a serving platter (or directly on the sliced lamb shoulder) so they undulate across the plate.

Spoon the buttery peas and their sauce evenly over the lettuce. Squeeze the lemon half over the salad and season with flaky salt. Garnish with the chives and parsley and serve immediately.

HOW TO PLAN THIS MEAL:

1 day before: Make lamb broth. Score, tie, and dry-brine lamb shoulder.

3 hours before: Braise lamb shoulder.

1 hour before: Blanch peas.

40 minutes before: Rest lamb.

10 minutes before: Slice and plate lamb. Make salad.

6

CRISP PORK BELLY BRAISED IN MILK

SERVES 8

Braising pork in milk is a classic Italian technique. While loin is most often employed, I think belly, a well-marbled cut, works better still. The cut's fat melts into the meat it laces, lending the sauce an over-the-top indulgence.

After cooking, the braised pork rests in its liquid overnight, to guarantee that the marriage between it and the milk is complete. Then we sear pieces off in a ripping hot pan, until the skin crackles and pops. Spring garlic, grassy and fresh, and a snap pea salad provide relief to an otherwise rich-on-rich pairing. While this is certainly not a dish for the faint of heart, the composition is balanced and elegant.

If you can find a bone-in belly, snatch it up—its nutty pork flavor is especially pronounced.

---

1 5-pound bone-in pork belly (if boneless, use 4 pounds)

Zest of 1 orange, removed in strips

7 fresh bay leaves

½ cup kosher salt

2 tablespoons sugar

5 tablespoons dry green peppercorns, toasted and roughly crushed

1 tablespoon fennel seeds, toasted and roughly crushed

1 tablespoon coriander seeds, toasted and roughly crushed

2 teaspoons ground nutmeg or mace

Olive oil, as needed

2 cups thinly sliced spring garlic or ½ cup thinly sliced garlic (2 heads)

2 cups finely diced fennel

1 cup finely diced celery

1 2-inch piece of lemongrass, bruised

1 lemon, zest removed in strips

2 quarts whole milk

Fine sea salt and freshly cracked black peppercorns

Chardonnay or cider vinegar to taste

SCORE AND DRY-BRINE THE PORK BELLY

Lay the pork belly skin side up on a clean work surface. Hold a razor blade or sharp paring knife at a 45-degree angle over the belly. Score the skin, running the blade at a diagonal from top to bottom, cutting just into the fat, not the meat. At this angle, continue making incisions about ¼ inch apart, making your way across the entire skin side.

Press down on the strips of orange peel and 5 of the fresh bay leaves with the broad side of a chef's knife to release their essential oils.

In a medium bowl, combine the kosher salt with the sugar, green peppercorns, fennel and coriander seeds, nutmeg, and pressed orange peel and bay leaves. Once well mixed, spread half of the salt mixture in a large roasting pan. Lay the belly on the salt and pour the remaining salt mixture over the meat. Thoroughly massage the salt into the pork's flesh, pressing it into the crevices, until the

meat feels roughed up. Transfer the pan to the refrigerator and let the belly rest, uncovered, for 2 days.

Remove the belly from the refrigerator and brush off the salt. Rinse off any remaining rub under cold running water and pat the belly dry. Place the belly on a cooling rack set over a rimmed baking sheet. Return the pork to the refrigerator and let it rest, uncovered, for 12 hours, or until the meat feels firm and tacky.

BRAISE THE BELLY

Remove the belly from the refrigerator and preheat the oven to 325°F.

Set a large heavy roasting pan over 2 side-by-side burners set to low heat. Brush the pork skin with 1 tablespoon olive oil and lay the belly in the pan skin side down. Once enough fat accumulates to slick the pan, increase the heat to medium and continue rendering the belly's fat for 12 minutes, or until it crisps and naturally releases from the pan. Stand back and use

a splatter guard to protect against sputtering fat while crisping the skin. Flip the belly and sear its underside for 8 minutes, or until it turns golden.

Transfer the rendered belly, skin side up, back to the cooling rack on the baking sheet. Loosely cover with aluminum foil and set aside.

Pour off all the accumulated fat from the roasting pan and wipe it completely clean. Set the pan back over the burners, both set to medium heat, and swirl in 3 tablespoons olive oil. Once the oil is shimmering-hot, stir in the garlic, fennel, celery, lemongrass, and 2 remaining bay leaves. Sauté the vegetables, scraping up any fond on the bottom of the pan, for 6 minutes, or until they begin to soften. Add the lemon peel and continue to sauté for 2 minutes more, or until the vegetables fully soften but pick up no color.

Return the belly, fat side up, to the pan and smear the sautéed vegetables all over the meat. Pour in enough milk to submerge two-thirds of the belly. Season the milk lightly with sea salt and black pepper.

Transfer the pan to the oven and braise the belly, uncovered, for 2½ hours, or until the thickest portion is easily pierced with the tip of a knife. Baste the belly every 30 minutes, and rotate the pan 180 degrees about halfway through cooking.

Once cooked, let the belly cool in the sauce for 1 hour at room temperature, or chill the pan by placing it in a sink of ice water. Cover and refrigerate the belly for 12 to 48 hours.

CLEAN AND PORTION THE BELLY

Remove the pan from the refrigerator. Lift the belly out of the liquid and wipe the meat clean.

Place the belly on a cutting board and cut it into 8 equal pieces, removing the bones if using a bone-in belly. With paper towels, wipe each piece clean, paying special attention to its fat side. Take a small sharp knife and, working with one piece at a time, scrape the belly's fat side until it is completely smooth and free of all milk residue. Repeat with the remaining belly pieces and set aside. Belly pieces can be cleaned and held in an airtight container in the refrigerator for up to 2 hours before serving, removing them at least 30 minutes before crisping.

MAKE THE MILK SAUCE

Remove the bay leaves and lemongrass from the braising liquid and discard. Spoon the liquid and vegetables into a blender or food processor and blend until completely smooth. Transfer the puree to a medium saucepan set over medium-low heat. Cook the sauce while stirring constantly for 5 minutes, or until it just warms through. Make sure the milk doesn't boil or it will scorch. Season the sauce with vinegar and sea salt and black pepper to taste. It

should be thick and taste bright but not vinegary. Hold the sauce, covered, in a warm place until ready to use.

CRISP THE BELLY AND SERVE

Set a large heavy sauté pan over medium-high heat. Slick the pan with 1 tablespoon olive oil. Once it is hot, lay 3 or 4 belly pieces, skin side down, in the pan, making sure not to crowd them. As the belly crisps it will sizzle and pop, so stand back and cover the pan with a splatter guard. After 5 to 7 minutes, once the fat puffs and crisps and releases easily from the pan, flip the pieces and sear the other side for 2 minutes, or until golden. Continue searing and rotating each piece until the belly is crisped all the way around and heated all the way through. Transfer the seared pieces, fat side up, to a cooling rack set over a rimmed baking sheet. Pour off all the fat from the pan and wipe it clean. Repeat the searing procedure with the remaining pieces.

To serve, spoon the warm milk sauce onto a large platter and arrange the belly pieces on top. Season the dish with a sprinkle of black pepper and a squeeze of lemon juice. If serving with Sugar Snap Peas with Celery and Shaved Mushrooms (recipe follows), arrange the seared celery hearts over the ribs so their blackened sides face up. Then, using both hands, scatter the dressed peas over the ribs. Garnish the plate with the mint and tarragon and shaved mushrooms.

SUGAR SNAP PEAS
WITH CELERY AND SHAVED MUSHROOMS

SERVES 8

Spring means ramps, spring garlic, and sugar snap peas. It's a bounty that rewards us for enduring what in New York always feels like an interminable winter. Once these ingredients finally show up at the farmer's market, for me, no task feels too laborious if it brings some freshness back into the kitchen. In making this salad, you must handle the snap peas individually. It is an exercise I am happy to lavish time on, so I'm hoping you won't mind, either.

4 bunches of celery

4 cups sugar snap peas

¼ cup olive oil

2 tablespoons lemon juice (from 1 lemon)

Fine sea salt and freshly cracked black peppercorns

1 cup whole mint leaves

Tarragon leaves, for garnish

6 small porcini mushrooms or 8 ounces other mushrooms, such as king trumpet or cremini

HOW TO PLAN THIS MEAL:

4–5 days before: Score and dry-brine pork belly.

2–3 days before: Dry belly.

1–2 days before: Braise belly.

2 hours before: Clean and portion belly. Puree milk sauce.

1 hour before: Clean and slice sugar snap peas. Temper pork.

20–30 minutes before: Warm and reseason milk sauce. Sear pork and celery. Arrange platter.

PREPARE THE VEGETABLES

Break off the outer ribs from the celery bunches until all that remains is their leafy, pale hearts. Reserve the ribs for another purpose.

Trim away the fibrous base of the hearts, making sure the bunches hold together. Halve the celery hearts lengthwise.

Working with 1 sugar snap pea at a time, peel away and discard the string that runs along the pea's larger arch. Carefully slice the peas lengthwise and place in a bowl. These can be prepared and refrigerated, covered by a damp paper towel, up to 1 hour in advance.

COOK AND ASSEMBLE

Set a large heavy sauté pan over medium-high heat and slick with 1 tablespoon of the oil. Once it is very hot, lay the halved celery hearts, cut side down, in the pan. Sear the hearts until browned and slightly tender, about 30 seconds. Remove from the heat.

Gently dress the peas with the remaining 3 tablespoons olive oil and season with the lemon juice and salt and pepper to taste.

If serving this salad as a garnish with the milk-braised pork belly (or any other protein), see the plating instructions in the preceding recipe.

If serving as a composed salad, arrange the celery hearts, seared side up, on a serving platter and sprinkle each with sea salt. Place the dressed peas in a mound around the hearts and scatter the mint and tarragon all around. Next, shave the mushrooms into paper-thin slices using a mandoline or sharp knife, and scatter the shavings over the salad. Serve immediately.

7

STOVETOP CASSOULET

SERVES 6

The classic cassoulet is a lusty stew of beans married to the flavors of cured pork and duck confit. It's crusty, hearty, salty, and funky—one of the truly great projects in cooking, especially if you choose to make all the sausages and duck confit yourself.

My version is a bit different from the French classic, though no less DIY or delicious. It pairs beans and confit duck legs as per the original. But, instead of slow-cooking the two together until tender, in this recipe they simmer quickly on the stovetop after being braised individually. Keeping the flavors separate until the very end, I find, maintains the ingredients' integrity. What emerges is looser, cleaner, and lighter than a classic cassoulet.

As for the braising liquid, it combines chicken broth with a smoky-sweet paste made with coarsely smashed blistered onions, tomatoes, and peppers. That paste thickens the simmering liquid and to me feels a bit Mexican in spirit, where vegetables are similarly blackened before turning into salsa.

Duck Leg Confit (recipe follows)

Braised Cranberry Beans, held in braising liquid (recipe follows)

2 medium spring onion bulbs

1 large tomato, halved equatorially

2 Italian long or finger hot peppers

2 garlic cloves

Kosher salt

¾ teaspoon finely grated lime zest (from 1 lime)

1 tablespoon olive oil

¼ cup coarse bread crumbs (see page 298)

1 tablespoon minced parsley stems

1 tablespoon duck fat

1 cup ¾-inch slices spicy pork sausage (see page 241)

1 cup ½-inch dice pancetta

6 cups Chicken Broth (page 288)

TEMPER THE CONFIT AND BEANS

Remove the duck legs and cranberry beans from the refrigerator and let come to room temperature.

CHAR THE ONION AND MAKE THE PEPPER-TOMATO PASTE

Halve the spring onions through their stem ends. Heat a large heavy sauté pan over medium-high heat until very hot. Lay the spring onion and tomato halves in the dry pan, cut sides down. Add the peppers.

Sear the tomato halves for 4 minutes, or until blackened. Turn and sear the reverse side until blackened in spots. Remove the tomato halves and set aside on a platter.

Continue to char and turn the peppers for 3 minutes more, or until blackened on all sides. Transfer to the platter with the tomato halves. Cover the plate with plastic wrap so the vegetables steam. Continue to char the onion, without flipping it, for 1 minute more, or until it blackens only on its cut side. Transfer the charred onion, cut side up, to a second plate and set it aside.

Working quickly with a paring knife, peel away the hot peppers' blistered skins and cut them open. Discard their skins, stems, and seeds. Peel and core the blistered tomato halves and discard the core. Return the peppers and tomato to the platter and re-cover with plastic wrap. Cut the charred onion halves into approximately 1-inch wedges. Cut away the root end of each wedge, so the layers are no longer connected. Separate the layers into individual petals and cover the plate with plastic wrap.

Using a large mortar and pestle or a food processor, smash or pulse the garlic and a generous pinch of salt together until a thick paste forms. Add the lime zest, half of the still-warm tomato, and all the peppers and continue smashing or pulsing everything together until a thick, chunky puree forms. Stir in the olive oil and season with salt. Set the paste aside. Cut the remaining tomato half into large chunks and set aside.

PULL THE DUCK MEAT OFF THE BONE

Lift the legs out of their fat. Scrape off as much of the fat from the duck legs as possible and set the fat aside for later use. Set the cleaned legs on a cutting board. Pull the skin off the legs and set it aside.

Next, carefully pull the meat off the bone, following the meat's natural seams, into plump, approximately 1-inch pieces, taking care not to shred the meat. Place the pulled meat in a medium bowl.

TOAST THE BREAD CRUMBS AND STRAIN THE BEANS

Spread the bread crumbs out in a heavy medium sauté pan set over low heat. Dry-toast the crumbs, tossing continuously, for 5 minutes, or until golden. Transfer the crumbs to a small bowl and stir in the minced parsley stems. Season the bread crumbs with salt to taste and set aside.

Strain the beans, reserving their cooking liquid. Discard the carrot, onion, celery, and bay leaf.

BUILD THE CASSOULET

Set a large Dutch oven over medium-high heat and stir in 1 tablespoon of duck fat. Once the fat sizzles, add the sausage rounds and brown on both sides, about 3 minutes. Transfer the sausage to a plate, leaving the drippings behind in the pot. Next, brown the pancetta in the pork drippings for 3 minutes, or until all sides turn light golden while the meat remains springy. Transfer the rendered pancetta to the plate with the sausage rounds. Then, lay in the duck skins, working in batches if necessary so as not to overcrowd the pan. Crisp the skins for 2 minutes on each side, or until golden brown on both sides. Transfer to a cutting board and julienne the skin. Place on the plate with the sausage and pancetta.

Spoon out half the fat from the pot, reserving it, and reduce the heat to medium. Add the drained beans to the pot and gently stir, scraping up all the fond. Pour in 1 cup of the reserved bean broth. Add enough chicken broth to cover the beans by 1/2 inch, bring the liquid to a steady, gentle simmer, and cook for 10 minutes. (You may not use all of the chicken broth.)

Stir the duck meat, julienned skin, browned sausage, and pancetta, along with all the plate's accumulated drippings, into the beans. Cook, stirring often, for 10 minutes, or until the meat heats through.

Stir the reserved roasted pepper–tomato paste into the cassoulet and simmer everything together for 2 minutes, or until aromatic. Add salt to taste or some of the reserved fat if the dish is a little lean.

FINISH AND SERVE

Remove the Dutch oven from the heat and quickly transfer its contents to a large 2- to 3-inch-deep pan, preferably a terra-cotta cazuela that can withstand heat, or a large cast-iron skillet. Pack the cassoulet into the dish and press the onion petals and reserved tomato pieces, ever so slightly, into the cassoulet's surface.

Place the pan over medium heat and bring everything up to a simmer until the cooking liquid tightens and thickens slightly, about 10 minutes. Scatter the reserved bread crumbs on top and serve immediately, directly from the hot pan.

DUCK LEG CONFIT

MAKES 6 DUCK LEGS

Duck confit is something of a braising offshoot. While purists may insist you need a water-based liquid to braise, this recipe lives here because I approach this confit process like a braise—first there is a brining step, then an air-dry, a thorough sear, a slow simmer, and finally a good rest.

As for the seasoning rubbed into the meat, since the pepper-tomato paste used to thicken the cassoulet reminds me of Mexico, the salt rub that flavors the meat looks there too. The Fresno chile, spices, and citrus zest perk up the duck with south-of-the-border charm.

---

10 garlic cloves, smashed and skins removed, plus 1 whole head, halved crosswise

2 Fresno chiles, finely grated

2 tablespoons dry green peppercorns

1 tablespoon fennel seeds

1 tablespoon coriander seeds

1 teaspoon finely grated orange zest (from ½ orange)

½ teaspoon finely grated lemon zest (from ½ lemon)

1 tablespoon sugar

¼ cup kosher salt

6 duck legs

4 cups duck fat, or as needed

½ red onion

15 fresh thyme sprigs

2 fresh bay leaves

DRY-BRINE THE DUCK LEGS

In a food processor or a large mortar and pestle, pulse or smash the 10 garlic cloves, the Fresno chiles, green peppercorns, fennel and coriander seeds, and orange and lemon zests until a damp paste forms. Transfer the mixture to a medium bowl and stir in the sugar and kosher salt.

Working over a roasting pan just large enough to hold the legs in one layer, rub the spiced salt mixture all over the legs, spending extra time and elbow grease to massage the rub deep into the legs' thickest portions. When properly rubbed, the meat should feel slightly frayed.

Arrange the legs so they fit snugly in the pan. Dry-brine the legs, uncovered, in the refrigerator for 24 hours.

Remove the legs from the refrigerator and brush off the salt rub, then rinse under cold water. Pat the legs very dry and arrange them on a cooling rack set over a rimmed baking sheet. Refrigerate the legs again, uncovered, for 12 hours, or until they feel very dry and tacky to the touch.

PREPARE THE FAT AND BROWN THE LEGS

Preheat the oven to 250°F. Place the duck fat in a medium saucepan and set it over medium-low heat until it melts. Turn off the heat and let the fat cool to just above room temperature. You want to keep the fat just warm enough to remain pourable.

Meanwhile, set a large Dutch oven over medium heat. Lay in as many of the duck legs as will fit comfortably in one layer, skin side down. When the legs' fat starts to render, increase the heat to medium-high and cook the legs for 7 minutes, or until the skins brown and easily release from the pot. Flip the legs and sear the meat side for 4 minutes, or until they brown. Transfer the legs to a warm platter, pour off most of the fat in the pan, and repeat the searing process with the remaining legs.

Pour off all but 1 tablespoon of the fat. Set the Dutch oven over medium-high heat. Once the fat is so hot it shimmers, lay in the onion half, cut side down. Sear the onion, without moving it, for 8 minutes, or until it chars and softens. Remove the pot from the heat and set the onion aside on a plate.

Return all the duck legs to the pot, arranging them so they fit in an even layer. Add the blackened onion, the thyme sprigs, split garlic head, and bay leaves to the pot. Carefully pour the warm duck fat over the legs and seasonings. Press down on the legs as needed to fully submerge them in fat.

CONFIT THE DUCK LEGS

Cut a piece of parchment paper to fit snugly inside the Dutch oven. Set the pot back over medium heat. Once

small bubbles start forming around the legs, carefully cover them with the parchment paper. Cover with the lid and slide the pot onto the oven's center rack.

Cook the duck legs for about 2 hours, until the meat plumps and shrinks down the bone; the top of the leg bones will be exposed, and the fattest portion of the meat should slide easily on the bone when prodded. Every 30 minutes while cooking, rotate the pot 90 degrees. When the legs are cooked through and the meat is bouncy-tender, carefully remove the pot from the oven.

NOTE: *Be careful when pinching the legs to check for doneness. The legs and the fat will be very hot.*

Discard the parchment paper. Using a slotted spoon, transfer the legs to a rimmed baking sheet to cool. Once the fat has cooled to room temperature but before it congeals, place the legs in a clean, lidded container and pour in the fat until they are completely submerged. Cover and rest the legs in the refrigerator for at least 12 hours; this will let the flavor of both the meat and the fat bloom. The legs will hold in the refrigerator, under fat, for up to 1 month.

BRAISED CRANBERRY BEANS

SERVES 4 TO 6

Fresh borlotti, or cranberry, beans are in farmer's markets in the early fall and late summer months. Pink and white speckled, these shell beans quickly lose their beautiful mottled pattern when braised, but the creamy earthiness they take on more than makes up for it.

I treat this humble bean with as much care as I lavish on the duck confit. A good bean, cooked to plump perfection, is just as essential to a great cassoulet, so make sure to cook these gently all the way through. To test for doneness, remove one bean from its liquid and gently press on it with the tines of a fork. With just a bit of pressure, the skin should burst and the soft interior should spill out.

Holding these beans in their cooking liquid once tender keeps them moist and extra soft. Dried cranberry beans will work instead of fresh, but they must be soaked overnight in two or three times their volume of water before cooking. Depending on how old they are, the dried and soaked beans will need a longer cooking time than fresh, perhaps an hour or so more.

---

2 tablespoons olive oil

1 red onion, halved equatorially

1 medium carrot, halved lengthwise

1 pound fresh cranberry or borlotti beans, shelled, or ¾ pound dried cranberry beans, soaked in water overnight and drained

1 large celery stalk

1 fresh bay leaf

Kosher salt

HOW TO PLAN THIS MEAL:

2 days before: Dry-brine duck legs. Soak dried beans, if using.

1 day before: Make duck confit and braised cranberry beans.

2 hours before: Temper duck and beans. Make pepper-tomato paste and bread crumbs. Pull duck meat.

1 hour before: Finish cassoulet.

Slick a medium heavy sauté pan with the olive oil and set over high heat. Once the oil is shimmering-hot, lay the onion and carrot halves, cut sides down, in the pan. Sear the carrot for 5 minutes, or until blackened on one side. Continue searing the onion until blackened all along its cut side, about 3 minutes more.

Place the beans, blackened vegetables, celery, and bay leaf in a large Dutch oven. Pour in enough water to cover the beans by 2 inches. Bring to a gentle simmer over medium heat. Skim the simmering liquid often during the first 10 minutes.

Cover the pot and lower the heat slightly to continue simmering the beans for 25 to 30 minutes (1 to 1½ hours for dried beans), or until they are tender and collapse when gently pressed with the tines of a fork. Throughout the cooking process, jostle and stir the beans to make sure they cook evenly, and keep an eye on the heat, adjusting it to make sure it maintains a gentle simmer. When the beans are fully tender, season with salt.

Remove the pot from heat, uncover, and let the beans cool to room temperature in their braising liquid. (This is best done by placing the pot in a sink filled with ice water.) Cover and refrigerate the beans in their liquid for 12 hours. Braised beans hold for up to 3 days in the refrigerator.

8

BLACK RICE WITH SQUID AND SAUSAGE

SERVES 6

Spanish paellas always look great. Served in huge, round, shallow dishes, the saffron-tinted rice brims with shellfish, artichokes, chicken, sausage, you name it . . . It's the sort of meal that encourages feasting in a dramatic, generous way. But, here's the rub: Something usually disappoints. Maybe the cooking liquid for the rice doesn't have much depth, or one element or another is either undercooked or overcooked, whether it is a mushy bite of rice or a tough piece of shellfish.

In this meal, good looks are matched with great taste. To guarantee big flavor, the braising liquid, a shrimp and prosciutto "tea," imbues every grain with a stunning, smoky-sweet jolt. It's the secret weapon that marries the pork to the squid, tying this paella together. Though the liquid is limited and ultimately disappears, that does not mean it isn't transformative. And so, with this ever-thinning pool of broth, what better way to introduce the practice of shallow braising?

You may need to look for black rice (it's the grain that colors this dish) in a specialty store, but it is worth the chase since it's super healthy and has a great, tense bite. My preferred variety comes from northern Italy, in the Po Valley near Milan. While most short-grain black or brown rices will do here, make sure not to buy Asian black sticky rice. That's a totally different grain and would end in a gooey disaster.

As for the braising vessel, terra-cotta cazuelas are best because their material conducts heat gently and keeps the grains moist. But, if you don't have one, a heavy, wide pan, like a cast-iron skillet or a Dutch oven, also does the job and ensures even cooking. What you want is a pan deep enough for the ingredients to pile up two to three inches high.

---

2 quarts water

½ cup kosher salt, plus more

2 cups ice

2 pounds whole squid, cleaned, heads and tentacles separated

2 or 3 whole canned Roma (plum) tomatoes

¼ cup olive oil, plus more for drizzling

2 pounds Italian sausage, skins pricked and cut into 2-inch links (see page 241)

2 medium red onions, finely diced

1 cup finely diced fennel plus ¼ small bulb fennel, thinly sliced or shaved crosswise

4 garlic cloves

1 teaspoon hot pepper flakes

½ teaspoon piment d'Espelette

3 tablespoons finely sliced fresh oregano leaves

2 cups short-grain black rice, preferably from Italy's Po Valley

1 quart Shrimp and Prosciutto Tea (recipe follows) or Dashi (page 286), warm

1 teaspoon finely grated Meyer lemon zest (from 1 lemon)

Meyer lemon juice to taste

2 tablespoons finely sliced fresh flat-leaf parsley leaves (optional)

2 tablespoons finely sliced fresh chives (optional)

BRINE THE SQUID

Pour the water into a deep container with ½ cup kosher salt and the ice. Submerge the squid in the brine and refrigerate for 2 hours.

Drain the squid and pat it very dry with paper towels. Transfer the squid to a paper towel–lined baking sheet and refrigerate.

BRAISE THE RICE

Preheat the oven to 375°F. Set a box grater in a wide, shallow bowl and grate the canned tomatoes on the medium holes until you get ½ cup pulp.

Set a high-walled, 12-inch cazuela, cast-iron skillet, or large Dutch oven over medium heat. Swirl in 2 tablespoons of the olive oil. Once it is shimmering-hot, add the sausages and gently brown the links on all sides for 8 minutes, or until the links are deep golden brown all over and the meat is half cooked. Set the seared sausages aside on a platter, leaving their drippings behind in the pan.

Reduce the heat to medium-low and swirl in the remaining 2 tablespoons olive oil. Stir in the onions, diced fennel, and garlic to dissolve all the fond in the pan. Gently sauté the vegetables for 15 minutes, or until they soften but do not color. Season lightly with salt. Stir in the hot pepper flakes, piment d'Espelette, and oregano. Sauté until aromatic, about 3 minutes. Stir in the reserved tomato pulp and gently simmer for 5 minutes, or until the pulp thickens and turns jammy.

Stir the rice into the pan and sauté the grains for 1 minute, or until coated in vegetable matter. Return the sausages and all their drippings to the pan, nestling the links into the rice.

Immediately pour in 3 cups of shrimp and prosciutto tea or dashi, raise the heat to medium-high, and bring the liquid up to a simmer. Taste the liquid for seasoning and add salt if necessary; this broth will season the grains so it should be flavorful but not salty.

Turn off the heat, spread out the grains, and carefully transfer the pan to the center rack of the oven. Cook the rice, uncovered, for about 40 minutes, or until the grains are al dente; check on the pan regularly and add extra splashes of prosciutto tea or water to keep the rice hydrated until the grains cook through. Rotate the pan 180 degrees halfway through to ensure even cooking.

Once the rice is just tender and there is just a little liquid pooling at the bottom of the rice, remove the pan from the oven. Press the squid into the rice, distributing it evenly around the pan. Return the pan to the oven for 5 minutes, or until the squid cooks through, the rice is fully cooked, and the liquid is absorbed.

FINISH AND SERVE

Garnish the rice with the Meyer lemon zest and a squeeze of Meyer lemon juice. Scatter the parsley and chives, if using, and sliced fennel all about and generously drizzle everything with olive oil. Serve immediately.

SHRIMP AND PROSCIUTTO TEA

MAKES ABOUT 2 QUARTS

This braising liquid is called a tea since it is more of an infusion than a stock. The gentle steeping of prosciutto trim and dried shrimp in dashi yields an elegant, nuanced broth. Many Italian delis are happy to sell prosciutto ends, and you can find dried shrimp in most Asian markets.

2 quarts Dashi (page 286)

½ pound prosciutto ends or trim, shaved or sliced very thin

1 cup whole dried shrimp

2 fresh bay leaves

1 tablespoon black peppercorns, toasted and cracked

2 dried chiles de árbol

Zest of 1 lemon, removed in strips with a vegetable peeler

MAKE THE TEA

In a medium pot, bring 1 quart of the dashi to a simmer, then remove from the heat. Place the shaved prosciutto in a deep, heatproof container. Pour the hot dashi over the prosciutto.

Cover the prosciutto dashi with plastic wrap and let infuse for 1 hour, or until a pronounced meaty scent blooms. Stir the dried shrimp, bay leaves, peppercorns, chiles, and lemon zest into the infusion.

Meanwhile, bring the remaining 1 quart dashi to a simmer and carefully pour it into the shrimp and prosciutto tea. Re-cover the container with plastic wrap and set it aside for 10 minutes, or until the aromatics infuse the broth.

STRAIN THE TEA

Line a sieve with cheesecloth and set it over the now-empty pot. Pour the broth through the sieve and press on the solids to extract as much flavor as possible. Use the shrimp and prosciutto tea immediately or cover and refrigerate for up to 1 day; you can also freeze it for up to 3 months.

HOW TO PLAN THIS MEAL:

2 days before: If making sausage, brine pork shoulder.

1 day before: Grind and stuff sausage, if making your own. Make shrimp and prosciutto tea.

4 hours before: Brine squid.

2 hours before: Prepare ingredients for rice.

1½ hours before: Braise rice.

9

BRAISED SNAPPER WITH GREMOLATA AND BEAN RAGU

SERVES 4

Now that we have entered the freewheeling world of shallow braising, where the cooking is done nearly as much by steam and direct contact with the pan as it is by hot liquid, let's dig a little deeper.

There are lots of reasons to shallow braise and in this dish we gently sear a whole snapper, then add a few splashes of cod broth to moisten and steam it through, protecting the fish's delicacy while producing a richly flavored pan sauce. Dusting the fish in flour before braising ensures that its exterior soaks up the pan's juices and enriches the stock.

This is a restrained method, cutting out the usual flavor-building steps between the crisping and the braising: no soffritto, tomato paste, or wine to complicate things. As a result, the sauce tastes clean and light, toeing the line between rustic and refined.

While some fish would turn mushy if braised, snapper, with its neutral flavor and slightly tense flesh, drinks up the moisture and turns all the better for it. Add only as much broth as will reduce to a thickened sauce by the time the fish is done. I also suggest spooning on some gremolata, a classic Italian sauce made with lemon, parsley, and garlic.

½ cup kosher salt, plus more to season

6 cups water

2 cups ice

1 3-pound whole snapper, scaled, cleaned, gutted, and gilled

5 fresh oregano sprigs

4 ¼-inch-thick Meyer lemon rounds, sliced from the center of the fruit

2 tablespoons Wondra or all-purpose flour

3 cups Cod Broth (page 292) or other fish broth

Olive oil, as needed

Gremolata (page 301)

BRINE AND STUFF THE SNAPPER

In a large, deep roasting pan, mix ½ cup kosher salt with the water and ice. Lay in the snapper and brine it, refrigerated, for 2 hours. If necessary, trim the fish's tail, without cutting into the snapper's meat, so the fish fits into the pan. If the fish is not fully submerged, add enough water to cover, plus an additional tablespoon of salt for every extra cup of water.

Press the oregano sprigs with the broad side of a chef's knife to release their essential oils. Remove the snapper from the brine and thoroughly pat it dry. Wipe the roasting pan dry as well. Lay the fish on a clean work surface and stuff its belly cavity with the oregano and lemon slices.

BRAISE THE SNAPPER

Cut a piece of parchment paper or foil to just fit inside the roasting pan. (If using foil, grease it thoroughly with butter or oil so it won't stick to the fish.)

Preheat the oven to 325°F. Gently dust the snapper all over with flour. Pour the cod broth into a medium saucepan set over medium-low heat. Bring the liquid up to a gentle simmer.

Place the roasting pan over 2 side-by-side burners set to medium-high heat. Swirl in enough olive oil to coat the pan with about ⅛ inch. Once the oil is shimmering-hot, lay in the snapper. Give the pan a shake so the fish doesn't stick. Cook the fish for 6 minutes, or until it easily releases from the pan and has turned golden and crispy. If the

flour browns too fast, reduce the heat to prevent burning. Using a spatula and your free hand, carefully flip the fish. Sear the reverse side for 4 minutes, or until golden brown.

Slowly pour in the fish broth until a third of the fish is submerged in liquid. You may not use all of the broth. Bring the broth up to a steady simmer while gently basting the snapper.

Cover the fish with the parchment. Slide the roasting pan onto the oven's center rack and gently braise for 20 minutes, or until the flesh is flaky and just cooked through. The best place to check for doneness is just behind the head; if that meat gives easily when prodded,

the fish is done. About 10 minutes into cooking, pull out the pan, lift up the parchment, and baste the snapper with the pan juices. Re-cover the pan, rotate it 180 degrees, and return to the oven. When the fish is done the bottom of the pan should be covered in enriched, reduced broth.

SERVE

Remove the roasting pan from the oven. Using two spatulas, carefully transfer the whole snapper to a large, warm serving platter. Spoon the pan drippings all over the fish. Fillet the fish at the table and serve it with Bean Ragu (recipe follows) and Gremolata (page 301) alongside.

BEAN RAGU

SERVES 4 TO 6 (MAKES ABOUT 6 CUPS)

To get dried beans to cook up plump and creamy, it is essential that they rehydrate in water until they expand and fill their skins. A bit of baking soda in the soaking water helps them along, guaranteeing proper softening. It's an old-school trick I picked up from Richard Olney.

Once simmered, the beans then rest in their liquid, like most proper braises should, to guarantee tenderness. Just before serving, they simmer again with a blanched soffritto. This procedure, really a bean ragu deconstruction and reassembly, keeps the flavors distinct. My preferred bean for this recipe is the risina, a small, earthy white bean from Umbria. But any small white bean, like rice or navy, will work. I also love to use black-eyed peas, a Southern mainstay, whose earthy, aromatic flavor plays beautifully with braised meats and fish.

---

2 cups dried risina, navy beans, or black-eyed peas

1 teaspoon baking soda

Zest of ½ lemon, removed in strips with a vegetable peeler

10 fresh thyme sprigs

3 garlic cloves

Kosher salt

¼ cup finely diced red onion

2 tablespoons finely diced carrot

2 tablespoons finely diced celery

1 tablespoon finely sliced fresh chives

1 tablespoon finely sliced fresh flat-leaf parsley leaves

Olive oil, for drizzling

SOAK THE BEANS

Place the beans in a deep container and cover with 6 cups water. Stir in the baking soda, refrigerate, and let soak for 24 hours, or until the beans swell and fill their skins.

BRAISE THE BEANS

Drain the beans and rinse them under cold water. Transfer the beans to a medium Dutch oven or large saucepan and add fresh water to cover by 2 inches.

Press on the lemon strips with the broad side of a chef's knife to release their essential oils. Toss the lemon zest, thyme, and garlic into the pot. Set over medium heat and bring the water to a steady, gentle simmer.

Simmer the beans, uncovered, for 45 minutes, or until they are tender but fully intact. Add extra water as needed

so the beans are always covered by at least 1 inch of liquid. Season the cooked beans to taste with salt, then let cool and rest in the braising liquid for at least 3 hours. These can be made 1 day in advance and stored in the refrigerator.

FINISH THE BEANS

Bring a small pot of water to a boil over medium-high heat. Salt the water until it tastes like the ocean. Set up an ice bath next to the stove.

Blanch the onion, carrot, and celery until brightly colored, about 30 seconds. Transfer the vegetables to a strainer and submerge the strainer in the ice bath. When the vegetables are cool, lift them out, shake them dry, and transfer to a small bowl.

(recipe continues)

Set a colander over a large bowl and pour the beans through the colander, catching the cooking liquid in the bowl. Discard the garlic, thyme, and lemon peel. Scoop out ½ cup of the beans and mash them in a small bowl with a few splashes of the reserved cooking liquid until a thick, uniform paste forms.

Set the bean cooking pot back over medium heat. Add the strained beans, 1 cup of the reserved bean cooking liquid, and the bean paste. Bring everything up to a simmer. Taste and season with salt.

Once the beans are heated through and the cooking liquid tightens slightly, stir in the blanched vegetables. Simmer the ragu for 2 minutes. Taste and adjust seasoning with salt if necessary. Turn off the heat and stir in the chives and parsley. Drizzle the beans with a generous amount of olive oil and serve.

HOW TO PLAN THIS MEAL:

1 day before: Soak beans and make cod broth and gremolata.

5 hours before: Braise beans.

3 hours before: Brine snapper.

1 hour before: Dry and stuff snapper.

45 minutes before: Braise snapper and finish braised beans.

10

WINTERTIME CLAMS IN AVOCADO-CHILE BUTTER

SERVES 4

Winter clams are typically chubbier and more saline than their summer relatives. In this recipe, their extra-rich juices get put to good use. Once coaxed out of their shells, they provide this dish with its braising liquid and much of its character. Only a splash of water is added to help these clams steam-braise.

Rounding out the clam's briny drippings is a rich avocado butter. Once emulsified, it injects a lush, vegetal quality to the sauce. The trick to nailing the emulsifying process is moderate heat, whisking in the butter incrementally to form a smooth sauce, and taking it off the heat as soon as it's done.

This is a shallow, quick braise at its most elemental: tender "meat," a clever sauce, and nothing else. Well, except for some grated chorizo and serrano chile oil, because what's better than clams with a little salty, spicy spicy pork?

It is important to steam the clams open in a single, even layer. Using a wide pan instead of a tall pot helps keep the steam in dense contact with the clams.

Serve these clams with lots of crusty bread to soak up the sauce and a hearty salad, such as Year-Round Chicory Salad (page 179) or Charred Escarole with Spicy Brown Butter–Hazelnut Vinaigrette (page 245).

---

2 quarts water

½ cup kosher salt

2 cups ice

4 pounds littleneck clams, scrubbed clean

1 ounce dry-cured Spanish chorizo (optional)

2 tablespoons olive oil

¾ cup Avocado-Chile Butter (recipe follows), chilled

2 tablespoons Meyer lemon juice (from 1 Meyer lemon)

Fine sea salt

2 tablespoons thinly sliced fresh chives

Serrano Chile Oil (page 294), for finishing

¼ orange, for finishing

CLEAN AND BRINE THE CLAMS

Pour the water into a large, deep container that will fit in the refrigerator. Stir in the kosher salt. Once dissolved, stir in the ice. Add the clams and refrigerate for 3 hours.

Fill a second deep container with cold water. Remove the clams from the brine, making sure their sediment stays behind, and transfer to the fresh water bath. Shake to dislodge any remaining grit. Transfer the clams to a colander. These can hold in the refrigerator for 1 hour.

BRAISE THE CLAMS

If using, place the chorizo in the freezer to make it easy to grate later.

Heat a large, heavy, lidded pan over medium-high heat. (Prior to cooking, see if all the clams will fit in one layer; if not, work in batches, dividing the olive oil and water accordingly. However, you can likely combine the batches of clam drippings and finish the sauce all at once.)

Swirl in the olive oil, and when shimmering-hot, add the clams. Stir to coat the shells in oil, then shake the pan to arrange the clams into an even single layer. Pour 1 cup water into the pan and cover with the lid. Steam-braise the clams for 5 to 7 minutes, or until their shells fully open.

(recipe continues)

With a slotted spoon, quickly transfer the clams to a large bowl, leaving all the drippings behind in the pan. If some clams are more stubborn, remove the opened ones, cover the pan, and steam the closed ones for another minute or two. If they still don't open, discard them.

EMULSIFY THE AVOCADO BUTTER AND SERVE

Lower the heat to maintain a gentle simmer. Vigorously whisk in the chilled avocado butter a few tablespoons at a time. Add more butter to the pan only when the previous addition has emulsified. Stop whisking once all the butter is incorporated and the sauce is thick enough to coat the back of a spoon. Season with lemon juice and sea salt, remembering that the clams themselves are salty. Return the clams to the pan and toss just to heat them through again. Remove from the heat and stir in the chives.

Serve immediately, garnishing the clams with a healthy drizzle of serrano chile oil, a squeeze of fresh orange juice, and a fine grating of chorizo on top.

AVOCADO-CHILE BUTTER

MAKES ABOUT 1 CUP

This compound butter takes advantage of avocado's addictive fatty, creamy qualities.

1 small garlic clove

1 serrano chile, stemmed

1 very ripe avocado, halved and pitted

½ teaspoon grated lime zest

¼ pound butter (1 stick), softened

Finely grate the garlic and chile into a medium bowl. Working over the bowl, push the avocado's flesh through a potato ricer or use a spatula to push it through a coarse sieve. Fold in the lime zest until everything is just incorporated.

In a stand mixer fitted with a paddle attachment, beat the butter on low speed for 1 minute, or until it becomes smooth. With the machine running, add half the avocado puree and continue beating for 1 minute, or until just incorporated. Add the second half of the puree and beat 1 minute more, or until fully incorporated.

Scrape the butter onto waxed paper and wrap it into a cylinder. Refrigerate the avocado butter for 3 hours, or until firm. Frozen butter keeps for 1 month wrapped in waxed paper and plastic.

HOW TO PLAN THIS MEAL:

3 days before: Make serrano chile oil.

3½ hours before: Brine clams and make avocado butter.

20 minutes before: Braise clams and assemble dish.

11

SUMMER CLAMS IN CORN MILK WITH FRESH CORN RELISH

SERVES 4

Braises are rarely thought of in midsummer, when we need something fresh, fast, and light. But that is precisely what this recipe provides, plus the depth that comes from marrying a sweet cooking liquid—in this case corn milk, the juice of fresh corn kernels—to briny clams. Once the dairy-free milk cooks down with the clams' juices, the soupy sauce becomes sweet, salty, unctuous, sharp, and a touch creamy, thanks to the starch and sugar in the corn milk. The raw corn relish, spiked with chile, brings pop and texture.

This is great with crusty bread to soak up the juices and a lean, flavorful vegetable, like the Grilled Zucchini with Fried Shallot Bread Crumbs (page 226).

---

2 quarts water

½ cup kosher salt

2 cups ice

4 pounds littleneck clams

1 large ear of sweet corn, shucked

2 teaspoons olive oil

1 red Fresno chile, stemmed and sliced into thin rings

1 tablespoon plus 2 teaspoons sliced fresh chives

1 tablespoon plus 2 teaspoons finely sliced fresh flat-leaf parsley leaves

Fine sea salt

2 tablespoons lime juice (from 1 lime), or to taste

4 tablespoons (½ stick) butter

2 tablespoons finely diced shallots

3 cups Corn Milk (recipe follows)

White peppercorns, toasted and freshly cracked

CLEAN AND BRINE THE CLAMS

Pour the water into a large, deep pot. Stir in the kosher salt and ice. Add the clams and brine them in the refrigerator for 3 hours.

Fill a second deep container with cold water. Remove the clams from the brine, making sure their sediment stays behind, and transfer them to the fresh water bath. Shake to dislodge any remaining grit. Transfer the clams to a colander. Refrigerate until ready to use, up to 1 hour.

MAKE THE RELISH

Trim the top and bottom off the shucked corn. Hold the ear straight up on a work surface. With a sharp or serrated knife, cut off the kernels. Try to keep the kernels as close to whole as possible.

Transfer the kernels to a small bowl and toss with the olive oil, chile, 2 teaspoons of the chives, 2 teaspoons of the parsley, and sea salt and lime juice to taste. Let the relish stand for at least 10 minutes at room temperature.

BRAISE THE CLAMS

Heat a large, heavy, lidded pan over medium-low heat. (Prior to cooking, see if all the clams will fit in one layer; if not, work in batches, dividing the butter, shallots, and corn milk accordingly.)

Swirl in 2 tablespoons of the butter. Once it begins to foam, add the shallots and gently sweat for 3 minutes, or until translucent but not colored.

Increase the heat to high and add the clams. Stir to coat the shells in butter and shake the pan to arrange the clams in a snug single layer. Cover the pan and steam the clams for 3 to 5 minutes, or until their shells *just* open. If you smell browning butter, take a peek—if no clams have opened to release juice and produce steam, add a few splashes of water and re-cover the pan to help them along.

With a slotted spoon, quickly transfer the clams to a large bowl, leaving their drippings in the pan. If some clams are more stubborn, remove the opened ones, cover the pan, and steam the

closed clams for another minute or two. If they still don't open, discard them. Repeat with the remaining clams, if necessary.

Immediately reduce the heat to medium and pour the corn milk into the pan. Simmer, whisking frequently, for 8 minutes, or until the milk thickens. Whisk the remaining 2 tablespoons butter into the corn milk and, once it is melted, return all the cooked clams to the pan. While tossing to coat, finish braising the clams, uncovered, for 1 to 2 minutes more, or until their shells fully open and the meat firms slightly.

Remove the pan from the heat and stir in the remaining 1 tablespoon chives and 1 tablespoon parsley. Season with more lime juice, sea salt, and pepper to taste. The braising liquid should toe the line between sweet, briny, and creamy. Serve immediately, garnished with the corn relish.

CORN MILK

MAKES ABOUT 3 CUPS

This vegan "milk" captures the explosive sweetness of perfect summer corn. It couldn't be more straightforward: Saw off the kernels and juice them. A healthy, vegetal alternative to dairy or cream, corn milk can be used in a host of other dishes, bringing flavor and an ability to thicken when cooked. (It's where cornstarch comes from, after all.) Imagine this stirred into a clam chowder or polenta or . . . play around and see.

8 large ears of sweet corn, shucked

Trim the tops and bottoms off the corn. Hold one ear straight up on a clean work surface. With a sharp or serrated knife, cut off the kernels. Repeat with the remaining ears. Place the kernels in a large bowl. Working over the bowl, hold the blade of your knife across the now-kernel-less cobs, as if you were about to cut through them, and scrape all the way down to dig out any remaining juices.

If you have a juicer, juice the corn kernels. Otherwise, using a food processor or blender, puree the kernels for 2 minutes, or until evenly smooth and soupy. Working over a bowl, pass the corn puree through a sieve and press down on the solids to extract as much liquid as possible. Discard the solids. Use the milk immediately or refrigerate for up to 3 hours.

HOW TO PLAN THIS MEAL:

$3\frac{1}{2}$ hours before: Brine clams. Make corn milk.

30 minutes before: Drain clams and make corn relish.

20 minutes before: Braise clams and garnish.

12

CHICKEN LEGS BRAISED IN PEPERONATA

SERVES 4 TO 6

When the farmer's market fills with summer fruits and vegetables, the possibilities seem endless. It's an abundance that makes me giddy, and this recipe, built on sweet peppers, springs from that enthusiasm. As with the clams in the two previous recipes, part of the braising liquid comes from one of the dish's main elements itself, in this case sweet red peppers.

Peperonata is a traditional Italian stew of peppers; here, we intentionally over-crowd a pot with red pepper, onion, and garlic so that they wilt into their own juices. Once the vegetables are nice and soupy, we nestle in some browned chicken legs so everything cooks down together. The pepper juice is lean, vegetal, and sweet, and it makes for an unexpected braising liquid. This is rustic, seasonal eating at its best.

---

2 quarts water

½ cup kosher salt, plus more

2 fresh bay leaves

½ cup fresh oregano sprigs

½ cup fresh flat-leaf parsley stems

1½ lemons

2 tablespoons dark honey

1 head of garlic, halved crosswise

2 tablespoons black peppercorns, toasted and lightly crushed, plus more for seasoning

6 whole chicken legs, skin on (about 3 pounds total)

3 tablespoons olive oil

1 tablespoon butter

5 large red bell peppers, cored and finely julienned

3 large red onions, sliced very thin

8 garlic cloves, grated fine

1½ pounds beefsteak tomatoes, halved

2 tablespoons finely chopped fresh oregano leaves

1 teaspoon hot pepper flakes

½ teaspoon piment d'Espelette or hot paprika (optional)

2 tablespoons red wine vinegar

1 tablespoon finely grated orange zest (from 1 orange)

⅓ cup orange juice (from 1 orange)

BRINE THE LEGS

Pour the water into a large container and stir in the kosher salt. Press the bay leaves, oregano sprigs, and parsley stems with the broad side of a chef's knife to release their essential oils. Squeeze the lemons into the brine and add the lemon rinds as well, along with the herbs, honey, garlic head, and peppercorns. Stir to combine. Submerge the legs in the brine and refrigerate for 12 to 24 hours.

Remove the chicken from the brine and pat the legs very dry. Arrange the meat in one layer on a cooling rack set over a rimmed baking sheet. Transfer the meat to the refrigerator and let it rest, uncovered, for 12 to 24 hours, or until the skin feels tacky.

BRAISE THE LEGS

Season the legs lightly with salt and cracked pepper.

(recipe continues)

Warm a large Dutch oven over medium-high heat and swirl in the olive oil. (If you will need to work in batches to avoid overcrowding the pot, divide the oil accordingly.) Once the oil shimmers, lay the chicken in the pot, skin side down. Reduce the heat to medium and sear both sides at a moderate sizzle, for 10 minutes total, or until the skin and meat turn a deep golden brown.

Pour off all the fat from the pot, leaving the caramelized fond in place. Set the pot back over medium-low heat and swirl in the butter. Once it melts, add the peppers, onions, and grated garlic. Sweat the vegetables, which will overcrowd the pot, while stirring and scraping up the fond. Gently cook the peperonata for 20 minutes, or until the peppers turn very soft but pick up no color.

While the vegetables cook down, grate the tomatoes by rubbing their cut sides on the medium holes of a box grater set over a wide, shallow bowl. Discard the skins.

Stir the oregano, hot pepper flakes, and piment d'Espelette, if using, into the pot. Next, stir in the vinegar, grated tomato, and orange zest and juice. Gently simmer over medium heat for 2 minutes. Taste and season lightly with salt if the liquid tastes flat, but remember that it will reduce, concentrating the salt.

Return the legs to the pan, snuggling them into the peppers. Spoon the peppers over the legs and pour in just enough water to cover the legs three-fourths of the way, about 1 cup.

Gently simmer the legs, uncovered, while basting them regularly. After 35 to 40 minutes, once the thigh meat easily slides on its bone, turn off the heat. Let the legs cool in the peperonata until they come to room temperature. Cooling is best done by placing the pot in a sink filled with ice water.

Cover the pot and refrigerate for 12 to 24 hours. (You can serve the chicken now, but it's much better the following day.)

REWARM AND SERVE

Remove the pot from the refrigerator and uncover. If any fat is congealed on the surface of the braise, skim it off. Set the pot over medium heat and gently bring the liquid up to a simmer. Gently simmer until the legs heat through to the bone, but be careful not to cook the chicken much further; you want the meat to still have a little bounciness.

To serve, distribute the braised chicken legs and peperonata among plates. Serve with fresh bread or Herbed Potatoes with Preserved Lemon (recipe follows) alongside.

HERBED POTATOES WITH PRESERVED LEMON

SERVES 4 TO 6

These potatoes are simple indeed. Boiled until tender, they're tossed with good butter, herbs, and, for an intriguing aroma, a touch of preserved lemon peel. When cut, their thin skins snap and a pearly interior, just the tiniest bit sweet and seasoned straight through, reveals itself.

---

2 pounds small Yukon Gold potatoes, scrubbed clean but unpeeled

Kosher salt

4 tablespoons (½ stick) butter, softened to room temperature

2 tablespoons finely sliced fresh flat-leaf parsley leaves

2 tablespoons finely sliced fresh oregano leaves

1 tablespoon finely sliced Preserved Lemons (page 302)

½ teaspoon agave or honey

Freshly cracked black peppercorns, to season

BOIL THE POTATOES

Place the potatoes in a large, wide pot and add cold water to cover by 2 inches. Season with salt until the water tastes of the sea. Bring the water to a simmer over medium-high heat, then reduce the heat to medium-low and gently simmer the potatoes for 20 to 25 minutes, or until they are easily pierced with the tip of a knife. Drain the potatoes and shake off the excess water.

DRESS THE POTATOES

While the potatoes boil, mix the butter with the parsley, oregano, preserved lemon peel, and agave in a large serving bowl.

Place the dry, hot potatoes in the bowl and toss until coated with melted butter. Season with salt and freshly cracked pepper. Serve immediately.

HOW TO PLAN THIS MEAL:

2–3 days before: Brine legs.

36–48 hours before: Dry legs.

1 day before: Braise legs.

30 minutes before: Rewarm legs and make potatoes.

13

RICOTTA GNUDI AND BRAISED SPRING VEGETABLES

SERVES 6 TO 8

Gnudi, pronounced *nu-dee*, is what Italians call pillow-soft ricotta dumplings. The word actually does mean "naked," and the reason for that is twofold. The first is that these dumplings are reminiscent of ricotta ravioli, minus their pasta cloak. The second is that they are best enjoyed in the buff, wearing nothing more than a slick of butter sauce.

Making these gnudi is a trip; you don't have to make a dough with flour. Once formed, the dumplings sit in a bed of semolina overnight. The flour drinks up the ricotta's moisture, and a thin skin forms around the gnudi, encasing the creamy interior.

I love to serve these with a mix of braised spring vegetables: crispy olive oil–cured artichokes, leeks cooked in orange juice, and baby favas braised in a cheese broth. The dumplings anchor this generous spread, and the mixed vegetables invite diners to choose their own adventure—"dressing" their gnudi as they see fit.

1 quart whole-milk Fresh Ricotta (page 312)

2 large eggs

2 large egg yolks

1 cup finely grated Parmesan, plus more for garnish

Kosher salt and freshly cracked black peppercorns

1 teaspoon roughly chopped fresh thyme leaves

2 teaspoons finely grated lemon zest (from about 2 lemons; Meyer lemons preferred)

½ teaspoon finely grated nutmeg

1½ pounds semolina flour

½ pound (2 sticks) butter, diced and chilled

DRAIN THE RICOTTA

Set a fine-mesh strainer lined with damp cheesecloth over a container deep enough to suspend the strainer. Scoop the ricotta into the strainer and set a few small plates over the cheese. The plates will apply pressure and help the ricotta drain. Refrigerate the ricotta until much of its liquid is pressed out and the strained cheese has the density of a fresh goat cheese—soft and a little crumbly, breakable, and spreadable—about 24 hours. (The whey makes a fine braising liquid.)

MAKE THE GNUDI DOUGH

Place the drained ricotta in a large bowl, so it forms a small mound. The ricotta should occupy only half the bowl, affording you plenty of work space.

Create a 4-inch-wide well in the top of the ricotta. Place the eggs, yolks, Parmesan, 1 teaspoon salt, 1 teaspoon cracked peppercorns, the thyme leaves, 1 teaspoon of the lemon zest, and the nutmeg into the well. With a spatula, gently fold the ricotta over and into these ingredients until evenly combined. Do not overmix or the ricotta's curds will lose their soft mouthfeel.

FORM THE GNUDI

Line a large rimmed baking sheet with parchment paper. Shake ¾ pound, or about 3 cups, of the semolina across the paper. Scoop about 1½ tablespoons of the ricotta mixture from the bowl. Slide the spoonful onto the semolina. Repeat, spacing the dumplings about ½ inch apart in a single layer, until all the ricotta mixture is used up. You should have about 50 dumplings.

(recipe continues)

Next, dust clean, dry hands with semolina. Working with one dumpling at a time, gently roll each dollop of ricotta between your hands into a ball. Return the balls to their former place on the semolina. Dust your hands with extra semolina as needed.

Pour the remaining semolina over the gnudi, making sure all dumplings are evenly and thoroughly coated in the flour. Refrigerate the dumplings, uncovered, for 24 hours, or until they are firm to the touch and do not dent when gently prodded.

BOIL THE WATER AND MAKE THE BUTTER SAUCE

Remove the gnudi from their semolina covering and place them on a clean rimmed baking sheet. If you want to repurpose the semolina flour, sift it, transfer to a clean container, and store in the freezer.

Fill a large pot with well-salted water— it should taste distinctly but pleasantly salty—and bring to a boil over high heat.

Meanwhile, make the butter sauce. Set a small saucepan over high heat. Pour in ¼ inch of water. When the water begins to boil, reduce the heat to low and whisk in the chilled butter, 2 tablespoons at a time. Add more butter only when the previous addition has emulsified. Once all the butter is fully incorporated and the sauce thickens enough to coat the back of a spoon, remove it from the heat, add the remaining 1 teaspoon lemon zest, and season with salt to taste.

Fill a medium sauté pan with hot water. Place the saucepan with the butter sauce in the hot water to keep the sauce warm, off direct heat. If necessary, occasionally remove the saucepan, reheat the water, and replace the saucepan to keep the sauce warm. (Setting the butter sauce over direct heat may cause it to separate.)

COOK THE GNUDI

Drop a third of the gnudi into the pot of boiling water. Cook the gnudi at a steady but not too aggressive simmer for 5 minutes, or until the dumplings rise to the surface and their interiors are fluffy. Do not let any dumpling bob for more than 30 seconds or it will overcook and the ricotta will toughen. With a slotted spoon, transfer the poached gnudi to a large warm platter. If the gnudi are too wet, gently blot them dry with a kitchen towel. Repeat with the remaining gnudi.

DRESS THE GNUDI AND SERVE

Pour the warm butter sauce over the hot dumplings and season them with pepper and Parmesan lashings. Serve the gnudi platter immediately with Seared Oil-Cured Baby Artichokes, Leeks Braised with Oranges, and Young Favas Braised in Parmesan-Pecorino Broth (all recipes follow) alongside.

SEARED OIL-CURED BABY ARTICHOKES

**SERVES 6 TO 8 WITH GNUDI;
4 AS A STAND-ALONE SIDE**

Truth be told, most of the time I find preserved artichokes a bit soggy. That is why in this recipe I introduce textural contrast by caramelizing them before serving. The final touch: a sprinkling of almonds and parsley.

Technically, these artichokes aren't braised; though I think of this poach-preserve-and-sear technique as a close cousin, just in the opposite order of operations. The artichokes are first blanched and then submerged in olive oil, so they drink up the oil's raw, grassy, unaltered flavor (it pays to use a good oil here). The final sear gives them crispness and a rich caramelized edge.

3½ lemons

16 baby artichokes

Kosher salt

6 fresh thyme sprigs

1 quart olive oil, plus more as needed

½ cup Marcona almonds

1 tablespoon finely sliced fresh flat-leaf parsley leaves

PREPARE THE ARTICHOKES

Fill a large bowl with ice water. Halve 2 of the lemons, squeeze their juices into the ice bath, then toss in the squeezed halves.

With a sharp paring knife, cut off the top ½ to 1 inch of each artichoke, exposing the tender interior. Peel back the tough, dark outer leaves. Once only tender and pale green leaves remain, pare the artichoke's base, where its leaves were snapped off, until smooth.

Trim ¼ to ½ inch from the stem end, until it feels moist. With the tip of your knife or a vegetable peeler, cut away the stringy exterior from the stem of the artichoke, beginning at the base of the heart and carefully running down along its curve and onto the stem. Immediately place the peeled artichoke in the lemon water. Repeat the peeling procedure with the remaining artichokes.

BLANCH AND MARINATE

Bring a stockpot filled with salted water to a rolling boil over high heat. Just before blanching, taste the water to make sure it tastes like the ocean.

Remove the artichokes from the lemon water and blanch them for 3 to 5 minutes, or until they are brightly colored and their stems are easily pierced with the tip of a paring knife. Drain the artichokes and set them on a paper towel–lined plate.

Pat the artichokes dry and let them cool for about 10 minutes. Transfer the artichokes to a wide, lidded container and arrange them in a snug, single layer with their stems facing up.

With a vegetable peeler, remove the zest from 1 lemon in strips. Add the thyme sprigs and zest to the artichokes. Pour enough olive oil into the container to cover the artichokes completely.

Once the artichokes are completely cool, cover with the lid and refrigerate. Let them marinate for at least 2 days. Oil-cured artichokes will keep up for to 2 weeks in the refrigerator.

FINISH AND SERVE

Remove the artichokes from the refrigerator and let them come to room temperature. Remove them from the marinade, leaving as much olive oil behind as possible. Halve the artichokes lengthwise through their hearts and stems.

Set a large heavy sauté pan over medium-high heat. Once hot, slick the pan with 2 tablespoons of the artichoke-infused oil. Working in batches, lay the artichokes in the pan cut side down. Sear for 3 minutes, or until their cut sides richly caramelize.

Arrange the seared artichokes, cut side up, on a platter and scatter the almonds and parsley on top. Garnish with the finely grated zest of the remaining lemon half. Just before serving, season the artichokes with lemon juice (from the lemon half) and salt. Serve the artichokes warm or at room temperature.

HOW TO PLAN THIS MEAL:

2 days before: Make ricotta, if using homemade. Drain ricotta. Oil-cure artichokes.

1 day before: Make gnudi dough and form gnudi.

3 hours before: Make Parmesan broth and toast bread crumbs.

2 hours before: Braise favas. Braise leeks. Sear and dress artichokes. Arrange vegetables on separate platters and let stand at room temperature.

20 minutes before: Make butter sauce.

10 minutes before: Poach and dress gnudi.

LEEKS BRAISED WITH ORANGES

SERVES 6 TO 8 WITH GNUDI; 4 AS A STAND-ALONE SIDE
These spring leeks braise in orange juice and zest, under orange slices, until their mild flavor melds with the fruit's sweet acidity. The juice becomes a sweet-tart glaze for the buttery, delicate leeks.

4 medium leeks, light and pale green parts only

3 tablespoons olive oil, plus more for drizzling

2 oranges

2 fresh bay leaves

1 Thai bird chile or other medium-hot, small red chile, stemmed and thinly sliced into rounds

½ teaspoon dry green peppercorns, toasted and lightly crushed

Fine sea salt

CLEAN THE LEEKS

Halve the leeks lengthwise and trim away their root ends, making sure to keep the stems intact. Fill a large bowl with warm water and submerge the leeks, cut sides down. Shake the leeks vigorously, freeing their grit.

Fill a large bowl with ice water, and add the leeks. Chill for 5 minutes. Pat dry.

SEASON AND BRAISE THE LEEKS

Swirl 2 tablespoons of the olive oil in a large, high-walled skillet set over medium-high heat. Once the oil is shimmering-hot, lay in as many leeks as will fit comfortably in one layer, cut sides down. Sear the leeks for 3 to 5 minutes, or until golden. Flip the leeks and sear for 1 minute, or until lightly caramelized. Repeat with the remaining leeks if necessary.

Finely grate the zest of 1 orange and juice it into a small bowl; you should get about 1 tablespoon zest and ⅓ cup juice. Set the juice aside. Thinly slice the other orange into rounds. Return all the leeks to the skillet, arranging them in a snug single layer. Evenly scatter the bay leaves, chile slices, green peppercorns, and orange zest over the leeks. Pour the fresh orange juice, ½ cup water, and the remaining tablespoon of olive oil into the pan. The leeks should be nearly covered; if not, add more water. Season with salt. Arrange the orange rounds over the leeks. Cover the pan with a lid or foil, leaving it slightly open.

Set the pan over low heat. Bring the liquid up to a gentle simmer and braise the leeks for 30 minutes, or until they are completely soft but retain their shape. Periodically baste the leeks and re-cover the pan. Toward the end of the braising time, check in more regularly; if the leeks are almost tender but the liquid looks too dry (it should be a nice syrupy reduction), add a few splashes of water to stretch the sauce. When the leeks are fully tender, the juice and zest should cling to them, coating them in a pulpy syrup. Taste, and adjust the salt if necessary. Serve warm or at room temperature with a drizzle of olive oil.

YOUNG FAVAS BRAISED IN PARMESAN-PECORINO BROTH

SERVES 6 TO 8 WITH GNUDI; 4 AS A STAND-ALONE SIDE

When small and young, favas needn't be peeled once shelled. However, the window in early spring when they are at this point is narrow; if you can't find favas whose pods are just a few inches long, don't sweat it.

Though young favas are optimal, bigger beans whose skins have toughened are the norm. Either way, cooking them in the cheese broth brings forth their sweet nuttiness.

Olive oil, as needed

½ cup coarse bread crumbs (see page 298)

Kosher salt and freshly cracked black peppercorns

2 to 3 pounds young favas in their pods, or 1½ to 2 cups shelled

2 tablespoons butter

2 tablespoons finely diced shallots

4 oil-packed anchovy fillets, patted dry

2 cups Parmesan-Pecorino Broth (page 290) or Chicken Broth (page 288)

TOAST THE BREAD CRUMBS

Set a small sauté pan over medium heat with ¼ inch of olive oil. Once the oil is shimmering, add the crumbs.

Sauté the crumbs, stirring constantly, for 3 minutes, or until golden. With a slotted spoon, transfer the crumbs to a paper towel–lined plate. Season with salt and pepper and set aside until ready to use.

PREP THE FAVAS

Shell the fava beans. A young fava should be quite tender, but if you are using larger favas with a tough outer skin, prep them: Bring a pot of well-salted water to a boil over high heat. Set up an ice bath in a large bowl nearby. Blanch the beans for 1 minute, or until bright green. Transfer the blanched favas to the ice bath. When cool, drain the favas and shake them dry. Remove their tough outer skin by pinching the beans on the end opposite the stem, where they attached to the pod. Reserve the peeled favas.

BRAISE THE FAVAS

Set a large high-walled sauté pan or skillet over medium-high heat and swirl in 2 tablespoons olive oil. Once it warms, add the butter. When the butter starts to foam, stir in the shallots and sauté for 2 minutes, or until soft.

Stir in the anchovies, smashing the fillets with the back of a spoon. Once they disintegrate, reduce the heat to medium-low. Stir in the favas, thoroughly coating them in the anchovy-shallot mixture. Pour in the Parmesan broth. Bring the liquid up to a simmer and then reduce the heat slightly so the favas gently simmer for 10 minutes, or until very tender.

Remove the pan from the heat and season the favas to taste with salt and pepper. Serve the braised favas immediately or hold them, at room temperature, for 1 to 2 hours. (They're best just warm.) Just before serving, scoop the favas onto a platter, ladling some of the braising liquid over the beans to keep them moist. Scatter the bread crumbs on top and serve.

14

ZUPPA DI PESCE

SERVES 6 TO 8

Traditionally this seafood soup is made by cooking all the fish together. But this version, a play on one I make at Upland, builds the flavor layer by layer, steam-braising or poaching each type of seafood individually until just tender, concentrating their essences in the broth. We then finish with a fresh, gorgeous raw tomato water. Since we keep that tomato water relatively uncooked, it balances the rich broth with its bright acidity and aroma.

¼ cup olive oil, plus more

3 tablespoons butter

1 pound Manila clams, cleaned (see page 69)

1 pound mussels, bearded and cleaned (brined and cleaned as for clams)

1½ pounds halibut, 1-inch cubes

1 quart Tomato Water (page 293)

Fine sea salt

1 cup roughly chopped Roasted Tomatoes (recipe follows)

1 pound medium whole squid, cleaned and de-beaked, tentacles and bodies separated

1 pound large shrimp, preferably with heads and tails

1 teaspoon finely sliced fresh chives

1 teaspoon finely sliced fresh tarragon

1 teaspoon finely sliced fresh basil

2 tablespoons red verjus or vinegar

1 tablespoon finely diced peel from Preserved Lemons (page 302)

Lemon juice, to taste

Bruschetta, for serving (page 298)

Aioli, for serving (page 297)

STEAM THE SHELLFISH

Set a large Dutch oven over medium-high heat and swirl in the olive oil and butter. Once the butter foams, stir in the clams, coating them in the fat. Add a few splashes of water, cover the pot, and steam the clams for 4 minutes, or until their shells just pop open. With a slotted spoon, quickly transfer the clams to a large bowl, leaving their juices behind in the pot. If a few stubborn clams don't open, leave them in the pot and steam them for another minute or two; if they still don't open, discard.

Quickly stir the mussels into the Dutch oven. Re-cover the pot and steam the mussels for 3 minutes, or until their shells just pop open. Remove the pot from heat and, with a slotted spoon, quickly transfer the mussels to the bowl with the clams, leaving their drippings behind in the pot as well. Continue to steam any stubborn mussels for another minute or two; discard any that are still closed. Set the shellfish aside, tossing every now and again to keep the flesh moist.

STEAM-BRAISE THE HALIBUT

Check that the Dutch oven has at least ¼ inch of shellfish drippings. If it doesn't, add just enough water to compensate. Set the pot back over medium heat and, once the liquid gently simmers, stir in the halibut; the salt in the shellfish juices will season it.

Steam-braise the halibut, uncovered, for 2 to 3 minutes, or until the cubes turn opaque and begin to flake when prodded. Flip the halibut cubes halfway through cooking. Turn off the heat and, with a slotted spoon, quickly transfer the fish to a platter. Set the fish aside.

BUILD THE ZUPPA

Set a fine-mesh strainer lined with a damp cheesecloth over a medium bowl. Pour all the liquid from the Dutch oven through the strainer. Discard the strainer contents and wipe the Dutch oven clean.

(recipe continues)

Pour the strained broth back into the Dutch oven along with the tomato water and set over medium heat. Bring the liquid up to a gentle simmer and taste. If necessary, brighten with sea salt or, if too salty, dilute the broth with more tomato water or fresh water. There should be about 5 cups of liquid in the pot.

Stir the roasted tomatoes into the broth and bring everything up to a gentle simmer. Cook for 2 minutes. Lightly salt the squid and shrimp. If the shrimp are very large, add them to the broth a minute before the squid. Otherwise, add them together. Once the squid whitens and the shrimp does not yet curl, gently stir in the steamed clams and mussels. Cover and cook for 2 minutes, or until the shrimp turn opaque and start to curl. Gently fold in the halibut. Immediately remove the pot from the heat.

FINISH AND SERVE

Gently stir the chives, tarragon, basil, verjus, and preserved lemon peel into the zuppa. Taste and season with lemon juice and extra salt to taste. Drizzle generously with good olive oil. Serve with bruschetta and aioli alongside.

ROASTED TOMATOES

Roasting concentrates a tomato's umami flavor and converts its water-packed meat into something more chewy and substantial. Stirring these morsels into the zuppa, as directed here, is just one way to enjoy the roasted fruit. Spreading them over bruschetta with Fresh Ricotta (page 312) is another. I could go on, but really, the possibilities are endless.

---

1 pound Early Girl, Cherokee Purple, or beefsteak tomatoes, halved equatorially

3 tablespoons olive oil

Fine sea salt and freshly cracked black peppercorns

10 fresh thyme sprigs

5 garlic cloves, skin on and crushed open

Preheat the oven to 325°F and position the rack to the top third of the oven. Brush the tomatoes' cut sides with 1 tablespoon of the olive oil. Season with salt and pepper and set aside.

Brush the bottom of a medium heavy roasting pan with 1 tablespoon of the olive oil. Scatter the thyme and crushed garlic across the pan. Lay in the tomatoes, cut sides down, so they fit in a snug single layer. Brush the tomato tops with the remaining tablespoon of oil.

Transfer the pan to the top rack of the oven. Roast the tomatoes for 40 minutes, or until the skins are shriveled but the flesh is still meaty.

HOW TO PLAN THIS MEAL:

1 day before: Make tomato water.

4 hours before: Brine clams and mussels. Make aioli and roasted tomatoes.

30 minutes before: Make zuppa and bruschetta.

15

CARAMELIZED FIVE-ONION SOUP WITH SPINACH SALAD

SERVES 6 TO 8

If a braise is all about the marriage between a main ingredient and its cooking liquid, this is the ultimate inseparable union. Here, onion-slathered croutons literally melt into a hot broth so that a warming, thick, sweet-and-savory soup emerges.

Though you can make this five-onion soup with any combination of onions, I'm partial to the depth that comes from mixing winter and springtime alliums. Baby leeks and ramps, harbingers of spring, taste grassy and green, while the shallots and Vidalias, leftover stalwarts from the winter cellar, are sugar sweet. In the winter, I swap in mature leeks and scallions in lieu of the ramps.

Alongside, a crisp, surprisingly hearty Spinach and Goat Cheese Salad with Shallot Vinaigrette bridges the soup's flavor with a refreshing bite. The Spiced Rye Carta di Musica adds crunch to the meal.

---

1 pound rustic sourdough bread, preferably 1 to 2 days old

4 baby leeks

¼ cup olive oil, plus more

3 tablespoons butter

3 medium Vidalia or other sweet onions, halved and sliced very thin

5 large shallots, sliced thin

1 tablespoon sugar

1 tablespoon dry green peppercorns, toasted and cracked

2 bulbs spring garlic or 6 garlic cloves

½ pound ramps, tender portions, or 1 pound scallions, white and light green parts only, thinly sliced

10 cups Burnt-Onion Dashi (page 287) or Chicken Broth (page 288)

2 fresh bay leaves

Kosher salt and freshly cracked black pepper

PULL THE BREAD CRUMBS

Pull 2½ cups of rough, 1½-inch croutons from the interior of the bread. Spread the croutons out in a single layer on a rimmed baking sheet and set them aside. If your bread is fresh, let the croutons dry out, at room temperature, for 12 to 24 hours before proceeding.

CLEAN THE LEEKS

Halve the leeks lengthwise and trim away their root ends, making sure to keep the stems intact. Fill a large bowl with warm water and submerge the leeks, cut sides down. Shake the leeks vigorously, freeing grit from their inner walls. The warm water helps loosen the leek's layers so dirt is easily released.

Lift out the leeks and shake them dry. Lay the leeks, cut sides down, in a single layer on a towel-lined baking sheet and pat dry.

Cut away the dark portion of the leeks. Slice the white and light green portions into very thin half moons. You should have about 1 cup thinly sliced leeks.

CARAMELIZE THE ONIONS

Set a large Dutch oven over medium-high heat and stir in the olive oil and butter. Once the butter foams, stir in the Vidalia onions, leeks, shallots, sugar, and green peppercorns. Immediately lower the heat to medium-low and stew the onions, stirring often, for 50 minutes, or until they completely soften and turn a dark caramel color.

ADD THE REMAINING ALLIUMS

Meanwhile, prepare the spring garlic, if using: Discard the skin and trim away the stem end. Separate the white and light green portions from the stalk, discarding the tough green portion, and thinly slice them crosswise. (If using regular garlic, thinly slice the cloves.)

(recipe continues)

Stir the spring or regular garlic into the pot and cook for 5 minutes, or until its aroma blooms. Stir in the ramps or scallions and the croutons. Cook until the bread is thoroughly coated in the onion matter, 2 to 3 minutes. Let the mixture rest at room temperature for 30 minutes, or until the onions soften the bread.

BUILD THE SOUP

Set a medium pot over medium heat, pour in the dashi, and bring to a simmer.

Meanwhile, press the bay leaves with the broad side of a chef's knife and toss them into the Dutch oven with the bread and onions. Set the Dutch oven back over medium-low heat.

Pour enough broth into the Dutch oven to nearly cover the bread-onion mixture. Simmer, stirring often, for 30 minutes, or until the bread breaks down and the soup takes on a thick, porridge-like texture. Add extra splashes of warm broth or water as needed to keep the soup moist and loose, to your preference. Once a loose porridge comes together, season the mixture with salt and black pepper to taste.

FINISH AND SERVE

To serve, ladle the soup into warm bowls. Drizzle each serving with a generous amount of high-quality olive oil and season with more black pepper. Serve the soup with the Spinach and Goat Cheese Salad with Shallot Vinaigrette and the Spiced Rye Carta di Musica (recipes follow).

SPINACH AND GOAT CHEESE SALAD
WITH SHALLOT VINAIGRETTE

SERVES 4 TO 6

Salad greens are some of the most precious ingredients and investing in great ones always pays off. Whenever possible, I buy mine from Nevia No at Bodhitree Farm.

The pride Nevia takes in her greens is unmatched. I have seen her literally yell at customers for packing too much into one of her sturdy plastic bags. That attention to detail has shaped my entire approach to salad making.

In this spinach salad, the greens are tossed in a big bowl to prevent bruising. Then, they are served on a cool platter slathered in goat cheese, instead of weighing down the leaves. It also makes the salad more fun to eat—swiping your fork through to pick up some of the cheese feels more feastlike than more prim salads.

Olive oil, as needed

5 large shallots, finely diced

⅓ cup red wine vinegar

1 tablespoon fresh thyme leaves, roughly chopped

2 teaspoons Dijon mustard

Fine sea salt and freshly cracked black peppercorns to taste

¼ pound fresh goat cheese, softened to room temperature

½ pound broadleaf or baby spinach

MAKE THE VINAIGRETTE

Pour enough oil to just cover the shallots into a medium heavy pot fitted with a candy thermometer. Gently warm the oil over medium-low heat until tiny bubbles appear around the shallots' edges; the oil temperature should register 250°F. Keeping this temperature steady, cook the shallots for 40 minutes, or until they turn a rich caramel color.

Remove the pot from the heat and carefully pour in the vinegar. The oil will bubble vigorously, so stand back. Cool to lukewarm. Ladle or pour out as much of the oil as possible into a small bowl, reserving it. Transfer the shallot mixture to a medium bowl. Allow both bowls to cool to room temperature. Meanwhile, chill a large serving platter and salad bowl in the refrigerator.

Stir the thyme and mustard into the shallots. Season the mixture with salt and pepper. Gradually whisk the reserved oil into the shallots.

DRESS AND PLATE

On the serving platter, use a spatula to spread the goat cheese across the plates.

Fill a third of the chilled salad bowl with spinach and season with salt. Toss the greens, using both hands.

Whisk the shallot dressing again until emulsified. Pour some of the dressing along the salad bowl's upper edge. Using both hands, gently lift the spinach up along the bowl's walls and toss the greens inward. The objective is to scoop and lift the greens while delicately working the seasoning into each leaf. Taste and add more dressing, salt, or pepper as needed. Place the salad on the platter, mounding it over the cheese. Dress the remaining greens in the same way. Extra dressing keeps, refrigerated, for up to 2 weeks.

SPICED RYE CARTA DI MUSICA

MAKES SIX 10-INCH CRACKERS

Carta di musica, "music sheet" in Italian, is the charming name given to these long, freeform, paper-thin crackers, served whole at the table. Encourage guests to break off pieces as they work their way through a meal. My version is coated in spices and made with rye flour, adding kick. I also like to serve these spiced *carta* with cheese, preferably a young pecorino, at the end of a meal.

1 tablespoon caraway seeds, toasted

1 teaspoon fennel seeds, toasted

½ teaspoon coriander seeds, toasted

½ teaspoon dry green peppercorns, toasted

1 cup dark rye flour

1¾ cups all-purpose flour, plus more for dusting

1 teaspoon fine sea salt

1 cup warm water

Flaky sea salt

EQUIPMENT

Pizza stone

MAKE THE DOUGH

Combine the caraway, fennel, coriander, and green peppercorns in a spice grinder and pulse until finely crushed.

In a large bowl, mix the rye and all-purpose flours together with the ground spices and fine sea salt. Stir in the water until a shaggy dough comes together.

Turn the dough out onto a lightly floured work surface. Knead the dough until smooth and elastic. Form the dough into a ball and wrap it in plastic. Let stand at room temperature for 1 hour, so that the dough relaxes.

ROLL OUT AND BAKE

Set a pizza stone on the middle rack of the oven and preheat the oven to 450°F. Turn the dough out onto a lightly floured work surface and cut it into 6 equal parts, rounding each piece into a ball. Cover the balls with a lightly dampened cloth.

Lightly flour your work surface. Working with 1 piece of dough at a time, roll out the dough until it is very thin but does not tear; it should be ⅛ inch thick or less, and about 12 inches in diameter. Carefully transfer the stretched dough onto a large silicone baking mat or piece of parchment paper. Sprinkle the top of the stretched dough with flaky sea salt.

Slip the mat directly onto the pizza stone. Bake the cracker for 5 to 6 minutes, or until it is bubbly, golden, and crisp. Remove the cracker from the oven and transfer it to a cooling rack. Roll, season, and bake the remaining balls.

Serve the crackers in large sheets so guests can break off pieces as they like. These crackers are good for up to 1 week if stored in an airtight container.

HOW TO PLAN THIS MEAL:

1 day before: Prepare croutons if using fresh bread. Make burnt-onion dashi and spiced rye crackers.

2 hours before: Stew onions and season bread. Make shallot vinaigrette.

30 minutes before: Finish soup.

10 minutes before: Dress salad.

16

SICILIAN KALE-STUFFED TURKEY LEGS

SERVES 4 TO 6

Here, we slather a deboned turkey leg with sautéed greens, raisins, pancetta, and pistachios before rolling it up into a snug cylinder. The delicious, Sicily-inspired stuffing flavors the meat with its nutty, sweet, porky goodness. Once the two meld together, we brown the rolled legs, then poach them in chicken broth. While the steps are nearly identical to a classic braise, the large quantity of cooking liquid and relatively short cooking time keeps the result cleaner and lighter.

With some shaved turnips, their greens, and a golden broth, the elegant final plate does right by turkey, a much misunderstood bird. I love turkey's mild, versatile flavor, especially when paired with big, rich ingredients. While it's typically reserved for holiday time eating, this meal is one you will want to make year-round. (Ask your butcher to debone and butterfly the turkey legs for you.)

---

2 whole turkey legs (drumsticks and thighs attached), 2 pounds each, deboned and butterflied

Kosher salt and freshly cracked black peppercorns

3 cups Sicilian Kale Stuffing (recipe follows)

¼ cup olive oil, plus more for drizzling

3 quarts Chicken Broth (page 288)

6 Tokyo or baby turnips, greens separated and reserved

Red wine vinegar

Flaky sea salt

STUFF AND ROLL THE TURKEY LEGS

Open both turkey legs up like a book and lay them on a clean work surface, skin side down. Season the meat side of the legs generously with salt and pepper.

Using a spatula, evenly spread the stuffing over the meat, leaving an untouched ½-inch border. Roll up the turkey legs by tucking and rolling the skin side into the smeared meat to form a long cylinder.

Set both rolled legs, seam sides down, on the work surface. With butcher's twine, tie the legs at 1-inch intervals.

Pat the rolled legs very dry, then season the outsides with salt and pepper. Transfer the legs to a cooling rack set over a rimmed baking sheet. Refrigerate, uncovered, for 24 hours.

BROWN AND POACH THE TURKEY LEGS

Remove the turkey legs from the refrigerator. Set a large Dutch oven over medium heat. Swirl in 2 tablespoons of the olive oil. Once the oil is shimmering-hot, lay 1 turkey leg in the pot and brown on all sides for 12 to 15 minutes total, or until deeply caramelized. Set the leg back on the rack and pour off the fat. If necessary, deglaze the pot with a little bit of broth to dissolve any fond, and pour it back into the broth. Rinse and wipe the pot clean, then repeat the browning process with the second leg.

Pour off the fat and set the pot back over medium-high heat. Stir in the chicken broth and scrape up any fond. Bring the liquid up to a simmer and season lightly with salt. Carefully lay both rolled legs in the broth. Add more water or broth if necessary to just cover the turkey legs.

(recipe continues)

Reduce the heat to medium-low so the broth very gently simmers, steaming but not bubbling, and cover the pot. Poach the legs, basting about every 15 minutes, for 1 hour, or until the meat is cooked through. A thermometer inserted into the center of a roll should read 165°F.

Carefully transfer the legs to a large cooling rack set over a rimmed baking sheet (reserve the broth). Let the meat rest for at least 15 minutes.

PREPARE THE GARNISHES

Meanwhile, slice the turnips into paper-thin rounds using either a very sharp knife or a mandoline. Set up an ice water bath in a medium bowl. Place the rounds in the ice water and refrigerate until the slices crisp. These can be held for up to 2 hours.

Rinse the turnip greens in cold water and dry thoroughly. Roughly tear the leaves into bite-size pieces or leave them whole. If not using the greens immediately, wrap them in paper towels and refrigerate until ready to use.

STRAIN THE BROTH AND FINISH THE SOUP

Set a fine-mesh strainer lined with cheesecloth over a deep container. Pour the reserved broth through the strainer. Discard all captured sediment from the strainer. Wipe the pot clean.

Pour the strained broth back into the Dutch oven and bring it to a gentle simmer over medium heat. Season with salt and vinegar to taste.

SLICE THE MEAT AND SERVE

Just before serving the soup, remove the turnip slices from the ice water bath and pat them dry. Carefully slice the legs crosswise into $1/2$-inch slices.

Divide the turkey slices among warm shallow soup bowls. Add the turnip greens and slices to the bowls and ladle in enough hot broth to almost cover the meat. Garnish the bowls with a generous drizzle of good olive oil and flaky salt. I like to eat this simply, with a crusty baguette and Whole-Grain Mustard (page 296).

SICILIAN KALE STUFFING

MAKES 3 CUPS

This stuffing is terrific in turkey, but it has numerous applications. It can be served with a range of simply roasted meats or even tossed into a pasta. I also like to eat it plain, right out of a bowl.

½ cup green or golden raisins

¾ cup vin santo or water

2 tablespoons olive oil

¼ pound chanterelle or white mushrooms, finely chopped

¼ pound black trumpet or shiitake mushrooms, finely chopped

Kosher salt

2 tablespoons butter

¾ cup finely diced shallots

6 garlic cloves, finely grated

1 tablespoon finely chopped fresh oregano leaves

1 tablespoon finely chopped fresh sage leaves

3 cups finely sliced cavolo nero (black kale), stems first removed and discarded

¾ cup finely diced pancetta

1 cup coarse bread crumbs, lightly toasted (see page 298)

½ cup pistachios, toasted and roughly chopped

1 tablespoon finely grated orange zest (from 1 orange)

⅓ cup fresh orange juice (from 1 orange)

Freshly cracked black peppercorns

Place the raisins in a small bowl and cover with vin santo or water until completely submerged. Set aside and let the raisins plump.

Meanwhile, set a large heavy sauté pan over medium heat. Swirl in the olive oil. Once it is hot, add the chanterelles and sauté for 2 minutes, or until softened. Add the trumpet mushrooms and a few pinches of salt, and sauté for 6 minutes, or until their juices release, then evaporate, and the edges turn golden brown. Transfer the mushrooms to a platter and set aside.

Wipe the pan clean and set it back over medium heat. Add the butter and, once it foams, stir in the shallots. Sauté for 4 minutes, or until translucent. Stir in the garlic, oregano, and sage. Once the garlic is aromatic but not colored, after about 2 minutes, stir in the kale leaves and a few pinches of salt. Sauté for 6 minutes, or until the kale is just tender. Transfer the pan's contents to a large bowl and set it aside.

Wipe the pan clean and set it back over medium heat. Add the pancetta and brown it on all sides, about 5 minutes. Transfer the pancetta and 1 tablespoon of its drippings to the bowl with the greens.

Drain the raisins, reserving the vin santo for another use. Stir the bread crumbs, pistachios, sautéed mushrooms, drained raisins, orange zest, and orange juice into the bowl with the greens until well combined. Season with salt and pepper to taste. Let the stuffing cool before using it to stuff the turkey, or it can be made 1 day in advance and held in the refrigerator.

HOW TO PLAN THIS MEAL:

1 day before: Make kale stuffing. Stuff and roll turkey legs.

2 hours before: Sear and poach turkey. Prepare turnips.

15 minutes before: Strain and season broth. Slice turkey and assemble dishes.

17

RIVIERA SALAD WITH OIL-CURED TUNA AND TOMATO VINAIGRETTE

SERVES 4

In between working at Barbuto and teaming up with Donna at the Alimentari, I spent two summers as the chef at André Balazs's Sunset Beach, which overlooks a picturesque bay in Shelter Island, New York. Yachts from all over dock at this Hamptons hot spot, and throngs come ashore for a glass of rosé and a meal. It was during this time that I began making countless iterations of salad niçoise. Though I never got to sit down and enjoy one during those summers, this is what I dreamt of eating one day, when I too could luxuriate and look out across the water.

Putting a salad in a braising chapter is unorthodox; I won't deny it. But, like the duck confit in the cassoulet, a gentle immersion in fat transforms the tuna; it emerges from its olive oil bath soft and lush. When that tuna is broken over raw tomatoes, cucumber, radishes, blanched beans, tender potatoes, and a soft-boiled egg, this salad niçoise is, well, dreamy.

⅓ pound ripe red tomatoes, preferably Brandywine or beefsteak, halved equatorially

2 tablespoons olive oil, plus more

1 tablespoon red wine vinegar, or more to taste

Fine sea salt and freshly cracked black peppercorns

1 pound Olive Oil–Preserved Tuna Belly (recipe follows)

4 large eggs

½ Persian cucumber, sliced into thin rounds

2 radishes, sliced into thin rounds

½ pound fingerling potatoes

Kosher salt

¼ pound haricots verts, trimmed

4 Pickled Cipollini Onions (recipe follows)

1 to 2 tablespoons lemon juice (from 1 lemon), to taste

¾ pound heirloom tomatoes, cut into 1-inch wedges, preferably a mix

½ cup whole Taggiasca olives

8 squash blossoms, stems removed and flowers roughly torn (optional)

½ cup fresh basil leaves, roughly torn

MAKE THE TOMATO VINAIGRETTE

Set a box grater over a shallow bowl. On the medium holes, grate the cut sides of the red tomatoes until they yield ½ cup pulp. Stir in 2 tablespoons of the olive oil and the red wine vinegar. Season with sea salt and pepper and add extra oil or vinegar to taste. Set the tomato vinaigrette aside.

TEMPER THE TUNA AND EGGS

Remove the tuna and eggs from the refrigerator. Set the eggs aside and let come to room temperature. If the tuna's oil has congealed, allow it to become liquid, then remove the tuna from the oil and let it come to room temperature.

CRISP THE CUCUMBERS AND RADISHES

Place the cucumber and radish slices in a small bowl. Add ice cubes and cover with cold water. Refrigerate until ready to use. These can be held for up to 2 hours.

BOIL THE POTATOES AND BLANCH THE HARICOTS VERTS

Place the potatoes in a heavy medium pot. Add cold water to cover by 1 inch. Season the water with enough kosher salt so that it tastes like the ocean.

Bring the water to a gentle simmer over medium-high heat. Reduce the heat to maintain the simmer and cook the potatoes for 20 minutes, or until easily pierced with the tip of a knife. Remove the potatoes from the water (leave the water in the pot) and set aside to cool to room temperature.

Set the water back over high heat and bring to a boil. In a medium bowl, set up an ice water bath by the stove.

Blanch the haricots verts in the boiling water for 1 minute, or until they turn bright green and crisp. Drain and transfer to the ice water bath. Once the beans have completely cooled, remove them from the ice water and pat dry. For visual flare, split the beans in half lengthwise.

SOFT-BOIL THE EGGS

Place the eggs in a small pot, cover with cold water, and set over high heat. Bring the water to a boil, then turn off the heat and cover the pot. Let the eggs stand for 3 minutes, then remove and place in the ice water to cool. They will have thickened, runny yolks when cut. If you prefer a more solid yolk, let them stand in the boiled water for 5 minutes, or 9 for hard-boiled.

Once they completely cool, remove the eggs from the bath. Peel and set aside.

ASSEMBLE AND SERVE THE SALAD

Remove the radishes and cucumbers from the refrigerator, strain, and thoroughly dry. Lay both on towel-lined plates.

Quarter or halve the pickled onions into 1-inch pieces. Remove their cores and separate their layers into individual petals. Set the petals aside.

Crack the potatoes open and season their insides with sea salt and lemon juice.

Spoon the tomato vinaigrette onto the center of a large serving platter and spread it out so it coats the plate. Nestle the tomato wedges into the vinaigrette, distributing them evenly around the platter. Place the cucumber slices over and around the tomatoes and sprinkle with sea salt.

Flake the tuna into large, smooth pieces and drape them over and around the tomato wedges. Tuck the olives, haricots verts, and onion petals in and around the tomatoes and tuna. Fill in the holes of the salad with the eggs and potatoes.

Tuck the radish rounds, torn squash blossoms, if using, and basil in and around the salad. Drizzle with olive oil and serve immediately.

OLIVE OIL–PRESERVED TUNA BELLY

MAKES 1 POUND

Preserving an ingredient à la Grecque, the French term for "in the Greek style," involves holding it in vinegar, spices, and oil. With this recipe, I play with that principle some and add way more olive oil than vinegar to the poached tuna. The uncooked oil remains pungent and fresh, and, due to extra-virgin olive oil's unique ability to bond with the tuna's muscle fibers, the marinade produces silky bites that are a pure indulgence.

1 quart water

¼ cup kosher salt, plus more to season

1 pound tuna belly, cut into two 1-inch-thick slabs

2 strips of lemon peel, removed with a vegetable peeler

10 fresh thyme sprigs

1 fresh bay leaf

3 tablespoons champagne vinegar

Olive oil, as needed

1 tablespoon black peppercorns, toasted

BRINE THE TUNA

Pour the water and ¼ cup kosher salt into a 1-gallon zip-top bag. Submerge the tuna slabs in the brine and refrigerate for 3 hours.

POACH THE TUNA

Remove the tuna from the refrigerator, lift it out of the brine, and pat it completely dry.

Set a wide, large pot with 2 quarts water over high heat. Bring to a gentle simmer, then reduce the heat to low, so the water steams, but doesn't bubble. Season the water generously with salt so it tastes like the sea.

Submerge the tuna in the hot water. If it doesn't fit comfortably in one layer, cook the tuna in 2 batches. Poach the tuna for 7 minutes, or until its flesh is easily pierced with the tip of a sharp knife or cake tester. At this point the fish should be cooked with a hint of pink in the center. With a slotted spoon, transfer the tuna to a cooling rack. Let it cool slightly.

PRESERVE THE TUNA

Press the lemon peel, thyme, and bay leaf with the broad side of a chef's knife to release their essential oils.

Pat the tuna dry and brush with champagne vinegar. Lay the tuna in a glass container just large enough to hold it snugly. Pour in enough olive oil, to completely submerge the tuna. Add the toasted peppercorns, lemon peel, and pressed thyme and bay leaf to the oil. Once the fish is at room temperature, cover and refrigerate for at least 24 hours, or until the tuna is well flavored.

PICKLED CIPOLLINI ONIONS

MAKES ABOUT 2 PINTS, INCLUDING PICKLING LIQUID
Quartering, then separating the layers of the onions after pickling turns them into elegant petals for scattering about.

½ cup champagne vinegar

½ cup rice wine vinegar

Kosher salt

2 tablespoons sugar

4 cilantro stems

1 kaffir lime leaf (optional)

1½ teaspoons dry green peppercorns, toasted

1½ teaspoons coriander seeds, toasted

½ teaspoon fennel seeds, toasted

1 pound cipollini onions, peeled

In a medium bowl, whisk the champagne and rice vinegars with ½ cup water, 1 tablespoon salt, and the sugar until dissolved.

Press the cilantro stems and, if using, the kaffir lime leaf with the broad side of a chef's knife to release their essential oils. Stir the herbs, peppercorns, and coriander and fennel seeds into the vinegar mixture.

Fill a large saucepan with water and bring to a boil over high heat. Season it with enough salt so it tastes like the ocean. Blanch the onions for 3 minutes, or until their outer layers soften slightly. With a slotted spoon, transfer the onions to 2 pint jars or 1 quart jar.

Pour the vinegar mixture over the onions to cover and let cool to room temperature. Secure the lids on the jars and refrigerate. Let the onions pickle for at least 1 day. I like these best after 1 week, but they hold for up to 1 month in the refrigerator.

HOW TO PLAN THIS MEAL:

1–2 days before: Make tuna belly and pickled onions.

1 hour before: Make vinaigrette and remove tuna and eggs from refrigerator. Crisp vegetables. Boil potatoes and haricots verts; soft-boil eggs.

15 minutes before: Assemble salad.

ROASTING

A WEEK BEFORE OPENING IL BUCO ALIMENTARI, WE WERE RECIPE TESTING LIKE crazy. We had no beef dish on the menu and I'd been racking my brain for one that could work. Whatever it was to be, it had to be beefy to the extreme—people love their red meat big and unapologetic. To give this TBD entrée its requisite intensity, I began thinking of roasts.

No technique articulates the flavor of an ingredient better than a roast. With grilling, smoke perfumes the cut and with braising, liquid alters it. With roasting, however, that same ingredient emerges more flavorful, more complex, and more *itself*.

After the meat had spent a few hours wrapped up tight in the oven, I pulled out a rack of pepper-covered short ribs and slid a knife along one of the tanned, protruding bones; the meat jiggled just as I wanted it to—a sign that these ribs were tender but still had bounce to their bite. I went in for a taste. Trapping the steam in the roasting pan kept them incredibly juicy. Part brisket, part corned beef, part pot roast, and part steak au poivre, this was getting there.

I slicked a hot skillet with oil and laid in a rib. The spices sizzled and popped and set hard against the meat before I transferred the pan to the oven, so every corner of this roast could crisp up right. When I pulled out the rib a few minutes later, the peppercorn crust seized in the air and I couldn't help but smile.

As the first order went out that night, a second immediately followed, then more, and we quickly sold out. I watched as every single plate returned to the kitchen clean, with just a lonely bone lying flat upon it. To me that bone exclaimed triumphant pleasure.

A few months later, the *New York Times* restaurant critic Pete Wells called us to fact-check: a sign the review—the last word in restaurant reviews in this town—was a few nerve-wracking days away.

We got three stars, a tremendous honor. Three stars meant we, an informal Italian place, joined the company of just a few dozen elite restaurants in the city. Those short ribs, Wells said, were "one of the best new dishes in town." He rapped rhapsodic about a lot in that review, giving our owner Donna her just due. But those ribs trumpeted the virtues of methodical and deliberate roasting, and the *Times* had noticed.

Overnight, the short ribs became our most popular entrée. In the beginning, we sold one hundred pounds a week; by the time I left the Alimentari a few years later, over a thousand pounds of short ribs would come and go through our kitchen every seven days and they were on my menu at Upland on day one.

Looking back now, it's not a stretch to say that this dish jump-started my career, and all it took was a few back-pocket roasting tricks . . . and a whole lot of beef.

ROASTING: TECHNIQUE AND DETAIL

Most people think of roasting strictly as an in-oven affair, but to me it comprises two elements—cooking both in the oven and on the stovetop. Of course, in many recipes, the two work together. But beyond that, they share a philosophy: Both transmit a neutral, dry heat, and the key to mastering them is understanding how to manipulate temperature and the moisture inherent in your food. In this chapter, the recipes explore the results of radiant heat, searing surfaces, and the steam they can produce.

THE BASIC TECHNIQUE

While nearly half the meals in the Braising chapter followed the same basic process, roasting is a bit more diverse—there is no one fundamental way to roast, as every ingredient or dish can follow a variety of paths. But there are some (nearly) universal rules or steps I keep in mind.

Brining is a constant in my cooking, and in this chapter, I take pre-seasoning a step further with rubs, thick smears painted on with the back of a spoon or stiff pastry brush. The beauty of these rubs is not just the intense flavor they impart to the roast, but, after some drying in the refrigerator, they form gorgeous crusts when cooked, lending texture and depth.

Then, before searing, I let my cuts sit at room temperature until they lose the refrigerator's chill. This helps prevent the outer portions of the roast from overcooking while the interior remains stubbornly raw.

TOUCHING AND JOSTLING

I always jostle and lavish attention upon a roast while it cooks. Though it may be the most approachable technique, roasting is not the most forgiving, and touching your food often cues you in to its transformation, telling you what the ingredient needs.

When standing over a pan, touch the food to get a sense of how taut or tender it's becoming; turn and move and flip it to control how much direct contact each inch of the food is getting with the pan. Watch, listen, and smell. Turn the heat up, turn it down, rotate the pan, flip the meat, hold that stubborn curved edge down to give it a good sear. The benefit of stovetop roasting is that you can be a control freak, so own it and make sure your roast sizzles, steams, and browns as it ought to throughout the cooking process.

While oven roasting, you still shouldn't walk away until a timer calls you back into the kitchen. Go ahead and open your oven to flip your meat (for even caramelization) or to baste it (if juices have accumulated). Rotate the pan often, to account for hot spots, and maybe even relocate it to a different rack. If you want to crisp the top of your roast, slip it onto the top rack and take advantage of the oven's reflective heat. And if the bottom of the dish needs crisping, why not roast it right on the oven floor? A seasoned roaster can confidently play with the oven to get a perfect result.

All this requires vigilance, as I have said. It also asks that you engage all your senses, which is one of the great pleasures of cooking. In each of these recipes, I'll help you see, hear, and feel what to look for as the dishes cook.

MANIPULATING HEAT BY CHOOSING THE RIGHT PAN

Another important and often overlooked element of roasting relates to your roasting vessel. Cooking, after all, is about how heat is harnessed and deployed, and different materials and shapes do those things differently.

In the following meals, heavy pans are often called for, which in my kitchen means cast iron. Nothing carries strong heat better or more evenly than cast iron. Though you needn't use the same, do reach for a pan or roasting tray with heft.

Heavy materials soak up and transmit an even heat; thinner pans waver—too hot in spots, cooling down too quickly in others—and they can be the culprit if your food ends up burnt or under-browned.

Terra-cotta transmits a gentle, wet heat that makes for elegant, delicate bites. When meat or fish roasts in terra-cotta, its moisture is absorbed into the material, creating a subtle steaming effect that helps keep the food supple, if that's your desire.

Size matters too. In general you don't want to overcrowd your roasting pan. If you do, you will create steam, inhibiting browning, and you only want to do that intentionally. Unless instructed otherwise, always reach for a pan that affords your roast plenty of room, meaning it should have a few inches around the edges, at least. And if you are cooking multiple items, like leeks or chicken legs, space these out to give each some breathing room.

The other consideration when choosing your roasting vessel is shape. Obviously, a covered pan traps steam, which helps cook food through. But even an uncovered, high-walled pan will keep some moisture circulating inside. That is pretty much what happens in the Pan-Roasted Pork Chops with Blistered Avocado and Chives (page 169). There, the cast-iron skillet browns the thick cut while the walls ensure the meat stays juicy as it cooks through. A deep pan captures more moisture and promotes even, all-around cooking.

On the other hand are planchas, pizza stones, griddles, and skillets that are much larger than the food you're cooking. These surfaces are flat and heavy. In practical terms, that means they give off a strong, superdry heat. With such flat surfaces, no moisture is trapped in the pan, and so what comes off these surfaces can be extremely seared, as the heat is focused entirely on surface contact. Try searing a steak on a plancha and then in a high-walled pan and the difference, in terms of char, will surprise you. The best char, time and again, comes off of a low- to no-walled surface.

But I'm a realist, and I know that not every kitchen comes fully stocked—and that, for many people, the difference between something seared on a flat surface versus a skillet may not seem like much. But when you cook and cook often, it's learning to observe the details that makes it so continually exciting, and the above thoughts are simply meant to shed light on why certain specifications are made in the following recipes. And when you strike out on your own, I hope you will have a better understanding of what your choices will get you.

HOW THIS CHAPTER IS ORGANIZED

These recipes start off by exploring straightforward oven roasts. Then we move to stovetop roasting and, finally, to meals that combine both.

The following meals look at all aspects of the roasting process—from searing and caramelizing to steam roasting and baking—and the range of recipes takes maximum advantage of the oven, from the stovetop to the oven's floor.

1

PANLESS ROAST DUCK WITH SQUASH, CIPOLLINI ONIONS, AND CAPER OIL

SERVES 4 TO 6

Amber-colored ducks hanging in steamy windows of bustling Chinese restaurants are a favorite late-night sight—it's the image I keep in mind whenever ducks come through my kitchen. What the best of those birds possess is a lacquered skin and a dense, succulent bite.

Those ducks roast in special hanging ovens, so their fat renders and rolls down their bronzing bodies, landing into a drip pan below. Inspired by that setup, I developed this technique for a standard oven, and it's the best way I know to get a comparably delicious result. To guarantee gorgeous skin, the duck in this recipe lies flat directly on the oven grate so hot air circulates all around; there's no pan contact to heat the meat unevenly. And moisture, which would build up in a roasting pan, does not interfere with the bird's browning.

As for the precooking steps, first brine and then rub your duck with plenty of green peppercorns, which lend spice and mystery. Then the duck rests, to dry the skin; the tackier the skin is before you start, the more browned it will get. Since steam rises from the drip pan—which holds a bit of water to prevent the rendered fat from scorching—this drying step is especially important.

Be warned: This isn't the tidiest of roasting techniques no matter what you do. Go in prepared for a messy oven grate at the least. If this concerns you, you can roast this duck on an elevated rack fitted inside a roasting pan. But, with this option, the browning won't be nearly as even or lush.

---

1 gallon water

1 cup kosher salt

½ cup sugar

1 lemon, thinly sliced

1 fresh bay leaf

4 fresh thyme sprigs

¼ cup dry green peppercorns, toasted and roughly crushed

1 6-pound Long Island duck, rinsed and dried

Toasted Caper Oil (page 294), for serving

BRINE THE DUCK

In a large nonreactive container, combine the water, kosher salt, sugar, and lemon slices. Stir until the sugar and salt dissolve.

With the broad side of a chef's knife, press down on the bay leaf and thyme. Toss the pressed herbs and peppercorns into the brine.

Add the duck, making sure it is fully submerged. Brine in the refrigerator for 24 hours.

PREP THE DUCK

Lift the duck out of the brine and very thoroughly pat it dry with paper towels.

Place the duck, breast up, on a clean work surface. Press down on the top of its breastplate and flatten the midsection.

Grasp one of the duck's legs with one hand and steady its body with your free hand. Pull up and out on the leg, twisting it at its joints until both the drumstick and thigh audibly pop out of their sockets. The leg should hang loose at its joints. Repeat with the other leg. The duck should now lie flat on the work surface.

Transfer the duck to a large roasting pan so you can make sure the pan is large enough to hold the flattened duck with room to spare. Set the pan aside and return the duck to the work surface.

NOTE: *The roasting pan will catch the fat drippings, so make sure to choose the right size or dangerous flare-ups may occur if the fat falls to the oven floor.*

SCORE THE DUCK

With the tip of a sharp knife or a needle, prick the duck's skin all over at $1/2$-inch intervals. Make sure not to pierce through the fat to the meat.

Set a cooling rack in the roasting pan. Place the duck on the rack and transfer it to the refrigerator. Let the duck dry for 24 hours, or until its skin feels tacky. Midway through the drying, check on the duck's progress; flip it over to expose the underside if it is less dry than the top.

SET UP THE OVEN

Remove the duck from the refrigerator. Slide one of the oven's racks to the center position and a second to the lower third. Remove all other racks. Preheat the oven to 350°F.

Once the oven is hot, carefully pull out the center rack. Place the duck directly on the rack, breast up, so it lies flat. Next, pull out the lower rack and slide the roasting pan (without the cooling rack) directly below the duck. Pour $1/4$ inch of water into the roasting pan. Slide both racks back into place. Be sure the roasting pan is positioned directly below the duck so it catches all of the fat that will render.

ROAST AND REST

Roast the duck for about 2 hours, checking on it every 30 minutes. As the duck begins to render, fat in the drip pan will produce smoke if there is no water, so keep an eye on the water level, keeping it at about $1/4$ inch. Do not add too much, though, or too much steam will be created.

Halfway through roasting, use tongs to rotate (not flip) the duck 180 degrees, so its neck points in the opposite direction.

Once done, the duck should be golden brown and its joints should give freely when wiggled; it will be tender and cooked to medium-well doneness. Transfer the duck to a cooling rack set over a rimmed baking sheet and let it rest for 30 minutes before carving.

SERVE

Working on a large cutting board, gently pull on one of the legs and cut it off. Find the joint that connects the drumstick and the thigh with the tip of your knife and cut through to separate them. Using the same process, remove the wings. With a fork, pull bite-size pieces off the leg meat and its skin off the bone. Set the meat aside. Next, make a cut down the center of the breastbone and use your fingers or a fork to gently pull the left breast off to the left side, exposing where it sits on the carcass. Gently pull the breast off the bone and cut it into big chunks. Repeat with the right breast. Pull off any other meat still attached to the carcass with a fork, tongs, or fingers. Scatter all the pulled meat and skin across a large serving platter.

Serve the duck with the Roasted Squash and Cipollini Onions (recipe follows) scattered around the platter and the Toasted Caper Oil (page 294) alongside.

ROASTED SQUASH AND CIPOLLINI ONIONS

SERVES 4 TO 6

I like to cook duck when the leaves turn and the weather cools, since it is fatty and rich, so roasted fall vegetables are natural accompaniments. Cipollini, a squat, sweet onion, and winter squash fit the bill. Here the two roast stovetop until nicely caramelized, before oven roasting until tender. When served with duck, their sweetness dances off the bird's rich, musky flavor.

---

2 pounds butternut or delicata squash

Kosher salt

Olive oil, as needed

8 cipollini onions, peeled and halved equatorially

Leaves from 5 fresh marjoram sprigs

1 teaspoon hot pepper flakes

Flaky sea salt

HOW TO PLAN THIS MEAL:

2 days before: Brine duck.

1 day before: Dry duck. Make caper oil.

3½ hours before: Temper duck and caper oil.

2½ hours before: Roast duck.

1 hour before: Sear squash and onions.

30 minutes before: Roast squash and onions. Rest duck, then pull off duck meat and assemble platter.

PREPARE THE SQUASH

Preheat the oven to 350°F. If using butternut, peel away the tough skin; delicata skin can be eaten. Halve the squash lengthwise and scoop out the seeds. Cut the squash into ½-inch-wide crescents (1 inch if using delicata). Season well with kosher salt.

Set a large heavy pan over medium heat. Slick the pan with 2 tablespoons olive oil and, when it is shimmering-hot, add as many squash slices as will fit without overcrowding the pan. Roast the squash, cut sides down and without flipping, for 5 to 7 minutes, or until well browned in spots.

Transfer the squash to a platter, clean out the pan, and sear the remaining squash slices.

SEAR THE ONIONS

Wipe the pan clean and set it back over medium-high heat. Swirl in 2 tablespoons oil and season the onions with kosher salt. Once the oil is hot, add the onions, cut sides down, in one layer. Lower the heat to medium and sear the cipollini for 10 minutes, or until they almost blacken. Transfer the onions to a platter and wipe the pan clean. If working in batches, repeat with the remaining onions.

COMBINE AND ROAST

Wipe the pan clean. Working off the heat, arrange all the squash crescents back in the pan, standing them on edge so they point up. Arrange the onion halves between the crescents so their cut sides face up. If necessary, do this in a large roasting pan so that the vegetables all fit.

Sprinkle the vegetables with the marjoram, hot pepper flakes, and flaky sea salt. Roast in the oven for 15 minutes, or until the vegetables are tender.

2

TERRA COTTA-ROASTED SARDINES
WITH CUCUMBER, MINT, AND OLIVE SALAD

SERVES 4

Sardines are polarizing. Either you love them or . . . not. When sardines are very fresh, I'm in the love camp, and I love everything about them. Their flesh is rich and oily, round and unctuous. Their skin is silver and sleek, salty and a touch briny. To celebrate these qualities, I treat sardines as simply as possible, and that means straight oven roasting.

To get a touch of browning on their skins, these roast in a terra-cotta dish directly on the oven floor. Because the fish are small, they will cook quickly; the oven floor hits them with an intense direct heat that manages to get a little sizzle on them first.

While a number of roasting vessels will do here, I think terra-cotta interacts with the fish best—as its material transmits a gentle warmth that protects the fish's oils. My main objective whenever I cook sardines is to protect their high fat content. Metal would more likely hard-sear, and while that's not a bad thing, bringing the fish's fat to the smoking point and changing its flavor is not my goal here. Though still delicious, it is just not as pure.

Along with this most simple roast, a cucumber and olive salad, fragrant with mint, is perfect. Serve the Herbed Potatoes with Preserved Lemon (page 79) alongside if you'd like a little more heft to your meal.

2 lemons

6 fresh bay leaves, halved lengthwise (optional)

12 large very fresh sardines (about 2 pounds total), cleaned, gutted, and scaled

Coarse sea salt

Olive oil, as needed

Hot pepper flakes to taste

4 dill sprigs, torn

PREPARE AND SEASON THE SARDINES

Finely zest both lemons to get 2 teaspoons of zest. If you like, slice one of the lemons into thin rounds for stuffing the fish.

Preheat the oven to 475°F. If using the bay leaves and sliced lemons, stuff half of a bay leaf and a lemon round into the belly cavity of each fish.

Place the sardines in a large terra-cotta dish or other large, heavy roasting vessel. Season with salt and toss the sardines with oil, lemon zest, hot pepper flakes, and dill. Arrange the fish in a single, uncrowded layer; roast in batches if necessary.

ROAST THE SARDINES AND SERVE

Raise the oven temperature to 500°F and immediately set the sardines on the oven floor. Raising the temperature causes the flame to kick in and gives the oven floor a jolt of heat. Roast the sardines for 5 minutes, or until their eyes turn opaque and the flesh gives easily when pressed at its thickest point. Remove the sardines from the oven and serve immediately with Cucumber, Mint, and Olive Salad (recipe follows).

CUCUMBER, MINT, AND OLIVE SALAD

SERVES 4

Cool and refreshing, this salad is well suited to the roasted sardines. It's a little unusual in that the salad is never really tossed; the vinaigrette—also made with cucumbers—is pooled on a plate with the components scattered on top. The briny olives that dot the mix complement the fish's richness and the crisp cucumber is a fresh counterpoint.

½ English cucumber, peeled and seeded

½ jalapeño pepper

Finely grated zest and juice of 1 lime

1 teaspoon colatura or high-quality fish sauce, such as Red Boat

1 teaspoon agave or light honey

2 tablespoons olive oil

Flaky sea salt, as needed

1 cup oil-cured whole Taggiasca or other aromatic black olives, pitted and smashed

4 Persian cucumbers, sliced into very thin rounds

¼ cup fresh mint leaves, whole or roughly torn

MAKE THE CUCUMBER VINAIGRETTE

Working with a box grater set over a medium bowl, finely grate the English cucumber. Finely grate the jalapeño, stopping at its stem. Stir the pulps together to combine. Whisk in the lime zest and juice, colatura, agave, and olive oil. Season with salt if necessary. Hold the vinaigrette until serving.

PREPARE THE SALAD

Pour some vinaigrette onto a serving platter, creating a shallow pool. If serving with the sardines, arrange the roasted sardines over the vinaigrette and scatter the smashed olives and cucumber rounds over the fish. Or, simply top the vinaigrette with olives and cucumbers. Garnish with mint and serve immediately.

HOW TO PLAN THIS MEAL:

30 minutes before: Make cucumber vinaigrette. Prep salad. Stuff sardines, if you like.

10 minutes before: Roast and plate sardines and salad.

3

NANCY SILVERTON'S FOCACCIA DI STRACCHINO
WITH ARTICHOKE AND ARUGULA SALAD

SERVES 4

I first ate this pizza-like focaccia di stracchino at Nancy Silverton's Pizzeria Mozza in Los Angeles. It was instant seduction: When bitten, the cracker-like focaccia shattered and oozy cheese slipped out. Despite its richness, every bite was light and airy. Much to my surprise, once Nancy sent me the recipe, I realized how well it translates to home kitchens.

The olive oil–enriched dough is richly flavored and the cheese it encases, stracchino, is milky and mild—a dream when melted into the crust. If you can't find stracchino, fresh, soft mozzarella does well here too. Or you can use a careful amount of the more-assertive taleggio.

The dough needs only a half hour of rest after a quick knead. One helpful note from Nancy: A shallow, thin metal pan works best here. Since it holds little residual heat, a thin pan creates less steam and the end result crisps up just right.

Yes, this is a baking recipe living in a roasting chapter. But since this pie cooks off like a simple oven roast, why *not* include it here? Anyway, it *is* here and it's a gift. Thank you, Nancy.

---

4 cups (17 ounces) bread or all-purpose flour, plus more for dusting

1 teaspoon fine sea salt

½ cup plus 2 tablespoons olive oil, plus more for brushing

7 ounces stracchino or fresh mozzarella

Flaky sea salt

MAKE THE DOUGH

Mix the flour and fine sea salt together in a large wide bowl. Make a mound and punch a 4-inch-wide well in its center. Pour ½ cup of the olive oil and 1 cup plus 1½ tablespoons water into the well. Use a fork to slowly work the dry ingredients into the wet until a shaggy dough forms. Knead the dough in the bowl for 30 seconds, or until a cohesive mass forms.

Turn the dough out onto a clean, lightly floured work surface and knead it until smooth. Halve the dough and form 2 balls. Set the balls aside, covered with a lightly dampened kitchen towel, and let rest for 30 minutes.

ROLL OUT THE DOUGH

Preheat the oven to 500°F.

Lightly brush a large baking sheet (18 × 13 inches, the size of a half-sheet tray, or a 16-inch thin round pizza pan) with olive oil.

Return 1 ball of dough to a clean, lightly floured work surface. Keep the second ball of dough covered under the kitchen towel. Lightly dust a rolling pin with flour.

Flatten the ball slightly and stretch and press it so it resembles a disk.

For a rectanglar pan: Start rolling your pin back and forth and side to

side, until you have a rectangle about 12 × 10 inches. Carefully pick up the dough and stretch it out with the backs of your hands, until it is approximately 20 × 15 inches and $\frac{1}{8}$ inch thick. The dough should be just thin enough that you can see light through it. Lay the dough on the pan, centering it; there should be about 1 inch of overhanging dough on all sides.

For a round pan: Roll out the disk of dough from its center. Rotate the circle slightly, about 10 degrees, and repeat this action. Continue rolling the dough and turning it until you have a circle 12 inches in diameter. Then pick up the dough and stretch it, with the backs of your hands, until the circle is approximately 18 inches wide and $\frac{1}{8}$ inch thick. The dough should be just thin enough that you can see light through it. Lay the dough on the pan, centering it; there should be about $\frac{1}{2}$ inch of overhanging dough.

ASSEMBLE THE PIE

Dot the dough with the cheese, placing either small bits at $\frac{1}{2}$-inch intervals across its surface or large clumps intermittently, depending on whether you like every bite the same or prefer contrast between dough and cheese. Drizzle the top generously with about 2 tablespoons of the olive oil and sprinkle on some flaky salt.

Roll and stretch the second ball of dough in the same fashion as the first. Lay this dough over the pie, matching the first layer. Cinch together the 2 layers of dough along the edge of the pan so the pie is well sealed. Trim away the excess overhanging dough

With the tip of a knife, make $\frac{1}{2}$-inch slits in the top layer of dough at 1-inch intervals, leaving a 1-inch border untouched, or, if you used big clumps of cheese, make slits above the cheese clumps. Brush the pie with olive oil and sprinkle with more flaky salt.

BAKE AND SERVE THE PIE

Bake the focaccia on the oven's center rack for 10 to 12 minutes, or until golden and crisp. Tap it with a fork. If it sounds solid, your pie is done.

Remove the pan from the oven and serve the focaccia immediately with the artichoke and arugula salad and hazelnut pesto alongside (recipe follows).

SHAVED ARTICHOKE, ARUGULA, AND HAZELNUT PESTO SALAD

SERVES 4

The preceding focaccia, like most dishes from northern Italy, is elegant and minimal and wants a salad with similar qualities to accompany it.

Hazelnuts, which are prolific in the north, reference the focaccia's provenance and provide this loose pesto with its body. When dressing the salad, add just enough pesto to slick and flavor the mix. Any extra can do double duty as a dip for the crispy, stuffed focaccia.

If you're not a fan of raw artichokes, or if you can't find great-looking ones to feature raw, simply toss the shavings with salt, pepper, and enough olive oil to make them shine. Then, spread them out over a baking tray and roast them off at 400°F for 15 minutes, or until browned and crisp.

1½ lemons

5 baby artichokes

1 garlic clove

Kosher salt

10 sage leaves, finely sliced

1½ cups skinless hazelnuts, toasted

¼ cup coarsely grated Parmesan, plus more for shaving

1 cup olive oil

3 cups arugula

2 fresh mint sprigs, leaves removed and roughly torn

Freshly cracked black peppercorns

1 tablespoon aged balsamic vinegar (optional)

PREPARE THE ARTICHOKES

Set up an ice water bath. Cut 1 lemon in half, squeeze its juices into the ice bath, and toss in the squeezed fruit.

With a sharp paring knife, cut off the top ½ to 1 inch of the artichoke leaves to expose the tender interior. Peel back and remove the tough, dark outer leaves. When only tender and pale green leaves remain, pare the artichoke's base until smooth.

Trim ¼ to ½ inch from the stem end, until it feels moist. With the tip of your knife or a vegetable peeler, cut away the stringy exterior from the stem of the artichoke, beginning at the base of the heart and carefully running the blade along its curve and onto the stem. Once peeled and smooth, immediately place the artichoke in the ice bath and repeat the peeling procedure with the remaining artichokes.

Remove 1 artichoke from the ice water, pat it dry, and halve it lengthwise. With a sharp knife or mandoline, shave the artichoke into ¼-inch slivers. Put the shavings back in the ice water and repeat with the remaining artichokes.

Once all the artichokes are shaved, transfer the ice bath to the refrigerator. Chill for 15 to 30 minutes, or until the shavings' edges curl.

MAKE THE PESTO

Place the garlic and a pinch of salt in a large mortar. With a pestle, smash the garlic until a smooth paste forms. (Alternatively, do this on a cutting board with the blunt sides of your knife, transfer to a food processor, and continue the recipe in the food processor.) Add the sage and hazelnuts. Continue smashing until the hazelnuts break into a medium-fine crumb.

Grate the zest of the remaining lemon half and stir it, along with the grated Parmesan and olive oil, into the nut mixture (save the lemon half for seasoning the salad). Season to taste with salt and set the pesto aside. Pesto can be held at room temperature for up to 2 hours; for overnight or longer, store pesto, covered, in the refrigerator for up to 1 week.

ASSEMBLE THE SALAD

Lift the artichoke shavings from the ice water bath, drain, and pat dry. In a large salad bowl, place the artichoke shavings, arugula, and mint leaves. Season with a pinch of salt and pepper and gently toss with some hazelnut pesto. Add extra pesto, salt, or lemon juice, as needed, until the salad is lightly coated and well seasoned.

Drizzle aged balsamic vinegar, if using, over the salad and, if inclined, garnish with extra shavings of Parmesan. Serve immediately with the leftover pesto alongside.

HOW TO PLAN THIS MEAL:

2 hours before: Shave artichokes and make pesto.

1 hour before: Make focaccia dough.

45 minutes before: Preheat oven.

20 minutes before: Assemble focaccia.

10 minutes before: Bake focaccia and dress salad.

4

OLIVE OIL–CURED COD AND SUMMER TOMATO PANADE

SERVES 6 TO 8

Panades are savory bread puddings, but instead of being moistened with egg, milk, or cream, as is traditional, here a Mediterranean mix of grated tomatoes and olive oil does the trick, making for a complex casserole.

As the dish cooks, the juices fuse with the bread, binding the interior. To help this along, let the panade rest overnight before baking so the bread gets a head start on the softening process and the cod's flavor has a chance to mix with the tomato juices. Once baked, this panade has a wonderful contrast between its fluffy inside and crusty, roasty outside. The result is rich but bright, juicy and meaty from the tomatoes and salt cod.

For best results, choose the right roasting vessel (a heavy pan will crisp the panade's edges properly) and pack your dish just high enough to give you one part roasty goodness on the outside to two parts pillowy softness on the inside. And, of course, use great, ripe summer tomatoes.

Before you start layering, taste the cod for salinity and adjust the seasoning of the dish accordingly. Also, for extra oomph, use the garlic oil from the Garlic Confit (page 306) instead of raw olive oil. In such instances, I also toss in a few of the whole garlic cloves too, tucking them in somewhere between the tomato pulp, bread, and cod. Whatever you do, have fun with this one. Layering it together is good and messy.

1½ pounds Olive Oil–Cured Salt Cod, at room temperature (page 308)

Olive oil, as needed

8 ¾-inch slices of filone or other rustic country white bread

2 garlic cloves, peeled and halved

4 pounds large beefsteak tomatoes (about 5 tomatoes)

Kosher salt and freshly cracked black peppercorns

2 tablespoons roughly sliced fresh oregano leaves

10 Garlic Confit cloves plus their oil (page 306), optional but recommended

1 to 2 Fresno chiles, to taste, stemmed, seeded, and thinly sliced

2 teaspoons finely grated lemon zest (from about 2 lemons), or to taste

½ cup roughly sliced fresh flat-leaf parsley leaves

PREPARE THE COD, GRATED TOMATO, AND BREAD

Remove the codfish from the olive oil. Peel away and discard the skin and break the fillets into large pieces, following the fish's natural seams. Set aside.

Place a large heavy sauté pan over medium heat. Once the pan is hot, pour in ¼ cup olive oil and, when the oil shimmers, lay in as many bread slices as will fit comfortably in one layer. Fry both sides for 1 to 2 minutes each, or until golden and crisp. Remove the toast from the pan and, while hot, rub both sides with the cut, raw garlic. Set the toast aside and repeat the process with the remaining bread slices, adding extra oil as needed to coat the bottom of the pan.

Halve 3 of the tomatoes equatorially and grate them into a wide, medium bowl, stopping at their skins. You should have about 4 1/2 cups of pulp. Season the pulp with salt and pepper and set the bowl aside. Slice the remaining tomatoes into 3/4-inch rounds.

BUILD THE PANADE

Brush the bottom and sides of a 4-quart (13 × 9-inch) casserole dish with olive oil. Spread a thin layer of the tomato pulp over the bottom. Sprinkle on a few of the oregano leaves. If using garlic confit, smash 1 or 2 cloves and toss them into the dish.

Next, lay in the tomato slices, fitting them snugly across the dish (reserve a few for the top). Season the tomato with salt, pepper, another sprinkle of oregano, and some chile slices. Break up 2 of the toasts into bite-size chunks and scatter them on top of the tomato. Scatter half of the flaked cod and 4 garlic confit cloves, if using, around the bread.

Spoon more tomato pulp over the mixture and press down on the layers, compressing the panade.

Now add a solid layer of larger pieces of bread, followed by another scattering of oregano and chiles. Spoon around a little more tomato pulp. Gently press down to compress again.

Add a solid layer of the remaining cod, flaked into bite-size pieces. Scatter the remaining garlic confit and nestle in slices of tomato, as will fit. Season the tomatoes with salt and pepper.

Spoon over the remaining tomato pulp. Drizzle garlic confit oil or olive oil generously over the top, and finish with the remaining oregano, chile slices, and the lemon zest.

COVER AND REST

Tightly cover the casserole with plastic wrap and refrigerate for at least 12 hours so the flavors meld and the bread moistens.

BAKE AND SERVE THE PANADE

Preheat the oven to 400°F. Uncover the panade and bake on the center rack for 45 minutes, or until the top browns and the casserole is bubbling. Remove the panade from the oven and let it rest for 10 minutes. Top with the sliced parsley.

To serve, spoon the panade onto individual plates and serve with Herb and Scallion Salad (recipe follows) alongside, if desired.

HERB AND SCALLION SALAD

SERVES 6 TO 8 AS A GARNISH FOR THE PANADE

Even though this cod and tomato panade is lighter than most bread casseroles, it benefits from contrast. Enter this herb and scallion salad: Sharp and herbaceous, it works as a palate cleanser. Crisping the herbs in ice water perks up their flavor and snap.

¼ cup fresh flat-leaf parsley leaves

1 cup fresh mint leaves

2 tablespoons celery leaves

1 cup thinly sliced scallions, dark and light green parts, cut on the bias

Flaky sea salt and freshly ground black peppercorns

2 tablespoons olive oil

Juice and finely grated zest of ½ lemon

Chill a medium bowl. Fill a small bowl with an ice bath. Place the parsley, mint, and celery leaves in the bath and chill for at least 10 minutes. Remove and spin dry.

Transfer the herbs to the chilled bowl and toss in the scallions. Gently toss and season with salt and pepper. Let the mixture rest for 10 minutes, or until the herbs soften slightly.

Just before serving, dress the salad with olive oil, lemon juice, and zest to taste.

HOW TO PLAN THIS MEAL:

7 days before: Prepare semi-cured salt cod.

3 days before: Prepare olive oil–cured salt cod and garlic confit, if using.

1 day before: Build panade.

1 hour before: Bake panade and chill herbs.

10 minutes before: Make herb and scallion salad. Let panade rest.

5

SALT-ROASTED BASS WITH GREEN GRAPE SMASH

SERVES 4

Straight oven roasting yields a focused flavor and caramelized exterior. Salt roasting, however, complicates that equation by eliminating caramelization and improving succulence. It's a beautiful twist.

In this recipe, we cook whole black bass in a pink peppercorn salt crust, which insulates the fish, perfumes it, and conducts heat evenly around the fish. Under the salt crust, it steams in its own juice, turning extra tender and almost sticky. To wrap up the plate, the sweet-tart juices and pulpy fruit of a smashed green grape vinaigrette trickle down and pool around the fillets. If you like, you can roast a few extra grapes to serve whole with the fish as well.

A note on serving: The fish continues to roast in its crust even when removed from the oven, so you should account for that when planning your meal. Also, once filleted and plated, the meat cools rapidly. So, I suggest, before you start the dramatic act of unearthing the fish, have guests at the ready. Score some oohs and aahs, crack the crust, and serve.

---

1 4-pound whole black bass, gutted but not scaled

2 lemons

10 fresh thyme sprigs, bruised

3 fresh bay leaves, bruised

4 cups coarse sea salt

3 large egg whites, plus more if needed

¼ cup pink peppercorns, lightly toasted

1 cup seedless green grapes

¼ cup plus 2 tablespoons olive oil, plus more for drizzling

Flaky sea salt and freshly ground black peppercorns

1 tablespoon aged balsamic vinegar, preferably 10 years old (optional)

PREPARE THE FISH

Preheat the oven to 400°F. Under cold running water, rinse the bass, inside and out. Gently pat the fish dry. Lay the bass on a clean work surface. Slice 1 lemon into thin rounds and stuff the fish's cavity with the lemon rounds, thyme sprigs, and bay leaves.

MAKE THE SALT CRUST

In a medium bowl, mix together the coarse salt, egg whites, and pink peppercorns. The mixture should feel granular and be damp enough to hold together when pressed. If it's too wet, add more salt; if it's too dry to hold together, add part of an extra egg white.

ROAST THE FISH

Cover a cookie sheet or an inverted baking sheet with parchment paper. (Inverting the baking sheet lets you slide the fish off without a rim to get in the way.) Spread a ½-inch salt bed across the paper that is large enough to cover the bass's body; its head and tail need not rest on the salt. Lay the bass on the salt and pack the remaining salt over the fish, leaving the tail and head exposed. The body should be fully encased in a uniform ½-inch crust.

Slide the baking sheet onto the oven's middle rack. Roast the bass for 25 minutes, or until its eyes turn opaque and a cake tester inserted into the thickest part of the fish meets with no resistance and comes out very warm, but not quite hot to the touch. If you don't have a cake tester, you can also brush back the salt and prod the flesh just behind the fish's head. If that is juicy and almost flakes when pressed, the fish is done. Remove the bass from the oven and let it rest for 10 minutes so it finishes cooking and the juices settle.

(recipe continues)

MAKE THE GREEN GRAPE SMASH

With a mortar and pestle, smash the grapes into a coarse, pulpy mixture. (You can also do this in a bowl using a fork.) Whisk in the ¼ cup olive oil and season to taste with salt, pepper, and the juice from half of the remaining lemon (about 1 tablespoon).

CLEAN AND FILLET THE FISH

For dramatic effect, present the whole roasted fish at the table before removing the salt crust. Then, back in the kitchen, slide the bass off the baking sheet and onto a clean work surface. Flip the pan right side up and keep it nearby so you have a place to dispose of the salt crust and bones when filleting.

In a small bowl, mix the remaining 2 tablespoons olive oil with 2 tablespoons water.

With a large spoon or the heel of a chef's knife (the heel is where the blade meets the handle), tap down the length of the fish, cracking the crust in half at its center. Carefully peel away as much of the salt crust as possible and discard.

Next, dip a stiff pastry brush in the oil-water mixture and brush away any remaining salt from the fish. Brushing with oil and water helps dissolve any remaining bits of salt.

Once all the salt is cleared from the top of the fish, carefully flip the fish onto a perfectly clean work surface, so the salt crust faces up. Carefully pull away the parchment if it is stuck to the fish, and the salt crust too. Discard both. Using the pastry brush dipped in the oil and water mixture, wipe away any remaining salt particles.

Once your work area is completely salt free, use a fork to loosen the skin behind the gills, just behind the fish's head. Carefully lift this skin up and pull it back toward the tail, exposing the flesh. Discard the skin.

Using a serving spoon and knife, separate the fillets by cutting down the center line that runs the length of the body. This will divide the fillet into 2 long pieces. Working with one at a time, lift each of these fillets off the bones and place on a warm serving platter. Since the fish is cooked through, it should easily peel off the bone.

Next, grip the fish's tail and lift the spine up and away from the flesh below. Discard the spine and head. Gingerly split the bottom fillet into 2 long parts, as you did with the top fillet. Working with one at a time, lift each off the skin and transfer them to the serving platter.

Note: There will be bones in the fillets, in the belly area in particular. These are easy to remove at the table, but it's nice to let your guests know.

DRESS AND SERVE THE FISH

Spoon the green grape smash and its juices over the warm fish. Drizzle on the balsamic vinegar, if using. Finish with a squeeze of the remaining lemon half. Serve with Caramelized Parsnips (recipe follows).

CARAMELIZED PARSNIPS

SERVES 4

Serving these parsnips with the salt-roasted sea bass and grape vinaigrette brings a quiet, roasted charm to an otherwise juicy composition.

The mace lends a singular, musky warmth to the parsnips. Carrots (and a host of other winter root vegetables) work fine in place of the parsnips, too. If you like, you can even make a medley.

---

2 pounds parsnips, scrubbed and stem end removed

2 tablespoons olive oil

Kosher salt and freshly cracked black peppercorns

¼ teaspoon ground mace or nutmeg

Preheat the oven to 375°F. Cut the parsnips into long, ½-inch-thick planks.

In a medium bowl, toss the parsnips with the olive oil, a few generous pinches of salt and pepper, and mace or nutmeg.

Spread the parsnips on a rimmed baking sheet, so they fit comfortably in an even layer. Roast on the oven's center rack, flipping them halfway through, for 35 minutes, or until caramelized and tender. Remove from the oven and serve.

These can also be held at room temperature for up to 2 hours in advance and rewarmed just before serving.

HOW TO PLAN THIS MEAL:

75 minutes before: Roast parsnips.

1 hour before: Prepare fish and salt crust.

45 minutes before: Roast fish.

25 minutes before: Make grape smash.

20 minutes before: Let fish rest.

10 minutes before: Clean and fillet fish. Arrange platter.

6

FARRO PORRIDGE WITH SWEET AND SAVORY WINTER ANTIPASTO

SERVES 4 TO 6

Flipping through an old Italian cookbook, I came across a reference for cracked farro, also known as emmer—an ancient, nutty variety of wheat. Out of curiosity, I played with it and found it made a dark, wholesome, slightly chewy porridge—an ideal brunch with a host of roasted winter fruits and vegetables.

For variety, I suggest roasting each fruit and vegetable differently, exposing different sides of their character. Caramelize the pears and apples by using both the stovetop and oven. Steam-roast the beets and carrots by cooking them in foil-wrapped packets, and, finally, roast the chestnuts in their shells in the oven's dry heat.

Pecorino butter and quince mostarda melt into each bite, and the combination of sweet, sharp, and slightly salty is brunch at its brightest. Other fixings at home on this table include raw apple slivers and thin slices of prosciutto.

If you can't find cracked farro, slow-cooked polenta (page 35) or even coarse oats make great alternatives and hold their own against each of these offerings.

---

1 pound chestnuts

½ tablespoon butter, melted

Flaky sea salt and freshly cracked black peppercorns

Kosher salt

1½ cups cracked farro

Zest of 1 lemon

2 green apples

Sage-Roasted Pears and Apples (recipe follows)

Foil-Roasted Beets and Carrots (recipe follows)

1 cup Quince Mostarda (page 303)

4 ounces Pecorino Butter (page 310), chilled and sliced

½ pound thinly sliced prosciutto

ROAST THE CHESTNUTS

With a small paring knife, cut an X into the flat side of each chestnut shell. Spread the scored nuts on a rimmed baking sheet. This can be done up to 3 days ahead of time, and will help in peeling.

Preheat the oven to 350°F. Roast the chestnuts on the center rack for 35 minutes, or until aromatic and their flesh is easily pierced with the tip of a sharp knife. Remove the nuts from the oven and let them cool.

Wrap the chestnuts in a kitchen towel and place them on a flat work surface. Gently bang on the nuts with a mallet or heavy saucepan until their shells crack open. Peel off the shells and discard.

Wrap the chestnuts in another kitchen towel and rub them until their thin papery films release from their flesh. Place the skinned chestnuts in a small bowl and toss them with the melted butter and a few pinches of flaky sea salt and pepper. Set the chestnuts aside until ready to serve.

(recipe continues)

MAKE THE PORRIDGE

Pour 6 cups water into a medium
Dutch oven, add 2 teaspoons kosher
salt, and bring to a boil over high heat.
Reduce the heat to low and, whisking
constantly, slowly pour the cracked
farro into the simmering water. Add the
lemon zest.

Cook the farro, stirring often to ensure
the bottom doesn't scorch, for about
1 hour, or until the grains tenderize and
the porridge has a rich, creamy texture.
Add water to loosen or continue to cook
to tighten to your preference, but don't
cook all the chew out of the grains.
Turn off the heat and season with extra
kosher salt and pepper, enough to make
it a bit savory.

Cover the pot and keep the porridge
warm until serving. The farro can be
prepared up to 1 hour in advance. To
rewarm, loosen the farro with water, if
too tight, and warm it gently over low
heat, stirring often, until bubbling hot.

PREPARE THE APPLES

While the farro cooks, prepare the
fresh apples. Fill a small bowl with ice
water. Quarter, core, and thinly slice
the apples. Put the slices in the ice
water and refrigerate, uncovered, for
20 minutes, or until chilled and crisp.
The apples can be prepared up to 1 hour
ahead of time. Fifteen minutes before
serving, drain the apple slices and
pat dry.

SERVE

Put the chestnuts, roasted apples and
pears, and roasted beets and carrots in
individual serving bowls, or pile them
together in a large, warmed skillet. Set
out the apple slivers, quince mostarda,
pecorino butter, and a platter of
prosciutto. Serve the porridge, and let
guests garnish as desired.

SAGE-ROASTED PEARS AND APPLES

SERVES 4 TO 6 WITH FARRO

Simple pears and apples turn buttery-sweet when blasted at high heat. To get a pronounced caramelization, I first sear the fruit, cut sides down, in a cast-iron pan on the stovetop. Then the action moves to the oven, so the fruits tenderize. Sage leaves lend their warming, forest flavor.

2 Bosc pears, halved lengthwise

2 Pink Lady or Honeycrisp apples, halved lengthwise

¼ cup olive oil

Kosher salt

3 large fresh sage sprigs

Preheat the oven to 400°F. In a large bowl, toss the fruit with 2 tablespoons of the olive oil and a generous pinch of salt. Arrange the fruit, cut sides down, in a large cast-iron pan or other heavy, ovenproof sauté pan. Cook the fruit over medium-high heat for 3 to 5 minutes, or until browned along the fruit's edges.

Nestle the sage amid the pears and apples. Without flipping the fruit, transfer the pan to the oven's center rack and roast for 12 to 15 minutes, or until the skins wrinkle and are easily pierced with a knife. Remove the pan from the oven and transfer the fruit to a clean work surface.

When cool enough to handle, core the fruit and cut it into 1-inch wedges (or leave it whole, if you prefer). Place the pears and apples in a bowl and drizzle with the remaining 2 tablespoons olive oil. Cut up the sage leaves and sprinkle them over the fruit.

The roasted fruit can be served hot or at room temperature.

FOIL-ROASTED BEETS AND CARROTS

SERVES 4 TO 6 WITH FARRO

Wrapping carrots and beets in foil means the sugary vegetables steam in their own vapor. I love to cook these on the oven floor, to get a bit of uneven, rustic caramelization on their otherwise smooth surfaces. If their skins are tender, you can serve the roasted beets skin-on. Otherwise, rub them between lots of paper towels until their skins slip off.

1 pound baby beets, preferably Chioggia, scrubbed clean

1 pound medium carrots, greens trimmed, scrubbed clean

¼ cup olive oil

Kosher salt and freshly cracked black peppercorns

12 fresh thyme sprigs

2 tablespoons lemon juice (from 1 lemon), or to taste

SEASON THE VEGETABLES

Preheat the oven to 400°F. Place the beets in one large bowl and the carrots in another. Toss each with 2 tablespoons olive oil and salt and pepper to taste.

MAKE PACKETS

Rip off two 24-inch pieces of aluminum foil. Pile the beets on one piece of foil and the carrots on the other. Divide the thyme evenly between the piles. Fold the foil over and cinch it together along its edges to form tightly sealed packets.

ROAST THE VEGETABLES

Place the packets in a heavy roasting dish. Set the dish on the oven floor and roast for 15 minutes. Flip the packets and roast for another 15 minutes, or until the vegetables are just tender enough to be pierced easily with a knife. Depending on the vegetables' relative size, the beets may take longer to cook than the carrots.

Remove the vegetables from the oven and open the packets, being careful of the steam that will burst out. Let the vegetables cool until just warm to the touch. If the beets' skins are tough or thick, use paper towels to rub them off. Discard the skins.

Cut the carrots and beets into bite-size pieces (or in half, or leave them whole if you prefer). Transfer the vegetables to a bowl and season them with salt, pepper, and lemon juice to taste. Set the vegetables aside and let them cool to room temperature before serving.

HOW TO PLAN THIS MEAL:

3 days before: Cut chestnuts and let dry.

1 day before: Make quince mostarda.

3 hours before: Make pecorino butter and roast chestnuts.

90 minutes before: Make farro porridge. Prepare raw apple.

1 hour before: Roast pears and apples. Roast beets and carrots.

15 minutes before: Drain and dry apple slices. Rewarm porridge, if necessary.

10 minutes before: Set out bowls of roasted antipasti.

7

DIRTY ASPARAGUS WITH SALSA DI PANE AND POACHED EGG

SERVES 2 TO 4

As an introduction to stovetop roasting, this simple recipe extols the technique's virtues: The heat from below creates a deep sear along each asparagus spear—so severe that the asparagus ends up looking, well, dirty. If you're using white asparagus, which require a bit more preparation but taste sweeter and nuttier than green, the look is even more dramatic. Poached eggs and a rich, mellow sauce made from bread and garlic confit lend contrast and a bit of substance. It's a simple but compelling meal for brunch or a light dinner with crusty bread.

With this recipe, high heat and a low-walled pan are key. Otherwise, the moisture in the pan won't evaporate quickly enough and it may turn to steam. Trapped steam, which can gather as an ingredient releases its water, can either overcook the spears or inhibit an aggressive mark from forming on them.

As for the actual cooking, you'll know if you are on the right track from the moment the asparagus hit the pan. They should sizzle instantly and keep sizzling at an excited pace until nearly blackened.

---

12 jumbo asparagus (about 1 pound), white asparagus preferred

2 tablespoons olive oil

Kosher salt

4 tablespoons (½ stick) butter, diced

10 fresh thyme sprigs

10 fresh sage leaves

6 strips of lemon peel, removed with a vegetable peeler

1 tablespoon plus 1 teaspoon white wine vinegar

4 very fresh large eggs

Salsa di Pane (recipe follows)

Flaky sea salt

Freshly cracked black pepper

½ cup arugula (optional)

2 tablespoons finely cut fresh chives

PREPARE THE ASPARAGUS

Trim the woody ends off the asparagus spears until their bases are no longer fibrous. With a vegetable peeler, remove the stalks' tough outer skin until they feel tender.

In a medium bowl, toss the asparagus with the olive oil and 2 generous pinches of kosher salt. Set aside.

COOK THE ASPARAGUS

Set a heavy, large low-walled skillet over high heat until very hot. Lay the asparagus in the hot, dry pan; work in batches if you can't fit all of the spears comfortably in one layer. It is important not to overcrowd here, as that creates steam.

Sear the asparagus, without moving it, for 2 to 3 minutes, or until darkly browned on one side. Then turn the spears and roast all sides in the same fashion so they are uniformly charred.

In the last minute of cooking, add the butter, thyme, sage, and lemon peel to the pan. (If you are working in batches, divide accordingly.) Swish the asparagus around and, with a large spoon, vigorously baste the spears with the butter until the foam subsides.

Transfer the spears to a warm platter. Season with kosher salt and set aside.

POACH THE EGGS

Set a medium saucepan filled with 1 quart water, the white wine vinegar, and 1 teaspoon kosher salt over medium-high heat. Crack each egg into its own ramekin.

Bring the water to a boil, then reduce the heat to low, to maintain steam, but no bubbling. Lower 1 ramekin into the pot and tilt it so the egg slips into the water. Once the egg white begins to

set, add the next egg. Repeat with the remaining eggs.

Gently poach the eggs for 3 minutes, or until the whites set and the yolks firm up along their edges but remain runny at their centers. With a slotted spoon, lift the eggs out of the water, in the same order they were dropped in. Blot the eggs dry and set them aside on a plate.

ASSEMBLE THE DISH

Generously smear the salsa di pane across a large, warm serving platter.

Top the sauce with the seared asparagus and poached eggs. Sprinkle flaky salt and pepper over the top and garnish with the arugula, if using, and chives. Serve immediately.

SALSA DI PANE

MAKES 1½ CUPS

Bread isn't used enough as a thickener, but it works like a charm and always lends a voluptuous mouthfeel. Here, we blacken and blend slices into a hot liquid, creating a sauce with voluptuous body and funky depth.

To stop this sauce from cooking and protect the fried bread's flavor from getting lost, set it over an ice water bath once blended smooth. Then, whisk in the olive oil, preferably one with spicy, grassy notes.

---

4 ounces country bread, sliced ½ inch thick

1½ cups Burnt-Onion Dashi (page 287) or vegetable stock, warm

5 cloves Garlic Confit (page 306)

2 tablespoons olive oil

1 tablespoon sherry vinegar

Kosher salt and freshly cracked black pepper

CHAR THE BREAD

Heat a medium heavy pan over medium-high heat until hot. Lay in the bread and toast it for 3 minutes per side, or until well charred and nearly blackened. Remove the bread from the pan and, when cool enough to handle, roughly tear it into 1-inch pieces. There should be about 2 cups of torn bread.

MAKE THE SAUCE

Pour the warm dashi into a blender or food processor. Secure the lid and blend the dashi so it whizzes up the blender's sides. With the machine running, slowly add the garlic confit through the feeder. Once the sauce has emulsified, add the bread through the feeder. Continue blending until the sauce is smooth and resembles a loose aioli.

Set up an ice bath in a large bowl. Pour the bread sauce into a slightly smaller bowl and set it in the ice bath. Once it has cooled to room temperature, remove the sauce from the ice bath and whisk in the oil and vinegar. Season to taste with salt and pepper.

> **HOW TO PLAN THIS MEAL:**
>
> **3 hours before:** Make garlic confit and dashi.
>
> **30 minutes before:** Make salsa di pane.
>
> **10 minutes before:** Roast asparagus.
>
> **5 minutes before:** Poach eggs and arrange platter.

8

FLASH-SEARED SALMON WITH LEMON SALT, SPRING PEAS, AND CHANTERELLES

SERVES 4

Four-sided seared salmon is my western ode to teppanyaki, a Japanese method for quickly searing fresh ingredients on a very hot griddle. As with the asparagus on page 144, the pan matters. And here the walls should be even shorter if possible.

Fat-laced salmon reacts particularly well when browned all the way around: Fatty and rich, it caramelizes quickly while the inside remains moist. To ensure the salmon heats through, temper the fillets to room temperature before searing.

Accompanying the salmon is a lemon salt, made by evaporating lemon juice and zest directly on the salt crystals. It provides a sharp, sunny spike of flavor and salinity, and a punch to the salmon's natural unctuousness.

The quality of the fish you use here is important, since it's not seasoned until after cooking. Its natural flavor must shine. Understanding how to navigate through the various offerings out there isn't easy; I always opt for wild salmon caught in season: spring and summer. That's why spring chanterelles and sweet peas dress this dish. Round the meal out, if you'd like, with some steamed short-grain rice.

---

2 lemons

½ cup flaky sea salt

1½ pounds center-cut wild king salmon fillet, cut into 4 1-inch-thick portions

Olive oil, as needed

½ bunch watercress (about 3 ounces)

MAKE THE LEMON SALT

Finely grate the zest of 1 lemon and then juice it to produce ½ tablespoon of juice. In a small bowl, mix the salt, lemon zest, and juice. (Save the second lemon for garnishing.) Line a rimmed baking sheet with paper towels and spread the seasoned salt on it in a thin layer. Let it sit at room temperature for 12 hours, or until dry enough to sprinkle. Use the salt right away or store in an airtight container for up to 2 weeks.

SEAR THE FISH

Remove the salmon from the refrigerator at least 30 minutes before cooking and let it come to room temperature. Cut the remaining lemon into wedges, for serving.

Pat the salmon very dry with paper towels. Set a large heavy griddle or seasoned cast-iron pan over medium-high heat for 5 minutes, or until very hot. Turn heat to high. Brush the pan

with a thin coat of olive oil. When you see the first wisp of smoke, which will likely be right away, immediately lay in 2 pieces of salmon.

Pressing lightly on the fish, sear the salmon on all 4 sides, including the skin side, for just 1 minute per side, or until golden brown. When done, the salmon should be medium rare.

Transfer the seared salmon to a warm platter and sprinkle it all over with lemon salt. Clean out the pan and repeat with the remaining salmon. Cooked salmon may be kept warm in a 175°F oven, or serve immediately.

SERVE

Strain the Chanterelle and Pea Conserva (recipe follows) and scatter the vegetables over and around the salmon; scatter the watercress over the top. Serve with the lemon wedges and lemon salt alongside.

CHANTERELLE AND PEA CONSERVA

SERVES 4 AS A GARNISH OR SIDE

Simply cooked and then marinated in a colatura-spiked brine, these vegetables are a seasonal treat. In keeping with the supersimple cooking method we use for the salmon, these chanterelles are cooked minimally and a bit unusually—in a dry pan, no oil required. It's a technique inspired by the Mexican tradition of charring chiles, seeds, and vegetables on a blazing-hot comal. I find this toasts the chanterelles really nicely too, bringing out their almost cinnamon aroma and providing a little bit of scorched char.

---

2 cups small chanterelles, cleaned and torn into 1-inch pieces

Kosher salt and freshly cracked black peppercorns

2 cups shelled English peas

3 tablespoons red wine vinegar

1 teaspoon fresh savory leaves, lightly bruised

3 tablespoons colatura or high-quality fish sauce, such as Red Boat

1 cup olive oil

SEAR THE MUSHROOMS

Heat a medium heavy skillet or griddle over high heat until very hot. Add half of the mushrooms, making sure there is plenty of space between them so their moisture escapes readily. Let them toast until aromatic, then jostle them in the pan to let them cook all around. Transfer to a large bowl when tender and browned in spots, about 3 minutes, and season lightly with salt and pepper; their residual heat will let them continue to cook. Clean out the pan and repeat with remaining mushrooms.

BLANCH THE PEAS

Set up an ice bath in a bowl. Meanwhile, bring a small pot of well-salted water to a boil. Add the peas and blanch them for 1 minute, or until they turn bright green and plump. Using a small sieve, scoop out the peas and immediately plunge them into the ice bath. Once cool, lift out the peas, toss dry, and thoroughly blot them dry with a kitchen towel.

SEASON THE CONSERVA

Transfer the peas to the bowl with the chanterelles and stir in the red wine

vinegar, savory, and colatura. Let the vegetables marinate, stirring them occasionally, for 25 minutes. Stir in the olive oil and season with salt to taste; it may not need it.

If not using the conserva within a couple of hours, transfer the mixture to a jar, seal, and refrigerate. The conserva is best after marinating for 1 day, but it keeps up to 2 weeks.

Let the conserva come up to room temperature at least 1 hour before serving. To serve, strain the vegetables from the liquid, keeping the liquid for seasoning if desired.

HOW TO PLAN THIS MEAL:

1 day before: Make chanterelle and pea conserva. Make lemon salt.

2 hours before: Temper conserva.

45 minutes before: Temper salmon. Preheat oven to warm, if desired.

15 minutes before: Sear salmon and season with lemon salt. Assemble platter.

9

SHRIMP A LA PLANCHA WITH ROMESCO AND HERBED MELON AND CUCUMBER SALAD

SERVES 4 TO 6

Hot peel-and-eat shrimp, dunked in a nutty, garlicky romesco sauce, makes for messy communal eating, preferably outside on a hot summer's day.

Brining these shrimp makes them juicy and snappy. And cooking them whole on a griddle or low-walled pan is all about getting good color on their shells. If you have ever made stock with shrimp shells, you know how rich this flavor is, and that's the essence you want to capture in the meat.

Unlike in the preceding salmon recipe, I don't temper the shrimp ahead of time because I want a little bit of temperature resistance in the center while searing, to buy a little more time for the browning process before the shrimp are fully cooked. While you could argue that you'd want more time to caramelize the salmon, too, the difference there is that the outer flesh may overcook before the interior comes to temperature, whereas here the shells create a bit of a barrier to the meat.

Serve these shrimp with simple, sweet boiled baby potatoes or the Crispy Potato and Seared Pole Bean Salad (page 168), and no one will blame you for eating those with your hands too.

---

6 cups water

4 cups ice

½ cup kosher salt

½ stalk lemongrass, smashed open

Zest of ½ lime, removed in strips with a vegetable peeler

3 pounds whole jumbo shrimp (10 per pound)

3 tablespoons olive oil

Coarse sea salt

1 lemon, halved

1½ cups Romesco Sauce (recipe follows)

BRINE THE SHRIMP

Pour the water and ice into a deep container. Stir in the kosher salt and lemongrass. Press on the lime zest with the broad side of a chef's knife to release the essential oils and add it to the brine. Add the shrimp and transfer the container to the refrigerator for 3 hours.

Remove the shrimp from the brine and set them on a paper towel–lined tray. Dry thoroughly. If you have time, place the shrimp on a cooling rack and refrigerate them, uncovered, for up to 3 hours so they air-dry.

SEAR AND SERVE THE SHRIMP

In a large bowl, toss the shrimp with the olive oil. Set a large, low-walled pan, preferably a cast-iron griddle, over medium-high heat. Once the pan is

smoking hot, raise the heat to high and add half the shrimp, or as many as will fit with ½ inch of space between them. Sear the shrimp for 2 minutes, gently pressing them against the pan to ensure good contact, then flip. Sear the reverse side for another 2 minutes, or until both sides are well caramelized and the shrimp just begin to curl. Transfer the shrimp to a serving platter and repeat with the remaining shrimp. Season with coarse salt.

Turn the heat back to medium-high and lay in the lemon halves, cut sides down. Once they are nicely browned, about 1 minute, remove the lemon halves.

Serve the shrimp with romesco for dipping, seared lemon halves for squeezing, and the melon salad (recipes follow).

ROMESCO SAUCE

MAKES 1½ CUPS

½ cup Marcona almonds

1 slice of stale bread, toasted and torn into ½-inch pieces

¼ cup Garlic Confit cloves (page 306)

1 cup jarred piquillo pepper strips, or other roasted red peppers, drained

¼ cup crushed canned tomatoes, drained, preferably Salt Water–Brined Tomatoes (page 305)

2 tablespoons sherry vinegar

1 tablespoon pimentón (smoked paprika)

¼ cup olive oil

Fine sea salt

Pulse the almonds and bread in a food processor or blender until coarsely combined. Scrape the almond mixture into a medium bowl and set the food processor's bowl back into place.

Add the garlic, peppers, tomatoes, vinegar, and pimentón to the food processor. Process until smooth.

Scrape the pepper-tomato mixture into the bowl with the almonds and bread. Add the olive oil and stir to combine. Let the mixture stand for at least 10 minutes, or until the flavors meld. Season with salt to taste.

Hold the romesco at room temperature for up to 3 hours. Romesco keeps for up to 2 days, covered and refrigerated. Bring the sauce up to room temperature before serving.

HERBED MELON AND CUCUMBER SALAD

SERVES 6

Summer-ripe melon effortlessly transitions into a savory salad star. A great melon, while candy-sweet, also features a certain meatiness. Try it in place of tomatoes in a caprese to see how versatile it truly is.

The chilled melon in this composition takes on the hot chiles, herbs, and cucumber slices with grace. If you can't find Persian cucumbers, which are crisp and petite, just use a larger cucumber.

---

1 2-pound honeydew melon, chilled

1 Fresno chile, stemmed and thinly sliced

1 serrano chile, stemmed and thinly sliced

Fine sea salt

¼ cup olive oil

½ teaspoon finely grated lime zest (from 1 lime)

1 tablespoon lime juice (from 1 lime)

4 Persian cucumbers, sliced thin

¼ cup mint leaves, roughly torn

¼ cup fresh whole lemon verbena leaves (optional)

¼ cup fresh flat-leaf parsley leaves, roughly torn

PREPARE THE MELON

Peel and halve the melon. Scoop out all the seeds and slice the melon thinly. Arrange the fruit on a serving platter, cover tightly with plastic wrap, and refrigerate for 2 hours, or until very cold.

SEASON THE SALAD

Place the chiles in a small bowl and toss with ½ teaspoon salt. Let the chiles stand for 10 minutes, or until the salt dissolves. Stir in the olive oil and let the mixture stand at room temperature for 10 minutes, or until the oil tastes piquant.

Remove the melon from the refrigerator just before serving. Season with the lime zest and juice. Scatter the chiles and some of their oil all around the platter. Scatter the cucumber slices between the melon slices and finish with a scattering of the herbs and a sprinkling of salt.

HOW TO PLAN THIS MEAL:

$3\frac{1}{2}$–$6\frac{1}{2}$ **hours before:** Brine and dry shrimp.

2–3 hours before: Make romesco. Chill melon. Dry shrimp.

30 minutes before: Infuse chile oil.

10 minutes before: Assemble melon salad.

5 minutes before: Sear shrimp.

10

CARAMELIZED CAPONATA WITH CAPER VINAIGRETTE AND HERBED MOZZARELLA

SERVES 4 TO 6

I love honoring Italian classics while cleaning them up just a bit, like this caponata, a Sicilian stew made with eggplant, tomatoes, onion, and zucchini. Here, the bite and flavor of each remain distinct and the makeover, given Italians' tendency to stew vegetables together until homogenous, is fresh indeed.

To hone the caponata's flavor, each element gets seared individually until caramelized. One by one, the hot seared vegetables go into a big bowl, where they soak up the caper vinaigrette and soften in the steam of their residual heat. While steaming, the vegetables give up more juices, which puddle up and mix with the vinaigrette.

The vegetables' flavors stay bold and a touch acidic—very nice when piled on crusty bread or Bruschetta (page 298) and enjoyed with fresh herbed mozzarella.

¼ cup salt-packed capers

½ cup finely diced shallots

3 oil-packed anchovies, minced

¼ teaspoon finely grated lemon zest

1 serrano chile, finely grated

2 garlic cloves, finely grated

Fine sea salt and freshly cracked black peppercorns

¼ cup red wine vinegar

Olive oil, as needed

½ pound baby zucchini, cut into ½-inch slices

½ pound small spring onions, halved through their stems

½ pound sweet peppers, cut into 1-inch pieces

1 cup Castelvetrano olives, pitted

¾ pound cherry tomatoes

1 pound baby Japanese eggplant, cut into ½-inch-thick planks

PREPARE THE VINAIGRETTE

Rinse the capers under cold running water before placing in a small bowl. Cover with fresh water and soak for 15 minutes. Drain the capers, discarding the soaking water, and rinse again. Taste for salt. If they are still too salty, return the capers to the bowl and re-cover with fresh water. Soak for 15 minutes more. The longer the capers soak, the more muted their flavor becomes.

Remove the capers from their soaking liquid and drain them thoroughly. Roughly chop the capers and place in a medium bowl. Add the shallots, anchovies, lemon zest, chile, and garlic to the bowl. Season with salt and pepper. Whisk in the vinegar and ½ cup olive oil. Set the bowl aside for 1 hour, or until the flavors meld. The vinaigrette will keep in the refrigerator for 1 week.

SEAR THE ZUCCHINI, ONIONS, AND PEPPERS

Set a large heavy pan over medium-high heat until hot. Swirl in enough olive oil to coat the entire pan. When the oil shimmers, add as much zucchini as will fit comfortably in one layer. Cook for 2 to 3 minutes per side, or until deeply browned on both sides, then transfer the zucchini to a large bowl. Season lightly with salt and a few splashes of the caper vinaigrette. Toss to coat. Sear and season the remaining zucchini, cleaning the pan between batches if necessary.

Wipe the pan clean and set it back over medium heat. Once hot, swirl in enough oil to generously coat the entire surface. When the oil shimmers, add as many onions as will fit, cut side down. Sear, undisturbed, for 5 minutes, or until darkly browned and cooked through.

(recipe continues)

Add the onions to the bowl with the zucchini, season lightly with salt and some vinaigrette, and toss to combine. Sear and season the remaining onions, cleaning the pan between batches if necessary.

Set the pan back over high heat and slick the pan with more olive oil. When the oil is nearly smoking, add as many peppers as will fit comfortably in one layer, skin side down. Roast the peppers for 4 to 5 minutes, or until blistered and dark in spots. Transfer to the bowl with the zucchini and onions and season lightly with salt and some vinaigrette. Sear and season the remaining peppers, cleaning the pan between batches if necessary. Add the olives to the bowl and toss to combine.

SEAR THE EGGPLANT AND TOMATOES

Halve half of the cherry tomatoes and fold them into the bowl with the vegetables. Clean out the pan, set it back over medium-high heat, and generously slick it with olive oil. When it is shimmering-hot, add as much of the eggplant as will fit comfortably in one layer.

Sear the eggplant for 2 minutes per side, or until browned and tender. Transfer to the bowl and season lightly with salt and some vinaigrette. Repeat with the remaining eggplant, cleaning the pan between batches if necessary.

Set the pan back over medium-high heat. Coat the hot pan with olive oil. Add the remaining cherry tomatoes and roast, shaking often, for 3 minutes, or until their skins split and the tomatoes heat through. Add the blistered tomatoes to the bowl with the vegetables and fold to combine.

Allow the salt and vinaigrette a few minutes to seep in and flavor the vegetables before tasting; then add more of either to your liking.

MARINATE AND SERVE

Let the vegetables rest at room temperature for at least 1 hour, or until they are tender and their flavors meld. While the caponata marinates, gently fold it every 20 minutes to distribute its juices.

Serve the caponata at room temperature with the Herbed Mozzarella (recipe follows) and lots of crusty bread or Bruschetta (page 298).

HERBED MOZZARELLA

SERVES 4 TO 6

Springy, fresh-pulled mozzarella, the only kind worth buying, must be served at room temperature so you can taste the milk's sweet, grassy flavor. To pick a good ball, you have to squeeze for yourself and see. I always go with the squishiest—though sometimes the really fresh stuff is held in water behind the counter of an Italian grocer. That, you won't get to squeeze; buy it anyway.

The right ball is a beautiful thing, sliced and seasoned with salt. But embellished with the following seasonings, it's over-the-top good.

---

2 small, pale celery stalks, taken from the center of the bunch

2 large balls mozzarella (about 1½ pounds total), at room temperature

¼ cup fresh mint leaves, roughly torn

½ cup fresh basil leaves, roughly torn

½ cup fresh flat-leaf parsley leaves

Juice of ½ lemon

Flaky sea salt and freshly cracked black peppercorns

3 tablespoons olive oil, or to taste

Fill a medium bowl with ice water. With a vegetable peeler, shave the celery into long strips. Transfer to the ice water and crisp in the refrigerator for at least 1 hour and up to 3 hours. Remove from the bath and pat dry.

Tear the mozzarella into fat bites and scatter across a large, deep platter. Scatter the celery on top, followed by the mint, basil, and parsley. Season to taste with lemon juice, salt, pepper, and olive oil.

HOW TO PLAN THIS MEAL:

3 hours before: Make caper vinaigrette and prep vegetables.

2 hours before: Sear vegetables and assemble caponata.

1 hour before: Remove mozzarella from refrigerator.

20 minutes before: Assemble herbed mozzarella.

10 minutes before: Make bruschetta, if serving.

11

PANCETTA-WRAPPED HALIBUT
WITH GRATED TOMATO AND SUMMER SQUASH

SERVES 4

A play on saltimbocca, this is how I imagine an Italian surf and turf might look. Pancetta lines pounded halibut fillets, which quickly sear and crisp in a hot pan. Since this is such a quick-cooked meal, I pair it with a quick-marinated zucchini salad—a lovely light summertime lunch. Or, if you have more time, serve this with the Spiced Fried Rice (page 276).

Now, about tempering: Don't do it here. The reason for this anomaly is twofold. If the pancetta fat warms too much while sitting out, it may slip off the fish. Plus, cooking these cold buys you a little time when crisping the pork and helps prevent the halibut, which is thin and delicate, from overcooking.

1¼ pounds very ripe beefsteak tomatoes, halved equatorially

Olive oil, as needed

3 tablespoons sherry vinegar, or to taste

Flaky sea salt and freshly cracked black peppercorns

4 5-ounce halibut fillets

1½ tablespoons fresh thyme leaves, roughly chopped

16 to 24 ⅛-inch slices pancetta

MAKE THE TOMATO VINAIGRETTE

Holding a box grater over a wide bowl, grate the cut sides of the tomatoes on the largest holes until only their skins remain. You should have about 2 cups tomato pulp.

Stir ¼ cup olive oil and the sherry vinegar into the pulp. Season with salt, pepper, and extra vinegar and oil to taste. Hold the tomato vinaigrette at room temperature for up to 1½ hours. If necessary, this also keeps covered in the refrigerator for up to 3 days.

WRAP THE HALIBUT

Lay a 12-inch square of plastic wrap on a work surface. Leaving the rest of the halibut in the refrigerator, remove 1 fillet at a time and place it in the center of the plastic square. Cover the fish with a second square of plastic wrap.

With a mallet or small heavy pan, gently pound the fish to a uniform ½-inch thickness. Remove the top plastic wrap layer and set it aside. Lightly sprinkle the fish all over with salt and pepper and thyme leaves, reserving some thyme.

Lay 4 pancetta slices down on the work surface, shingling them slightly. The pancetta should be enough to wrap around the whole halibut fillet. Use a few more slices of pancetta if necessary.

Place the pounded, seasoned fillet on the pancetta and wrap the pancetta snugly around the fish so it is completely encased. If there is excess pancetta, cut it away.

Re-cover the fish with plastic wrap and gently whack it a little more to seal the parcel firmly shut. Place the pancetta-halibut parcel on a platter, with the plastic wrap protecting it, and refrigerate.

Repeat the process with the remaining fillets. Let all the parcels rest in the refrigerator for at least 35 minutes, or until the pancetta and fish cling together and are cold to the touch.

(recipe continues)

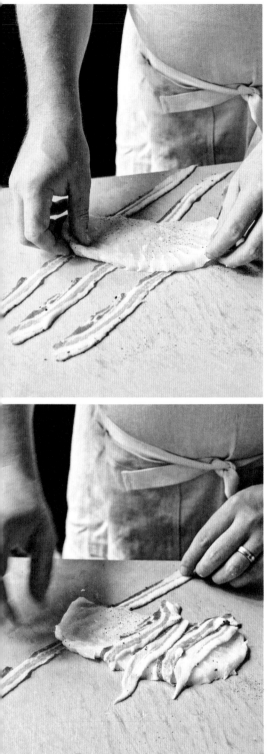

PAN-SEAR AND SERVE

Remove the halibut parcels from the refrigerator and sprinkle on the reserved thyme leaves. Set a large heavy, low-walled pan or griddle over medium heat. Swirl in 2 tablespoons olive oil. When the oil is shimmering-hot, lay in 2 of the parcels, making sure they have room between them. Cook, without flipping, for 3 minutes, or until the pancetta browns. Use a spatula to gently press edges onto the hot surface to brown.

Flip both parcels and cook their reverse sides, another 1 to 2 minutes, just to lightly brown the pancetta; the halibut will be cooked by this point.

Set the cooked fish aside and repeat with the remaining parcels.

Coat plates generously with tomato vinaigrette. Nestle the warm fillets into the vinaigrette. Serve immediately with the Shaved Zucchini Salad (recipe follows) on top or alongside.

SHAVED ZUCCHINI SALAD

SERVES 4

This salad involves shaving zucchini into broad ribbons and seasoning the tangle with lemon juice, vinegar, oil, and herbs. It eats like a simple, delicate slaw and it is the perfect accompaniment for the pancetta-wrapped halibut.

---

1 pound baby zucchini

2 tablespoons olive oil

½ teaspoon finely grated lemon zest (from ½ lemon)

1 tablespoon lemon juice (from ½ lemon)

1 tablespoon champagne vinegar

Flaky sea salt

2 tablespoons roughly torn fresh mint leaves

2 tablespoons roughly torn fresh basil leaves

2 teaspoons snipped fresh chives

2 zucchini flowers, stamen removed and petals roughly torn (optional)

Using a mandoline or vegetable peeler, shave the zucchini into long, thin strips. Place the strips in a medium bowl and toss with the olive oil, lemon zest and juice, vinegar, and a few pinches of salt.

Let the zucchini marinate for 15 minutes, or until softened and flavorful.

Arrange the zucchini ribbons on a serving platter. Scatter the mint, basil, chives, and zucchini flowers, if using, on top.

HOW TO PLAN THIS MEAL:

2 hours before: Form and pound pancetta-halibut parcels. Make tomato vinaigrette.

20 minutes before: Assemble zucchini salad.

10 minutes before: Sear parcels. Arrange platter.

12

SEARED BAY SCALLOPS WITH BAGNA CAUDA AND VEGETABLES

SERVES 4 TO 6

Bagna cauda, meaning "warm bath," is an Italian brew of olive oil, butter, garlic, and an unapologetic amount of anchovy. It's the centerpiece of Piemontese feasts, with a traditional crudité for dunking. To make a respectable pot, you will need good anchovies, the chubby ones packed in olive oil, tasty enough to be eaten right out of the jar.

Such spreads often celebrate humble winter vegetables. But when I heard that on fine tables in Alba, a Piemontese town known for its truffles and fine wines, white truffles are served with the sauce, I got to thinking about our most sumptuous cold-weather food here in New York. And that's how these bay scallops made their way into this meal.

Plucked from Long Island Sound, bay scallops—sweet, soft, and buttery—are precious. And with a bagna cauda dunk, their sweetness melds with the anchovy for a striking combination.

Seared in batches on one side only (to ensure caramelization without overcooking), these scallops should be cooked to order and brought to the table ripping hot. That means occasionally getting up to sear a few batches during the meal. Such come-as-you-are informality is at the heart of the bagna cauda tradition no matter how luxe you make it.

As for this spread's other bits: Sunchokes roast on the oven floor until their skins crackle and their insides collapse. The rest is raw, and you should buy whatever is best. If I make this in late fall and tomatoes and peppers are still around, I'll snatch some up. Otherwise, it's carrots, fennel, radicchio, radishes, and whatever else is in need of a hot bath.

---

2 pounds bay scallops (make sure they are "undipped," meaning preservative-free)

1 pound sunchokes

Olive oil, as needed

Kosher salt and freshly cracked black peppercorns

1 pound small fennel bulbs, sliced into ½-inch wedges

1 pound small carrots, halved lengthwise

½ pound radishes, preferably French breakfast, halved lengthwise

½ pound radicchio di Treviso or baby bok choy, leaves separated

1 pound (4 sticks) butter, cut into chunks

22 olive oil–packed high-quality anchovies, drained

6 tablespoons red wine vinegar

1 teaspoon hot pepper flakes

1 fresh bay leaf

1 tablespoon fresh thyme leaves

2 tablespoons lemon juice (from 1 lemon)

1 medium ciabatta loaf, sliced

CLEAN THE SCALLOPS

Place half the scallops in a colander and rinse them in cold water. Arrange the scallops in one layer on a paper towel–lined tray and repeat with the remaining half. Feel for grit and re-rinse any scallops that don't feel smooth. Thoroughly blot the scallops dry with paper towels.

Refrigerate the scallops, uncovered, for 3 hours. This will dry them so their surface sears well.

(recipe continues)

ROAST THE SUNCHOKES

Preheat the oven to 325°F. In a heavy roasting pan, rub the sunchokes with 2 tablespoons olive oil and a few generous pinches of salt and pepper. Set the pan on the oven floor and roast the sunchokes for 30 minutes, or until their skins are wrinkled and browned in spots and their flesh is fork-tender. Turn them at least once halfway through.

ARRANGE THE RAW VEGETABLES

Arrange the fennel, carrots, radishes, and radicchio on a large platter. Cover the platter with a lightly dampened towel until ready to serve.

MAKE THE BAGNA CAUDA

In a medium saucepan set over medium-high heat, cook the butter until it foams. Stir in the anchovies and sauté until they melt into the butter. Remove the pot from the heat and stir in 1 cup olive oil, the vinegar, hot pepper flakes, and bay leaf. Season with pepper; salt is probably unnecessary because of the anchovies.

Keep the pot warm over very low heat until serving. Just before serving, finish the bagna cauda with the thyme and lemon juice. Whisk it together just before serving, and rewarm and whisk it occasionally to bring it back together during the meal.

SEAR THE SCALLOPS AND SERVE

Remove the scallops from the refrigerator; if they don't feel tacky to the touch, blot them with a paper towel.

Lightly slick a large heavy pan with olive oil and set over high heat. When it is very hot, nearly smoking, add as many scallops as will fit comfortably, with some room between each. (Return the remaining scallops to the refrigerator until ready to cook.) Sear the scallops for 1½ minutes, without flipping, or until browned on their bottoms and cooked to medium doneness. Season with salt and pepper and serve immediately. Sear the remaining scallops in batches as needed.

Serve the seared scallops with the raw vegetables, roasted sunchokes, sliced bread, and warm bagna cauda.

HOW TO PLAN THIS MEAL:

3 hours before: Clean and dry scallops.

1 hour before: Prepare raw vegetables.

35 minutes before: Roast sunchokes. Prepare bagna cauda.

5 minutes before: Finish bagna cauda and sear scallops.

13

BLACK GARLIC–RUBBED HANGER STEAK
WITH CRISPY POTATO AND SEARED POLE BEAN SALAD

SERVES 4

Black garlic, a sweet, aromatic product of the Korean pantry, seems to inspire every chef who comes across it. For the uninitiated, it is garlic aged for weeks at a warm temperature, until it takes on a soft texture with a rich molasses flavor. Pounded into a paste, the cloves turn thick and gummy. Then, when rubbed onto this steak, the garlic's dark flavor and color slink into the meat's striations, forming a tasty second skin. It's readily available online and I've also spotted it at stores like Whole Foods. At Asian markets, it's a staple.

Since this meal serves as an introduction to my rubbing practice, let's review the basics: The steak must thoroughly dry before the paste is applied, so the rub can fully grip the meat. Then the two must rest together, becoming one. And make sure to gently press the meat into the pan, forcing the rub and meat to gel together before wrapping up the cooking of this dish in the oven.

2 heads of black garlic

1 tablespoon kosher salt

1 teaspoon freshly cracked black peppercorns

1 2-pound hanger steak

2 tablespoons olive oil

Flaky sea salt

MAKE THE RUB

Squeeze the black garlic cloves from their skins. Smash the cloves with the back of your knife until a rough paste forms; it's okay if large chunks dot the paste. Transfer to a small bowl and stir in the kosher salt and pepper. The rub should taste a touch salty and have a thick, pasty consistency.

RUB THE STEAK

Slice the steak in half, lengthwise, along the membrane that runs through it. Thoroughly dry with paper towels.

Rub the steaks all over with the black garlic paste, massaging it into the meat and coating the steaks with a ⅛-inch layer of paste. Set the steaks on a cooling rack set over a roasting pan. Transfer the meat to the refrigerator. Let it rest, uncovered, for 12 to 24 hours, until the rub hardens and feels tacky.

SEAR THE STEAKS

Preheat the oven to 400°F. Remove the steaks from the refrigerator and let them temper for about 20 minutes.

Set a large heavy pan, preferably cast iron, over medium-high heat until very hot. Slick the pan with the olive oil. When the oil comes to a light smoke, lay in the steaks and press on them gently with a spatula, so they are completely in contact with the hot surface. Sear for 3 to 4 minutes, or until the crust blackens and easily releases from the pan. Flip the steaks and transfer to the oven. Roast for 4 to 5 minutes, or until the interior is a blushing pink. Transfer the meat to a cooling rack to rest for 5 minutes.

Cut the steaks across the grain into ½-inch slices. Season the steaks with flaky salt. Pour any juices into the Crispy Potato and Seared Pole Bean Salad (recipe follows) and serve.

CRISPY POTATO AND SEARED POLE BEAN SALAD

SERVES 4

Roasting potatoes with rosemary and lemon zest is always lovely, but here we add seared pole beans and a brown-butter vinaigrette. This is a hot potato salad that would overshadow a less flavorful steak; here, both elements hold their own.

16 fingerling potatoes (about 1¼ pounds), halved lengthwise

Kosher salt and freshly cracked black peppercorns

1½ teaspoons coarsely chopped fresh rosemary leaves

½ teaspoon finely grated lemon zest (from ½ lemon)

1 tablespoon olive oil

4 tablespoons (½ stick) chilled butter, cut into ½-inch pieces

¼ pound wax pole beans or green beans, stemmed

½ serrano chile, stemmed, seeded, and finely chopped

1 tablespoon finely diced shallot

1 small handful watercress

1 tablespoon lemon juice (from ½ lemon)

1 tablespoon red wine vinegar

PREPARE THE POTATOES

Preheat the oven to 500°F. In a medium bowl, toss the potatoes with a few generous pinches of salt and pepper, the rosemary, lemon zest, and olive oil.

Arrange the potatoes, cut sides down, in a medium heavy roasting dish. They should fit in a snug single layer, or the butter may burn. Scatter the butter around the pan and transfer the dish to the oven's center rack.

Roast the potatoes, without stirring, for 30 minutes, or until they turn tender but crisp on the outside. Halfway through roasting, turn the pan 180 degrees. While they are hot, stir the potatoes to evenly coat with the browned butter. Set the dish aside and loosely cover it with aluminum foil to keep warm.

SEAR THE POLE BEANS

Set a large heavy sauté pan over high heat until very hot. Add the pole beans in one layer and the serrano chile. Dry-sear the beans without moving them for 3 minutes, or until blackened and wrinkly in spots. Season lightly with salt.

COMBINE AND SEASON

Using a slotted spoon, transfer the potatoes to a large serving bowl. Toss in a tablespoon of their butter and add the seared beans and chile. Add the shallot, watercress, lemon juice, and red wine vinegar. If serving with the hanger steak, pour in any runoff juices from the sliced meat. Taste and season the salad with extra salt, pepper, or lemon juice if necessary.

HOW TO PLAN THIS MEAL:

1 day before: Make black garlic rub. Rub steak.

45 minutes before: Roast potatoes.

35 minutes before: Temper steak.

15 minutes before: Roast steak.

5 minutes before: Blister beans, slice steak, and dress potatoes.

14

PAN-ROASTED PORK CHOPS WITH BLISTERED AVOCADO AND CHIVES

SERVES 4

Browned on the stovetop, these thick-cut pork chops then go into the oven to cook through. It's a classic pan roast, bringing together the burner's searing power with the oven's enveloping warmth. Keep in mind, though, that even while in the oven, the pork can cook unevenly—the side contacting the pan gets more heat. So for the most evenly textured results, flip the chops as they roast in the oven.

The recipe works a lot of flavor into the pork during precooking. First, as ever, a brine. Then a spice mix seasons the cut with bay, fennel, coriander, and oregano. It's not my usual thick rub, but the intense aroma of the spices slips into the meat.

Bits of lime, blistered creamy avocado, and seared chives round out these plates. For a heartier meal, I also like to serve Braised Cranberry Beans (page 59) or warm toasted bread for juice mopping and avocado smearing alongside. A batch of warm Old-World Polenta (page 35) is also nice here.

½ cup kosher salt

2 tablespoons honey

2 quarts water

6 fresh thyme sprigs

6 fresh flat-leaf parsley sprigs

1 tablespoon black peppercorns, toasted

½ lemon, sliced into thin rounds

4 1½-inch-thick bone-in pork chops, preferably T-bone (about 3 pounds total)

2 tablespoons Cochon Spice Blend (page 311)

2 limes

2 tablespoons plus 2 teaspoons olive oil

2 medium avocados

1 small bunch of chives (about 2 ounces)

Flaky sea salt and freshly cracked black peppercorns

BRINE AND SEASON THE PORK

In a deep medium container, whisk together the kosher salt, honey, and water until the salt dissolves. With the broad side of a chef's knife, press down on the thyme and parsley sprigs to release their oils, then add them to the brine. Toss in the peppercorns and lemon slices and submerge the pork. Transfer the container to the refrigerator and brine the meat for 12 to 24 hours.

Remove the pork from the brine. Pat the meat very dry with paper towels.

Sprinkle the cochon spice evenly all over, massaging it into the meat. Place the rubbed pork on a cooling rack set over a baking sheet and refrigerate it, uncovered, for 4 to 12 hours. When ready, the meat should be dry to the touch.

CUT THE LIMES

Slice off the tops and bottoms of the limes. Stand each lime straight up. With a sharp paring knife, cut away the peels and pith and discard.

Hold a lime in one hand and your paring knife in the other. Working over a small bowl, cut out the segments from the lime by slicing toward the core on each side of the segments' membranes. The segments should fall into the bowl. Once each lime is cut, squeeze the membrane to capture its juices in the bowl below. With a spoon, break the segments into approximately ½-inch pieces. Set the bowl aside.

TEMPER THE PORK

Remove the pork from the refrigerator and let stand at room temperature for 1 hour before roasting.

Preheat the oven to 375°F.

(recipe continues)

ROAST THE PORK

Heat a large cast-iron skillet over medium-high heat for 5 minutes. Rub each chop all over with ½ teaspoon oil. When the pan is very hot and smoking, turn the heat to high and carefully lay in the pork. If necessary, brown the meat in batches to avoid overcrowding. If you go this route, place a roasting pan in the oven to preheat.

Sear the meat without moving it for 3 minutes, or until light golden brown. Flip and sear the reverse sides for 3 minutes more, or until the pork is evenly seared. Flip the pork once more and transfer the skillet to the oven.

If searing the pork in batches, transfer the seared pork to the preheated roasting pan and continue using the skillet to sear the next batch. Rinse and wipe the skillet clean and thoroughly reheat between batches if necessary.

Roast the pork for 5 minutes, flipping it once halfway through. The chops should be deep golden brown all around, with a little blush at their centers.

Remove the pork from the oven and transfer to a cutting board. Let the pork rest for 5 minutes before slicing.

ROAST THE AVOCADOS AND CHIVES

While the pork rests, halve and pit the avocados, but leave their skins intact. Cut the halves into 1-inch wedges.

Rinse and wipe the skillet clean and reheat over medium-high heat until very hot. Place the chives in the dry pan and roast, without moving them, for 1 minute, or until blackened on one side. Remove the chives from the skillet and reserve.

Rinse and wipe the pan clean and place it back over medium-high heat, slicked with 1 tablespoon olive oil. When the oil shimmers, add the avocado wedges, cut side down, and sear for 90 seconds, or until deeply browned. Flip to sear the other side, another 90 seconds.

Transfer the avocado to a medium platter and sprinkle the wedges with sea salt.

CARVE THE PORK AND SERVE

With the tip of a sharp knife, cut around each pork chop's bones to free the meat. Cut the chops across the grain, into 1-inch slices. Arrange the pork on the platter with the avocados and chives. Lift the lime supremes from their juices and scatter the bits of fruit around the platter. Drizzle 1 tablespoon of the lime juice and the remaining 1 tablespoon olive oil over the top. Sprinkle everything with flaky sea salt and pepper and serve immediately.

15

THRICE-ROASTED CHICKEN WITH CUTTING-BOARD VINAIGRETTE AND YEAR-ROUND CHICORY SALAD

SERVES 2 TO 4

This isn't the simplest roast chicken recipe you'll ever see. It's a little particular, maybe even obsessive, in pursuit of juicy flesh and extra-flavorful skin.

To start with, if possible, buy a smaller bird; its muscles will likely be less worked. We go through the usual precooking steps: a brine, a rub, and a good long stint in the refrigerator to dry the rub onto the skin.

Then, it's a three-step roast. Start by searing the rub into the flesh until it's golden—this gives the skin a head start in crisping. Then transfer the pan to the oven to cook the meat through. Finally, bring it to the stovetop once more, to finish it with a browning baste of sizzling herbed butter.

One finicky detail I should explain involves breaking down the chicken and laying it into the pan in a specific fashion. Doing so helps ensure the pieces cook uniformly. Since the breasts are the thickest cut, they should lie near the handle, which conducts and focuses the heat of the oven. The devil is in the details, right?

A bird that celebrates all the heat an oven and stovetop have to offer, this chicken is hard to tire of. And to ensure you don't, four very different rubs are also provided.

---

2 fresh bay leaves

7 fresh thyme sprigs

1 gallon water

1 cup kosher salt, plus more to season

¼ cup sugar

1 lemon, thinly sliced

¼ cup black peppercorns, toasted and roughly crushed, plus more to season

1 2½-pound chicken

¼ cup rub (recipes follow; if using Rosemary-Anchovy, use 2 tablespoons)

¼ cup plus 1½ tablespoons olive oil

2 tablespoons butter

1 tablespoon champagne vinegar

1 tablespoon lemon juice (from ½ lemon), or more to taste

BRINE THE CHICKEN

With the broad side of a chef's knife, press down on 1 bay leaf and 4 of the thyme sprigs to release their essential oils.

Place the water, salt, sugar, lemon, peppercorns, and the pressed bay and thyme into a large nonreactive container. Stir until the sugar and salt dissolve. Add the chicken and make sure it is completely submerged. Cover and brine in the refrigerator for 12 hours.

BREAK DOWN THE CHICKEN

Remove the chicken from the brine and rinse it under cold running water. Set the chicken on a work surface and thoroughly pat it dry with paper towels.

With the chicken on its back, take a leg and gently pull it toward you. Cut the skin between the leg and the breast, exposing the inner thigh. Gently but

firmly force the thigh toward the back of the chicken, until the thigh bone pops out of the joint that connects it to the body. Repeat with the other thigh. With a sturdy knife or shears, cut the legs away at the thigh joint.

Turn the bird over and cut through the thin rib bones where they meet the back; this is the first step to freeing the breasts from the carcass. Put your hand in the cavity of the bird and hold the chicken down while you pull the breast back toward the neck; this should break the breast free. If necessary, cut it free near the neck and shoulders. Find the joint where the wings meet the drumettes with the tip of your knife and cut the wings free. At this point you should have 3 pieces: the whole breast and 2 legs. Save the carcass and wings for another use, like stock.

(recipe continues)

RUB AND DRY THE EXTERIOR

Pat the chicken dry once again. Once paper towels come away completely dry, lay the chicken on the work surface skin side up.

Smear the rub all over the skin until it's evenly coated in a distinct layer; you may not need the full 1/4 cup of rub (and with rosemary-anchovy rub, I generally use about 2 tablespoons).

Place the rubbed chicken, skin side up, on a cooling rack set over a rimmed baking sheet. Refrigerate the chicken for 12 to 24 hours, or until the rub dries and doesn't smudge easily when prodded. The crème fraîche rub will crack when dried, but the other rubs will remain more pliable.

ROAST THE CHICKEN

Remove the chicken from the refrigerator 1 hour before roasting. Preheat the oven to 400° F.

Slick a large heavy pan, preferably cast iron, with 1 1/2 tablespoons olive oil and set over medium heat. Place the handle at six o'clock. When the oil is shimmering-hot, lay the chicken breast, skin side down, in the pan, centering it with the pan's handle and placing the thickest part of the breast toward the pan's rim, so the tip of the breast points toward the pan's center. Next, add the legs, skin side down, with the thighs down by the point of the breast; the drumsticks should point back toward

the handle and the thick part of the breast. Press down slightly on all pieces so their skin is in maximum contact with the pan.

Increase the heat to medium-high and sear the chicken for 7 minutes, or until the edges turn golden brown. (If using the fennel, Meyer lemon, and honey rub, pay close attention, as the honey may darken quickly.) Without flipping the meat, transfer the pan to the oven and roast it for 17 minutes, or until the breast juices run clear and the drumsticks wiggle easily at their joints. When done, the meat should be 160 degrees at its thickest portion.

Carefully remove the pan from the oven and set it back over medium heat. Add the butter and remaining bay leaf and 3 thyme sprigs to the pan. As the butter begins to foam, protect your hand with a towel or an oven mitt and tip the pan slightly to pool the butter toward you. Use a spoon to baste the chicken all over in the foaming butter for 2 to 3 minutes, or until the butter browns. Make sure the butter does not blacken or it will taste acrid.

Remove the chicken pieces from the pan and place them, skin side up, on a cooling rack set over a large rimmed baking sheet. Let the chicken rest for 10 minutes so the juices settle and skin crisps.

CARVE THE CHICKEN

With a sharp, sturdy knife, cut through the breastbone lengthwise, separating the breast into 2 pieces. If you like, cut each breast piece in half crosswise as well. Next, break down the legs, separating the thighs from the drumsticks by opening the V between them and feeling for the joint with the tip of your knife. You should be able to cut through easily once you find it.

Transfer the chicken pieces to a warm serving platter, leaving their drippings behind. Pour all the drippings from the cutting board into a small mixing bowl, and add any accumulated juices from the roasting pan.

MAKE THE VINAIGRETTE

Whisk the vinegar, lemon juice, and 1/4 cup olive oil into the chicken juices. Season with salt, pepper, and extra lemon juice as needed.

SERVE

Serve the chicken with the vinaigrette and Year-Round Chicory Salad (page 179).

HARISSA RUB

MAKES ½ CUP (ENOUGH FOR 2 BIRDS)

A robust, terra cotta–colored North African spread that combines dried chiles, a host of toasted spices, garlic, and tomato paste, harissa can be used in everything from dips to rubs. Wherever it goes it gives a smoky, sweet, spicy boost. I break this rub out most often in the winter, when fresh produce is slim and bursts of bright flavor are welcome.

This harissa can be assembled in a blender or food processor, but I prefer the texture of a hand-smashed paste. A blender heats the spices and seeds, and I've found that tarnishes their subtlety a bit. So, if you can, make this by hand.

This recipe makes more than what you will use for the chicken, but leftovers are delicious as a rub for fish, or as a smoky-spicy condiment for just about anything.

---

4 dried pasilla chiles

4 dried sweet-mild hatch chiles, or 2 more pasilla chiles

½ teaspoon caraway seeds, toasted

¼ teaspoon coriander seeds, toasted

¼ teaspoon cumin seeds, toasted

¼ teaspoon sesame seeds, toasted

1 tablespoon tomato paste

1 teaspoon dried oregano

1 teaspoon piment d'Espelette or Aleppo pepper

2 tablespoons roughly chopped peel from Preserved Lemons (page 302)

3 garlic cloves, roughly chopped

Kosher salt

2 tablespoons olive oil

PREPARE THE CHILES AND SPICES

Heat a large heavy skillet over medium heat until hot. Add the pasilla and hatch chiles and toast on all sides for 3 minutes total, or until very aromatic. Remove the stem ends and shake out the seeds. Discard the stems and seeds unless you want a spicier harissa; then keep the seeds or add part of them to the mortar when smashing.

Place the chiles in a small bowl and cover with hot water. Let stand for 15 minutes, or until plumped and softened.

ASSEMBLE THE HARISSA

In a spice grinder or with a mortar and pestle, smash the caraway, coriander, cumin, and sesame seeds together until a coarse mixture forms. Transfer the mixture to a food processor or keep it in a mortar. (If your mortar is not very large but you want to hand-smash the harissa, smash up the elements incrementally and add them piecemeal to a bowl. Then stir them together to combine.)

Drain the chiles, pat them dry, and roughly chop. Transfer the chiles to the mortar or food processor and smash or pulse to combine with the seeds. Add the tomato paste, oregano, and piment d'Espelette and smash or pulse to combine once more. Add the preserved lemon, garlic, and a pinch of salt to the mixture and continue pulsing or smashing until a uniform, thick paste forms. Taste and adjust the seasoning as needed.

Transfer the harissa to a lidded container and top with olive oil. Stored in the refrigerator, this keeps for 1 month.

SPICED ORANGE CRÈME FRAÎCHE RUB

MAKES ½ CUP (ENOUGH FOR 2 BIRDS)

Creamy, tangy crème fraîche is a lush French staple—sweet or savory, there is nothing it cannot improve. Here it morphs into a rub with juniper, cardamom, and orange zest. Though this rub is great any time of year, I love using it in spring. That's when delicate young vegetables get a chance to dance off its creamy, floral flavors.

2 teaspoons juniper berries, toasted

½ teaspoon cardamom seeds, toasted

1 teaspoon finely grated orange zest

½ cup Crème Fraîche (page 310)

2 tablespoons finely sliced sage

½ teaspoon agave syrup or honey

Kosher salt

Place the juniper berries, cardamom, and orange zest in a mortar or spice grinder. Blend or smash the mixture with a pestle until coarsely ground. Transfer to a small mixing bowl.

Stir the crème fraîche, sage, and agave into the spice mixture. Season to taste with salt. This is best if made the day before using.

FENNEL, MEYER LEMON, AND HONEY RUB

MAKES ABOUT ½ CUP (ENOUGH FOR 2 BIRDS)

The honey in this sweet, anise-flavored rub caramelizes and forms a sticky glaze. When searing in this rub, keep an eye on the color of the chicken while it cooks and reduce the heat if the honey begins to brown too quickly. In the summer, when herbs are everywhere and fennel fronds are tender-sweet, this rub is a go-to.

3 tablespoons finely chopped fennel fronds

1 teaspoon finely grated Meyer lemon zest (from 1 Meyer lemon)

2 tablespoons Meyer lemon juice (from 1 Meyer lemon)

2 green garlic cloves or ½ standard garlic clove, finely grated

2 tablespoons wildflower honey

1 teaspoon coarsely cracked green or black peppercorns

2 tablespoons Whole-Grain Mustard (page 296)

Kosher salt

In a small bowl, mix the fennel fronds, Meyer lemon zest and juice, garlic, honey, pepper, and mustard. Season with salt to taste. The rub should taste pungent but not too salty. Covered in the refrigerator, this rub keeps for 3 days.

ROSEMARY-ANCHOVY RUB

MAKES ABOUT ½ CUP (ENOUGH FOR 4 BIRDS)

Rosemary and anchovy, two Italian mainstays, provide this chicken rub with its unflinching herbal, salty character. Vinegar and Dijon make it more pungent still. That's why I use this most often in the fall, when sugar-packed produce, like squash and sweet onions, want a savory punch.

Since this rub is loose and pungent, apply less of it to the chicken than the other rubs. Enough to just coat the bird should do it.

½ teaspoon freshly cracked black peppercorns, toasted

1½ tablespoons chopped fresh flat-leaf parsley leaves

1 tablespoon finely chopped fresh rosemary leaves

1½ teaspoons Dijon mustard

1½ tablespoons apple cider vinegar

½ teaspoon finely grated lemon zest (from ½ lemon)

1 tablespoon lemon juice (from ½ lemon)

½ garlic clove, finely grated

2 tablespoons Anchovy Paste (page 300)

1½ teaspoons olive oil

Kosher salt

Place the peppercorns, parsley, and rosemary in a mortar. Smash the mixture with a pestle until the peppercorns break into fine pieces. (Alternatively, blend the mixture in a spice grinder.) Transfer to a small bowl.

Stir the mustard, vinegar, lemon zest and juice, garlic, anchovy paste, and olive oil into the peppercorn mixture. Once a uniform paste is formed, season with salt if necessary. When stored, covered in the refrigerator, this rub holds 1 week.

HOW TO PLAN THIS MEAL:

24–36 hours before: Brine chicken. Make desired rub.

12–24 hours before: Rub chicken. Make tarragon vinegar, if using. Dehydrate anchovies, if using.

2 hours before: Make anchovy vinaigrette. Temper chicken.

40 minutes before: Sear and roast chicken.

10 minutes before: Dress and plate salad.

5 minutes before: Carve chicken. Make cutting-board vinaigrette. Arrange platter.

YEAR-ROUND CHICORY SALAD
WITH ANCHOVY VINAIGRETTE

SERVES 4

I love this salad and make it every place I go, any time of year, at any time of day. It's crisp and clean and full of personality. If you make the tarragon vinegar for the vinaigrette, its mild anise flavor will tone down the bracing anchovy in the dressing.

Dried anchovies are an umami flourish—think of them as briny bread crumbs. If you don't have the time to dehydrate the anchovies, skip it and try this salad anyway.

1 tablespoon red wine vinegar

½ garlic clove, finely grated

1 tablespoon Anchovy Paste (page 300)

½ teaspoon honey

1 teaspoon Dijon mustard

¼ Thai chile, sliced thin

¼ cup olive oil

½ small head of escarole, separated

½ head of radicchio di Treviso, separated

½ romaine heart, separated

½ small head curly endive, separated

Lemon juice to taste

Tarragon Vinegar (page 295) or champagne vinegar, to taste

Fine sea salt and freshly cracked black peppercorns

1½ fresh tarragon sprigs, leaves picked and roughly torn

Anchovy Powder to taste (page 299; optional)

MAKE THE DRESSING

In a medium bowl, whisk the red wine vinegar and garlic together. Let the vinegar infuse for 15 minutes. Meanwhile, chill a large salad bowl and serving platter.

Whisk the anchovy paste, honey, mustard, and chile into the vinegar until combined. Slowly whisk in the olive oil until emulsified.

Covered, the dressing keeps in the refrigerator for up to 1 week.

DRESS THE SALAD

In the chilled salad bowl, combine the escarole, radicchio, romaine, and endive leaves. The bowl should be no more than two-thirds full. If necessary, work in batches.

Drizzle some lemon juice and tarragon vinegar and 2 tablespoons of the anchovy dressing around the perimeter of the salad bowl. Lightly season the leaves with salt and pepper. Using both hands, toss the salad and mop up the dressing on the side of the bowl. Taste, then add more salt, pepper, dressing, lemon juice, or tarragon vinegar to taste.

ASSEMBLE AND SERVE

Lay the dressed lettuces on a chilled large platter. Scatter the tarragon leaves on top. Finish with a sprinkling of anchovy powder, if using. Serve immediately.

16

REAL PORCHETTA WITH ROASTED BEETS, GRAPEFRUIT, AND CRÈME FRAÎCHE

SERVES 12 TO 16

Porchetta is a great Italian celebration of pork that requires planning and, when it emerges in all its succulent glory, great feasting. Skin crisped to a crackling, perfumed with mustard, fennel, and herbs, roasted with garlic and enlivened by lemon, it is one of the truly great cooking projects.

If I can get a little philosophical, I think a true porchetta pays homage to the life of *one* pig and the unified flavor that comes from *one* lifetime of feed. If you can, have your butcher order a skin-on pork middle, about 8 pounds without the bones; this will ensure that it is from a young, tender pig. Since the fat lining in smaller animals is thinner, its fat will practically melt away, dissolving into the crackling and meat.

The middle, as the name implies, comes from the pig's midsection. It is the cut that attaches the pork loin to the belly. If bones are attached, simply ask your butcher to cut them out or do so yourself: Lift the bone racks away from the meat and, with a sharp knife, keep slicing underneath them to release the bones.

For large, rolled-up cuts such as this, I often forgo brining in favor of highly flavored rubs that "brine" the meat from the inside. Be generous when slathering it into place. Its sweet, sharp anise flavor pulls everything together.

The sauce, spooned over at the end, takes advantage of the pork drippings and the caramelized garlic cloves that roast beneath the porchetta. Served warm or at room temperature, this is my tribute to Italy's greatest pork creation.

8-pound skin-on boneless pork middle

1 cup Dijon mustard

6 garlic cloves, finely grated, plus 1 head, cloves separated but unpeeled for roasting

2 teaspoons finely grated orange zest (from ½ orange)

3 tablespoons fennel seeds, toasted and finely ground, or 1½ tablespoons fennel pollen

2 tablespoons black peppercorns, toasted and coarsely cracked

Kosher salt

3 tablespoons roughly chopped fresh rosemary leaves

3 tablespoons roughly chopped fresh sage leaves

3 tablespoons roughly chopped fresh oregano leaves

Olive oil, as needed

2 lemons

NOTE: *While I strongly suggest using a single pork middle for this, sometimes that is impossible. If so, you can wrap skin-on pork belly around a pork loin after they have both been seasoned and rubbed. Just be sure they total 8 pounds in weight.*

BUTCHER THE PORK MIDDLE

Set the middle on a work surface, skin side down. The loin is the long, rectangular muscle that runs down the thicker side. Cut the loin away from the skin beneath it by inserting your knife into the fat between the loin muscle and the skin. Cut in long strokes underneath the muscle while rolling it up and away from the skin, toward the center of the cut. Stop cutting the loin away from the belly once only 2 inches of uncut fat hinge the two together. The entire cut should now look like an open book, with the loin muscle something like the interior pages.

(recipe continues)

Flip the middle so its skin faces up. With a sharp knife, score the skin on the diagonal, working from the upper left corner to the lower right corner. Space each incision about 1 inch apart, just cutting through the skin into the fat; be sure not to cut through the fat into the meat. (Alternatively, you can score the skin after the roast is rolled, but it's a little more difficult to control the cuts that way.)

RUB AND ROLL

Flip the pork so it is now skin side down. Using the back of a spoon, smear the mustard evenly over the meat, including both sides of the loin. Sprinkle on the grated garlic, orange zest, fennel, and black pepper. Season the meat generously with salt. Sprinkle on all the rosemary, sage, and oregano.

Starting on the loin side, lift and roll the meat toward the other side, wrapping it snugly and rolling it over to form a tight cylinder. Using butcher's twine, tie the porchetta with a butcher's loop at 1-inch intervals. Rub salt over the porchetta's exterior.

Place the porchetta on a large roasting or cooling rack set over a rimmed baking sheet. Refrigerate, uncovered, for 48 hours.

Make sure you have a large, heavy roasting pan that can comfortably accommodate the porchetta. The pan should also be at least 2 inches deep, as you will be crisping the skin in oil in the pan.

ROAST THE PORCHETTA

Two hours before cooking, remove the porchetta from the refrigerator and let it stand, on its rack, at room temperature. Preheat the oven to 350°F. (If you are making the beets alongside, place a pizza stone on the oven floor, if you have one.)

Set the roasting pan over 2 side-by-side burners set to medium-high heat. Heat $1/4$ inch of olive oil until hot, but not smoking. Carefully lay the porchetta into the pan. Reduce the heat to medium.

Once the skin starts to puff and turns a light caramel color, after about 5 minutes, carefully rotate the porchetta a quarter turn. Crisp and brown it all the way around; the process should take 20 to 25 minutes total. The porchetta will release from the pan once it crisps, so don't force it or it will tear. A splatter guard may be needed when crisping the porchetta to protect you from sputtering hot fat.

Transfer the crisped porchetta back to its rack. Carefully pour off all the fat from the roasting pan. Pour 2 cups water into the pan, scraping up all the fond.

Place the roasting rack with the porchetta in the roasting pan and set it on the oven's center rack. Roast the porchetta, turning the pan 180 degrees every 30 minutes. Add splashes of extra water, if necessary, to maintain about $1/4$ inch of liquid in the pan (this prevents the drippings from scorching).

After 1 hour, quarter 1 of the lemons. Remove the porchetta from the oven. Add the lemon quarters to the pan and unpeeled garlic cloves to the roasting rack. Return the porchetta to the oven and roast it for 1 more hour, checking it regularly to ensure the skin is browning evenly and not burning in spots. Use a thermometer to check the temperature at its center; when it reaches 140°F and the outside is golden, the roast is done.

Transfer the porchetta on its rack to a cutting board. Loosely cover with foil and let it rest for at least 20 minutes before slicing.

MAKE THE PAN SAUCE AND SERVE

Once the garlic is cool enough to handle, pop the roasted cloves from their skins. Put the cloves in a medium bowl and smash them to a paste with a fork. Squeeze in the juice from the roasted lemon quarters and whisk in the pan drippings to create an emulsion. If necessary, season the sauce with salt, pepper, and fresh lemon juice from the remaining lemon.

Transfer the porchetta to a cutting board and, using a sharp knife, remove the string and slice the meat into 1-inch rounds. Fan the meat out on a serving platter. Spoon the pan sauce over the slices. Serve with the Stone-Roasted Beets with Grapefruit and Crème Fraîche (recipe follows) alongside.

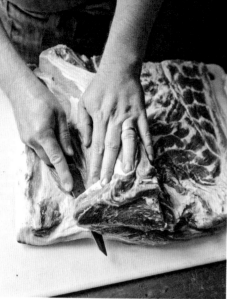
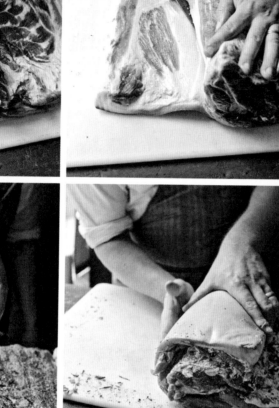

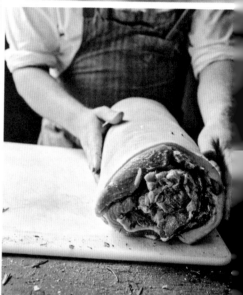

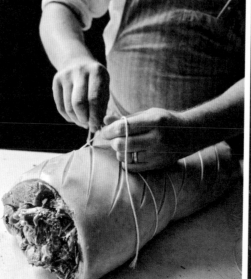

STONE-ROASTED BEETS
WITH GRAPEFRUIT AND CRÈME FRAÎCHE

SERVES 12 TO 16

Just as resolutely as I honor certain Italian traditions, I am quick to eschew others. So it is with this meal, in which porchetta, classically served with stewed beans, greens, and crispy potatoes, shakes off the weighty sides for a lighter, brighter riff.

---

4 pounds baby beets, without greens

¼ cup olive oil

Kosher salt and freshly cracked black peppercorns

1 pound radishes, greens removed

3 large grapefruit

Flaky sea salt

1 cup Crème Fraîche (page 310)

2 cups watercress

HOW TO PLAN THIS MEAL:

2 days before: Butcher porchetta. Score, rub, and tie porchetta.

5 hours before: Remove porchetta from refrigerator.

3 hours before: Sear and roast porchetta.

1½ hours before: Roast beets, prepare radishes, season crème fraîche, supreme grapefruit.

30 minutes before: While porchetta rests, make sauce and season beets.

10 minutes before: Slice porchetta and arrange on platter with sauce. Plate salad.

ROAST THE BEETS

If you have a pizza stone, set it on the oven floor. Preheat the oven to 350°F for 30 minutes.

Halve the beets; if they are substantially larger than a Ping-Pong ball, cut them into 1-inch wedges. In a large bowl, toss the beets with the olive oil and season generously with kosher salt and pepper. Divide them among sheets of foil and wrap the packets up snugly, sealing them completely. Lay the packets across a heavy baking dish (don't use glass).

Slide the dish onto the pizza stone or directly onto the oven floor. Roast for 40 minutes, flipping occasionally, or until the beets are easily pierced with the tip of a knife but remain slightly resistant at their centers. Unwrap the packets and set the beets aside to cool slightly.

PREPARE THE SALAD

Slice the radishes into very thin rounds. Transfer to a small bowl of ice water and refrigerate until very crisp. Radishes can be held in water for up to 1 hour. Dry them 10 minutes before serving.

Peel the grapefruit, cutting off all the white pith. Working over a bowl, hold the fruit in one hand and, with a sharp paring knife in the other, cut out the segments from the grapefruit by slicing toward the core on each side of the segments' membranes. The segments should fall into the bowl. Cut each segment into bite-size pieces. Season with flaky salt.

Season the crème fraîche with kosher salt and pepper. While the beets are still warm, rub off their skins with a paper towel. Place the beets in a large bowl and season with flaky salt and splashes of grapefruit juice. Let them marinate for at least 15 minutes.

Spread the crème fraîche across a large platter, coating it lushly. Arrange the roasted beets over the crème fraîche. In between the beets, scatter the grapefruit segments. Scatter the radish slices across the salad and sprinkle flaky salt on top. Garnish with watercress.

17

PEPPERCORN-CRUSTED SHORT RIBS

SERVES 6

From the moment we were reviewed by the *New York Times* at the Alimentari, these crackling, succulent, beefy short ribs became my signature. A few years later, when I left to open Upland, I thought long and hard about whether to include them on my new menu. In the end, I realized I couldn't *not* have them: Guests expected them to follow me wherever I would go. More than any dish in my repertoire, these ribs developed a life of their own, announcing my love of rustic, big flavors and slow cooking.

These short ribs are steam-roasted, a technique that up to now in this book we have only explored with vegetable sides, like the beets roasted in foil packets for the porchetta. The same principle is applied and taken a step further: These ribs roast in a high-walled pan, covered, at a moderate temperature for hours. Inside, the meat generates enough steam to keep itself plump and its peppercorn rub moist, so it doesn't scorch. Check on its progress from time to time. If the fond appears to be getting too dark, add a splash of water to prevent it from burning.

One note on buying the meat: These ribs roast as a whole slab, so make sure to place a special order with your butcher in advance to get the right cut. And, since you're putting in a request anyway, ask for a center cut (typically the amount called for here comes with 3 bones in). Keeping the slabs whole protects their succulence.

Over time, I've tried altering the original celery-walnut jumble that tops each helping, but guests have wanted nothing to change. Honestly, though, some of those toppings were just as good as the original and I've included those alternatives. I'm happy to say it's time for you to make these ribs at home and claim them as your own.

Olive oil, as needed (about 3½ cups)

1 red onion, halved equatorially

1 gallon water

1 cup kosher salt

¼ cup sugar

1 cup plus 2 tablespoons black peppercorns, toasted

2 tablespoons coriander seeds, toasted

2 tablespoons fennel seeds, toasted

3 fresh bay leaves

1 lemon, halved

1 8-pound bone-in beef short rib rack (3 whole ribs from the center cut preferred)

½ cup dry green peppercorns, toasted

¼ cup pink peppercorns, toasted

¼ cup white peppercorns, toasted

Colatura or high-quality fish sauce, such as Red Boat, to taste

BRINE THE SHORT RIBS

Set a medium heavy sauté pan over medium-high heat and slick it with 1 tablespoon olive oil. Once the oil is hot, lay the onion halves, cut sides down, in the pan. Sear the onion for 8 minutes, or until blackened.

Pour the water into a large nonreactive container. Stir in the kosher salt and sugar until dissolved. Add the burnt onion, 2 tablespoons black peppercorns, and the coriander and fennel seeds. Bruise the bay leaves and add them to

the brine. Squeeze the lemon into the brine, tossing the squeezed halves in as well.

Submerge the short ribs in the brine. Transfer the container to the refrigerator and brine the meat for 48 hours.

CONFIT THE PEPPERCORNS

Place 1 cup black peppercorns and the green, pink, and white peppercorns in a medium pot and pour in 3 cups of olive oil. Set the pot over low heat and bring the oil to a light bubble. Once bubbling, gently cook the peppercorns for 20 minutes, or until the pink peppercorns smash easily when pressed. Remove from the heat and let the confit come to room temperature.

Cover the pot and refrigerate for 12 hours. The confit will keep, covered, for 1 month in the refrigerator.

MAKE AND APPLY THE RUB

Remove the peppercorn confit from the refrigerator and let it come to room temperature.

Lift the peppercorns from the oil, place in a large mortar, and smash with a pestle until a wet, gravel-like paste forms, adding oil as necessary to achieve the consistency of wet sand. If your mortar is small, do this in batches and transfer the smashed spices to a bowl. Alternatively, you can pulse the peppercorns in a food processor. Set the remaining oil aside for another use. (As a finishing oil, this has a lot of heat. In a good way.)

Remove the ribs from the brine and hoist the meat onto a work surface. Thoroughly pat the meat dry with paper towels.

Slather the peppercorn paste all over the meaty portion of the short ribs. Place the ribs, meaty side up, on a cooling rack set over a rimmed baking sheet and refrigerate. Let the meat rest, uncovered, for 12 to 24 hours, or until the rub hardens and feels leathery to the touch.

STEAM-ROAST THE RIBS

One hour before roasting, remove the short ribs from the refrigerator and let stand at room temperature. Preheat the oven to 350°F.

Place the ribs peppercorn side up in a large Dutch oven or a deep roasting pan. Seal the pot with a double layer of aluminum foil before securing the lid into place. Slide the pot onto the oven's center rack. Roast the ribs for 3 hours, or until the meat is plump and bouncy, offering little resistance when pierced with a cake tester or paring knife at its thickest portion. Each hour or so throughout roasting, see if the meaty residue on the bottom of the pot looks dry or too dark. If so, add small splashes of water to loosen it. Reseal the pot with foil and return it to the oven, rotating it 180 degrees. Stick around the oven and let your nose tell you when to peek in—if you smell any roasty, browning smells, take a look to see what's going on.

Remove the ribs from the oven and take off the lid. Loosen the foil but don't remove it, and let the meat rest, undisturbed, for at least 1 hour. Transfer the ribs to a work surface and, while securing the meat with one hand, pull out the bones. They should easily slide out. Set the bones aside. At this point, the short ribs and bones can hold, covered, in the refrigerator for up to 12 hours.

SECTION AND SEAR
THE RIBS

If the meat and bones have been refrigerated, remove them 1 hour before serving. Preheat the oven to 400°F. Place the bones in a small roasting pan and set aside.

Set a large heavy sauté pan or skillet over medium-high heat. Swirl in enough olive oil to submerge the crust, about $1/8$ inch. Once the oil is shimmering-hot, lay the short ribs in the pan with the peppercorns facing down. Sear at a steady sizzle for 4 to 5 minutes, or until browned and just crisp. While searing the ribs, take care to roll them on their arch so the meat browns evenly all the way across the rubbed surface.

Once a thick peppercorn crust forms, transfer the pan to the oven and roast the ribs, without flipping, for 15 minutes, or until the crust sets hard but does not burn. When the intercostal meat, which lines the area where the bones once were, turns golden brown, the meat is ready and the crust is set.

(recipe continues)

Remove the ribs from the oven and transfer the meat, crust side up, to a cutting board. Let the ribs rest for 5 minutes. Meanwhile, place the bones in the oven to warm.

DICE, SEASON, AND SERVE

Cut away the ribs' intercostal meat. Carefully flip the ribs and cut through them, in between where the rib bones once were. The whole slab will be separated into individual pieces. Then take each rib and cut it crosswise into 2-inch cubes. Slice the intercostal meat into ½-inch julienne.

Arrange the warmed bones on a warm serving platter. Place the meat over the bones, re-forming the ribs' original shape. Scatter the julienned intercostal meat over the ribs and sprinkle colatura on top, to taste. Top the ribs with a seasonal salad (recipes follow) and serve immediately.

HOW TO PLAN THIS MEAL:

For the ribs:

3 days before: Brine short ribs.

2 days before: Confit peppercorns.

1 day before: Rub and dry short ribs.

5 hours before: Roast ribs.

25 minutes before: Section and sear ribs.

5 minutes before: Dice, season, and garnish ribs.

For the salads:

Celery, Castelvetrano, Horseradish, and Walnut

1–2 hours before: Slice celery and toast walnuts.

5 minutes before: Assemble and plate.

Asparagus, Lemon, and Pecorino Salad

1 day before: Marinate pecorino.

1–2 hours before: Temper pecorino.

30 minutes before: Shave asparagus and supreme lemons.

5 minutes before: Assemble and plate.

Pickled Cherry Peppers, Charred Scallions, and White Anchovy

At least 1 day before: Pickle cherry peppers.

1 hour before: Temper peppers.

10 minutes before: Sear scallions.

5 minutes before: Assemble and plate.

Butternut Squash, Dates, and Pumpkin Seeds

20 minutes before: Shave and marinate squash.

5 minutes before: Assemble and plate.

CELERY, CASTELVETRANO OLIVE, FRESH HORSERADISH, AND TOASTED WALNUT SALAD

SERVES 6 AS AN ACCOMPANIMENT FOR THE SHORT RIBS

Crunchy, round, hot, and briny, this mix of butter-toasted walnuts, crushed meaty olives, grated horseradish, and slivered celery is the original topping for these beefy ribs. It's a salad that refreshes the palate and contrasts the meat's richness between bites.

This is served as a garnish, but to bulk it up and make it a stand-alone side, add more celery and play with the balance among the other parts until it eats right to you.

---

4 large celery stalks, from the outside of a bunch, trimmed

1 cup walnuts

4 tablespoons (½ stick) chilled butter, cut into ⅓-inch pieces

Flaky sea salt

1 cup Castelvetrano olives, smashed, pitted, and roughly chopped

2 tablespoons finely sliced fresh curly parsley

1 tablespoon olive oil

1 tablespoon lemon juice (from ½ lemon)

Freshly cracked black peppercorns

Fresh horseradish, peeled and grated, to taste

Small handful of thin radish slices, for garnish

CRISP THE CELERY AND TOAST THE WALNUTS

Slice the celery at a 45-degree angle, cutting each stalk into ¼-inch wide pieces. (Alternatively, shave into ribbons with a vegetable peeler.) Place the celery in a bowl of ice water and refrigerate for 10 minutes, or until crisp. Remove the celery from the ice water and pat dry.

Place the walnuts and butter in a medium heavy skillet set over medium heat. Toss the nuts in the foaming butter until the butter begins to brown. Remove the nuts with a slotted spoon and drain on a paper towel–lined plate. Transfer the nuts to a work surface and give them a rough chop. Season with salt and set aside.

ASSEMBLE THE SALAD

In a medium bowl, gently toss the celery with the walnuts, olives, and parsley. Season the salad with the olive oil, lemon juice, and salt and pepper to taste.

Place the salad on the plated short ribs and garnish everything with grated fresh horseradish.

SHAVED RAW ASPARAGUS WITH
MEYER LEMON AND MARINATED PECORINO

SERVES 6 AS AN ACCOMPANIMENT FOR THE SHORT RIBS

This raw spring salad, which pairs thin asparagus slivers with fruity olive oil and herb-marinated hunks of pecorino, is simple and wonderful. Bits of mild, sweet Meyer lemon wake up the combination. Spooned over the ribs, the lemon refreshes and the cheese complements the beef's fat-laced bite. Since this salad features whole bites of lemon, it is highly suggested that you make this only with Meyer lemons; standard lemons would be too sour for most palates.

3 ounces Pecorino Romano

½ teaspoon fresh thyme leaves

1 tablespoon whole black peppercorns, toasted and coarsely smashed

¾ cup olive oil

1 pound green asparagus, woody ends trimmed

2 Meyer lemons

Flaky sea salt

1 tablespoon colatura or high-quality fish sauce, such as Red Boat

MARINATE CHEESE

Using the tip of a knife, chisel off bites of the pecorino into rough ½-inch pieces. Place the hunks into a medium bowl and toss in the thyme, peppercorns, and olive oil to coat. Let the cheese marinate, covered, in the refrigerator for at least 24 hours, and up to 3 days.

SHAVE THE ASPARAGUS AND ASSEMBLE THE SALAD

At least 1 hour before serving, remove the pecorino from the refrigerator and let it come to room temperature so the oil is completely loose.

Using a mandoline or a vegetable peeler, shave the asparagus into long slivers. Place the slivers in a bowl of ice water and refrigerate for 10 minutes, or until the asparagus crisps. Drain, dry, and set aside.

Meanwhile, finely grate the zest of both lemons and set it aside. Cut away the lemons' peel and pith. Working over a small bowl, hold a lemon in one hand and a sharp paring knife in the other. Cut out the segments from each lemon by slicing toward the core on each side of the segments' membranes. The segments should fall into the bowl. Season the fruit lightly with salt.

Remove the cheese from its oil and transfer it to a medium bowl. Gently toss the pecorino with the asparagus shavings, lemon zest, and lemon segments, leaving any citrus juices behind in the small bowl. Season the salad with the colatura, pecorino oil, and salt to taste.

Scatter the asparagus salad over the short ribs or serve it in a bowl.

PICKLED CHERRY PEPPERS WITH CHARRED SCALLIONS AND WHITE ANCHOVY

SERVES 6 AS AN ACCOMPANIMENT FOR THE SHORT RIBS

Anchovies and sweet peppers are a terrific pairing. This recipe works a little finesse and charred scallions into the mix. While you can use store-bought pickled cherry peppers, this fresh option, provided below, is far more delicious.

½ pound sweet cherry peppers, stemmed, halved, and seeded

2 tablespoons palm, raw, or light brown sugar

2 tablespoons kosher salt

½ cup champagne vinegar

½ cup rice wine vinegar

1 fresh bay leaf, lightly bruised

2 garlic cloves, peeled and smashed

Zest of ½ lemon, removed with a vegetable peeler and bruised

8 large scallions, root end trimmed and outer layers removed

10 oil-packed white anchovy fillets

Colatura or high-quality fish sauce, such as Red Boat, to taste

1 cup fresh basil leaves, roughly torn

PICKLE THE PEPPERS

Place the cherry peppers in a medium bowl. Pour 1 cup water into a medium saucepan and stir in the sugar, kosher salt, champagne and rice wine vinegars, bay leaf, garlic, and lemon zest. Set the pot over medium-high heat and bring the brine to a boil. Reduce the heat and simmer for 2 minutes. Carefully pour the hot brine over the peppers.

Once the brine cools to room temperature, remove the garlic cloves and discard. Transfer the brine and peppers to a clean jar, secure the lid, and refrigerate for at least 24 hours. The peppers will keep in the refrigerator for up to 3 weeks.

ROAST THE SCALLIONS AND SERVE

Remove the peppers from the refrigerator and drain the peppers. Let them come to room temperature.

Once the pickles have tempered, heat a large skillet over high heat until very hot. Add the scallions and roast, turning them often, for 4 minutes total, or until the scallions char and blister on all sides.

To serve, drape the scallions over the short ribs. Drape the anchovies over the roasted scallions. Scatter the pickled peppers around the platter, and splash a little colatura over the vegetables. Finish with the torn basil leaves.

SHAVED BUTTERNUT SQUASH
WITH DATES AND PUMPKIN SEEDS

SERVES 6 AS AN ACCOMPANIMENT FOR THE SHORT RIBS

In the fall, when butternut squash are just picked and their flesh is still tender, try this salad. It takes advantage of that window and plays on the flesh's sweet, musky character by pitting it against dense, chewy dates and toasted pumpkin seeds. Buttermilk lends some bracing, creamy acidity.

1½ pounds young butternut squash, peeled, halved, and seeded

½ teaspoon finely grated lemon zest (from ½ lemon)

1 tablespoon lemon juice (from ½ lemon)

3 tablespoons olive oil

Pinch of sugar

Fine sea salt and freshly cracked black peppercorns

½ cup dates, pitted and roughly chopped

¼ cup buttermilk

2 tablespoons pumpkin seeds, toasted

SHAVE THE SQUASH

Cut the squash into 2-inch chunks. Using a mandoline or a vegetable peeler, shave the chunks into thin slivers (about ⅛ inch, or thinner if the squash isn't very tender).

Transfer the shavings to a large bowl and season with the lemon zest and juice, olive oil, sugar, and a few generous pinches of salt and pepper. Toss to evenly coat. Let macerate for 10 minutes, or until the shavings tenderize. Taste and adjust the seasonings.

ASSEMBLE THE PLATTER

Toss the squash with the dates and season as needed with salt and pepper.

In a small bowl, season the buttermilk with salt and pepper. Smear the seasoned buttermilk across a serving platter. Top the buttermilk with the short ribs and then scatter the squash shavings over the meat. Garnish with the toasted pumpkin seeds.

18

CRISPY LAMB RIBS WITH PICKLED NECTARINES

SERVES 4

Thanks to their salty-sweet dry rub and an initial sear, these lamb ribs develop a compelling crust to go with their slightly gamy meat. They then confit in olive oil until the meat is soft enough to pull off the bone. Last, the ribs re-roast in the oven until crisp. It's a multistep process that results in irresistible tenderness and an addictive crackle.

Because this is too good not to be made year-round, if nectarines are not in season, try pairing the ribs with Stone-Roasted Beets with Grapefruit and Crème Fraîche (page 184) instead. In the summer, while just the meat and fruit are enough for me, you may want to round out the meal with a salad, like the Year-Round Chicory Salad (page 179) or the Spinach and Goat Cheese Salad with Shallot Vinaigrette (page 94). You'll want to match these rich ribs with a light accompaniment whatever time of year—even just a little warm bread or flatbread—so that the focus stays on the delicious ribs and sweet pickles.

---

1 tablespoon coriander seeds, toasted

1 tablespoon celery seeds, toasted

2 tablespoons kosher salt

2 teaspoons sugar

1½ tablespoons piment d' Espelette or hot paprika

6 pounds lamb ribs, cut into 2-pound racks

Olive oil, as needed (2 quarts or more)

12 fresh cilantro sprigs, thick ends trimmed

1 cup baby mustard greens

DRY-BRINE THE RIBS

Place the coriander and celery seeds in a mortar and smash them with a pestle until ground medium-fine (or use a spice grinder). Transfer the seeds to a medium bowl and mix in the kosher salt, sugar, and piment d'Espelette.

Lay the ribs on a clean work surface, so their meaty arch faces up. Pat them very dry with paper towels. Vigorously massage the salt mixture into the meat. When you're done, the meat should feel slightly frayed.

Place the ribs on a cooling rack set over a roasting pan. Transfer everything to the refrigerator and dry-brine the ribs for 12 hours.

SEAR THE RIBS

Let the ribs stand at room temperature for 1 hour before searing. Once the ribs are tempered, set a large heavy skillet over medium heat. Heat a ⅛-inch-deep pool of olive oil until shimmering-hot, then lay 1 rack of ribs, arch side down, in the pan.

Sear the ribs, rolling them on their arch as they brown, for 5 minutes, or until well crisped. Lower the heat as needed to ensure the spice rub does not burn.

Transfer the meat back to the cooling rack. Clean the pan and repeat the browning process with the remaining ribs.

CONFIT THE RIBS

Preheat the oven to 300°F. Transfer the ribs to a large, deep roasting pan or Dutch oven. Arrange them so the seared side faces up. Pour in 2 quarts olive oil, or enough to completely submerge the ribs.

(recipe continues)

Carefully set the pan, uncovered, on the oven's center rack. Cook the ribs for 2 hours, or until the meat is tender and a cake tester inserted into the meat's thickest part encounters little resistance. Check on the ribs after about 45 minutes; if the oil is bubbling actively, reduce the heat to maintain a lazy bubble.

REST THE RIBS IN OIL

Carefully remove the ribs from the oven and set aside to cool. Once the oil feels just warm to the touch, lift out the ribs and set them aside on a large rimmed baking sheet.

Set a strainer over a heatproof, deep container. Line the strainer with cheesecloth and carefully pour the confit oil through the strainer, catching any debris. Discard the debris.

Clean the roasting pan and return the ribs to it. Pour the strained oil back over the ribs to submerge and cover with aluminum foil. Transfer the ribs to the refrigerator and let the meat rest for 2 days.

CRISP THE RIBS

Remove the ribs from the refrigerator 2 hours before serving. When the oil is liquid again, lift out the ribs and place them on a cutting board. Set the oil aside. With a chef's knife, cut between the ribs. Using paper towels, blot as much oil off the ribs as you can without removing the spice rub.

Preheat the oven to 500°F. Working in batches, or using separate pans, slick the bottom of a large heavy roasting pan with some of the lamb confit oil. Lay in 1 rack of the lamb ribs, meaty side down. Roast for 10 to 15 minutes, or until crispy and caramelized on the outsides and heated through. Let the meat rest for 5 minutes before serving.

PLATE AND SERVE

To serve, arrange the lamb ribs on a large cutting board. Dot the arrangement with fresh or Pickled Nectarines (recipe follows). Garnish the ribs with the cilantro and mustard greens, and drizzle some of the lamb oil and nectarines' pickling liquid over and around the platter. Serve immediately with warm bread or pita.

PICKLED NECTARINES

MAKES 3 PINTS

I love lightening rich meats with fruit. Here I've called for pickling it first, and this brine is my most trusted pickling liquid for preserving fruit. If you can't get great nectarines, use any stone fruit.

---

4 medium-large ripe nectarines or peaches (about 1½ pounds total)

1 fresh bay leaf

Zest of 1 lemon, removed with a vegetable peeler

¼ cup kosher salt

1 tablespoon coriander seeds, toasted

1½ cups champagne vinegar

1½ cups rice wine vinegar

½ cup palm or raw sugar

Pit and quarter the nectarines. Using the broad side of a chef's knife, press down on the bay leaf and lemon zest to release their essential oils.

In a large nonreactive container, toss the nectarines with the salt, bay leaf, coriander seeds, and lemon zest. Set the fruit aside and let it macerate for 1 hour.

In a small bowl, mix the champagne and rice wine vinegars. Stir in the sugar until it dissolves. Pour the liquid over the peaches and toss to coat.

Cover the fruit and let pickle for 1 day, covered in the refrigerator. These pickles hold up to 2 weeks in the refrigerator.

HOW TO PLAN THIS MEAL:

3 days before: Dry-brine lamb ribs.

2 days before: Sear and confit lamb ribs.

1 day before: Pickle nectarines.

2½ hours before: Temper lamb ribs. Temper pickled fruit.

30 minutes before: Clean lamb ribs and recrisp in the oven.

10 minutes before: Arrange platter.

GRILLING

ABOUT SIX MONTHS AFTER I'D LEFT THE IL BUCO FAMILY, I SHOWED BACK UP TO help with their annual pig roast. It was a bit after midnight and I was coming off of a fourteen-hour run at my new restaurant, Upland. Lower Manhattan was wide awake and my friends and old colleagues were scrambling, setting up the grill. The scene, though, did not remind me of pig roasts I'd cooked with them in the past. Instead, I recalled a different time altogether. A time when this neighborhood went dark.

Hours before Hurricane Sandy came crashing into New York City, we were battening down the hatches at the Alimentari, putting a week's worth of meat and fish on ice, just in case.

The next morning, four and a half feet of water was surging against my garage door. Finally, Donna, the Alimentari's owner, called. Power was out all over lower Manhattan, she said. Water was scarce; few, if any, stores were open, and our neighbors needed help, especially the guys at the homeless shelter and the fire station. A meal, we thought, could provide some relief and use up some of our ingredients before they spoiled.

When I arrived, everything was in tatters. Signs and branches were down, debris everywhere, and the neighborhood felt utterly topsy-turvy.

We set up a grill outside and got the fire blazing. People started circling as we laid down some silver-skinned branzini. Next, octopus and sausages sizzled alongside the fish, and the smell that rose up as their fat splattered against the coals breathed some life back into our block.

People gathered as we worked: artists, guys from the shelter, firemen, yuppies, fashionistas, and shop owners. They lingered out in the fresh air and dragged out some chairs and tables to sit and finally relax for a moment.

We passed around day-old bread, a bit tough but still good. The food—elemental, hot, and charred—met everyone's hunger head on. Friends from The Wren, a restaurant a few blocks away, showed up with wine. Guys from Bohemian, a restaurant around the corner, came with hot miso soup.

Going home that night, my work felt more essential than ever before, leaving a ravaged neighborhood, and me, a bit better off in the midst of a hard time.

As I stood again on the same block, almost two years on, the city was thriving and Sandy seemed to be fading into a distant memory—in this neighborhood, at least. For me, though, the takeaway remained much the same: My job is to feed people well and nurture community.

And while the context of that day was obviously a hard one, I think it also showed, in retrospect, not just what I love about feeding people but what I love about grilling. Grilling speaks to a part of us that craves elemental satisfaction. Smoke, fire, food, and gathering. It is a craving dialed deep into our DNA in bad times and good.

GRILLING: TECHNIQUE AND DETAIL

My passion for grilling has everything to do with the rusticity of the technique—how effortlessly it adds flavor and lends a smoky, sweet char. Plus, the primal thrill I get from taming a fire just appeases my inner caveman.

My cooks have told me that I grill like I roast. What I think they mean by that is the food that comes off my grill rarely wears seared-black marks. That's a good thing, since I find this branding often tastes acrid and signals inconsistent cooking.

Instead, I aim to create an even crust all over, the sort that looks like it came out of a ripping hot pan. The way I do this is simple: turn the meat often, so it does not stick or cook too long over any one spot. What I get by grilling in this way is even caramelization and smoke distribution.

EQUIPMENT

I don't call for fancy gear in my grill setup, but it is important to understand your tools, and to have the right ones.

THE GRILL

The heart of the operation, of course, is the grill. I work with charcoal- or wood-burning grills, because I love the alluring smell and the sensory experience of dealing with live fire. Nevertheless, gas grills are convenient and what many home cooks use. Though the following recipes are written for charcoal, most *will* work with gas. When adjusting the recipes for a gas grill, skip the coal bed portion of the directions and just set the heat to the specified levels. (The one thing gas grills won't allow for is coal roasting, which is called for in some of the following meals. I suggest you roast those items in the oven instead.)

The recipes in this chapter were tested over two standard charcoal grills: a 24 × 18-inch rectangular one with a grate (resembling an oil barrel turned on its side) and a round 22-inch kettle grill (your standard-issue Weber). Any size grill in this general ballpark should work fine for the following meals, save for the suckling pig (see page 278). For that, you will need a grill with a cooking surface that is at least 30 × 20 inches and preferably with an adjustable grate. More on that later.

THE GRATE

Though I entertain fantasies of building my own souped-up grill setup one of these days, my home grill is relatively average and perfectly satisfactory. Well, except for the grate. My grate, like most grates out there, is made of stainless steel. In a perfect world, it would be cast iron. A cast-iron grate conducts heat well, prevents sticking, and, perhaps best of all, imparts a killer sear. If you have a choice, get a cast-iron grate for your grill.

CHARCOAL

All charcoal is made of the same stuff: wood. This said, not all charcoal is created equal, and I choose to use hardwood lump charcoal—not briquettes and certainly not instant-light briquettes.

The downside of hardwood lump charcoal (which isn't so bad, if you ask me) is that it is irregularly sized.

Briquettes, on the other hand, are formed by an industrial process that presses the wood into a standardized shape. In doing so, manufacturers often introduce additives and that's when the pure, clean smell of charcoal gets a little lost. What's more, briquettes don't burn as hot or as long as hardwood lump charcoal. But they are admittedly easier to work with.

Whichever you choose, just don't use ones soaked in lighter fluid. That petroleum is toxic stuff. On that score, don't use lighter fluid at all. Since good-smelling hardwood lump charcoal is the only kind I truly endorse, it is what we used while testing these recipes.

CHIMNEY STARTER

A chimney starter with a handle on the side for easy pouring is mandatory when using natural charcoal. These starters are straightforward: You stack coals into the long cage, stuff paper into the small cavity below, and you light the paper.

The chimney starter we used holds about 5 pounds of hardwood lump charcoal; the cage's dimensions are about 12 × 8 inches. A chimney-full burns for about an hour, with a medium-high heat that lasts about 40 minutes. To get the full burn out of hardwood lump, you may need to re-rake your coals to get them going again and reintroduce oxygen to the pile from time to time. Also, if you grill often, you may find it useful to get two chimneys. That way, if you need to make a bigger coal bed, it is easily done.

The other thing you will need is newspaper and long matches, or one of those long lighters, to get the whole thing going.

RAKES, SPATULAS, AND TONGS

Let's start with the rakes, useful for moving your coals about to create different temperature zones. The rake should be metal, 12 inches long, with a metal slab at its base. Since it will distribute hot coals across a grill bed, it should also be heavy duty. The ones I use at restaurants are typically cast iron and look pretty old school. At home, though, I just use a long-handled, heavy-duty spatula, and that does fine. The key term here is "long-handled," since you want to keep your arm safe. In some of the following preparations, you'll want a heavy-duty spatula for flipping delicate cuts. And you will almost always need at least one pair of heavy-duty metal tongs. Ideally, you will have two. Make sure your tongs are at least 12 inches long and strong enough to lift up a hot grate if necessary. Unless otherwise specified, tongs are what you should use to turn all the food in this chapter's recipes.

KITCHEN TOWELS

I always keep plenty of thick, dry kitchen towels handy for grabbing support. Make sure they're dry; a wet towel on hot metal will send burning hot steam right through to your hand. Also, one of those kitchen towels should be raggedy so you can dirty it when oiling the grill.

GRILL BRUSH

It is important to work on a clean grill, so that the heat is conducted properly, and food won't stick. You'll need a long-handled metal grill brush to scrape the grate clean. Do this when the grate is hot, right before you start grilling, and again just after you are done.

SETTING UP THE FIRE

Once all your equipment is ready to go, start the fire. Here's how:

1. Pour about 5 pounds of charcoal into the chimney starter, filling it to the top.

2. Bunch up 2 or 3 sheets of newspaper and lightly pack it into the chimney starter's small lower cavity.

3. Set the chimney on the empty grill and light the paper through the slots so the paper flares and sparks the coals.

4. When the coals in the chimney light up, flames will initially spew and sparks will fly. Don't be alarmed; these will subside. Once the coals glow bright red and lightly ash over, pour them out into the grill. Heating the chimney takes anywhere from 20 to 35 minutes, depending on your charcoal and the ambient temperature.

   If you are building a large coal bed, fill two starters up at the same time. If this isn't possible, you will need to replenish the coals using just the one starter immediately after they have been dumped into the grill. To do so, set the newly emptied starter down on a safe place, like a piece of slate or other flame-resistant surface (make sure no brush or leaves are near). Repeat the process detailed above and pour the hot coals into the grill once they are ready.

5. Once the coals are poured out, rake the specified bed into place. Each of the following recipes will tell you exactly what the bed should look like. The shape of these vary depending on what you are cooking and how.

6. Set your grate in place above the coal bed as soon as possible so it starts heating up. Note: On the grill used in testing these recipes, the grate sat about 4 inches above a flat coal bed; the different styles of coal beds will alter this distance, bringing some coals higher up and some lower to give you different temperature zones.

7. Once the grill grate is securely in place, let the metal heat up for 5 to 10 minutes, then scrape it clean using a grill brush. If the grate catches fire while warming up, let the flames burn out. That's just old food burning off the grate.

8. Apply oil to the grill's grate by moistening a kitchen towel with olive oil. Using long tongs, rub the grate with the oiled towel until it glistens. Be generous here, because an oiled grate really does prevent food from sticking.

PLAYING WITH SMOKE AND FIRE

To play up the smoky element of the grill, find ways to lift your meat up off the grate and rely on the radiant heat to smoke-roast the food—that's what I do with my Veal Meatballs (page 267). Because there's no contact with hot metal, the browning is gentle and the smoke flavor is purer. To turn your grill into a smoker, cover it with a lid and trap the smoke below. If you are smoking something for more than just a few minutes, make sure the flue is open so you don't snuff out the fire and to let the more bitter elements of the smoke out.

In a few instances, I fiddle with how the sear is imparted by lowering the grill grate and bringing it closer to the fire. Lowering a grate dramatically increases the temperature and deepens the char. Only some grills let you adjust the grate height, though. If yours does not, just build up a higher coal bed beneath your grate.

The other way I play with searing in the following pages is cooking directly on hot coals. I love the rich perfume that this contact creates and the ashy, crackly crust that forms.

COAL BEDS

The shape of your coal bed varies depending on what needs to be done. A flat, even coal bed, for example, allows for steady, even cooking all over the grate. A sloping bed creates heat zones: Where the coals are higher, the heat is more intense. This allows you to crisp or char in one zone, and gently cook the food through over a cooler zone. A channel-shaped bed, where the coals are pushed toward the sides of the grill, maximizes indirect, radiant heat—turning the grill essentially into an oven. Each of the following recipes will call for a specific shape of coal bed.

GAUGING HEAT AND MANAGING FLARE-UPS

Before laying food onto a grate, gauge the grill's heat. To do so, use a laser thermometer or let your hand be the judge.

I typically feel for heat with my hand 10 inches above the coal bed; usually this means 6 inches above the grate. I place my hand palm side down and count the seconds until I have to pull away my hand. Of course, this count varies for everyone and my palms are more callused than most, but do this a few times and you'll learn your own timing. Here is a range that's generally useful to keep in mind:

Flare-ups will likely occur at some point as oils and fats

	Heat feels unbearable after	Temperature of grate (4" above coals)
High heat	2–3 seconds	500°–600°F
Medium-high	3–4 seconds	400°–500°F
Medium heat	5 seconds	350°–400°F
Medium-low	6 seconds	300°–350°F
Low heat	7–8 seconds	250°–300°F

drip onto the coal bed. The problem with flare-ups is that they send up wild flames that impart an undesirable acrid flavor. The good news is, flare-ups are easily handled: Just move your food to a lower heat zone or remove it from the grill until the flames die down.

BALANCING GRILLED MEALS

You will notice these meals are more pared down than the braised or roasted menus. That's how I like my grilled food. Simple and robust, tasting of itself plus smoke and fire. Often just one, sometimes two, light accompaniments are needed to round out the plate. Those tend to be bright, acidic, and raw, bringing freshness to the dark flavors of the fire. But of course, feel free to add or mix and match sides and accompaniments from other areas of this book, or from your repertoire.

HOW THIS CHAPTER IS ORGANIZED

This chapter starts off with recipes that call for simpler cuts, simply seared over an even, flat coal bed. Typically, these are boneless and more or less uniformly shaped.

We then move on to sloping coal beds, working over multiple heat zones, in which the food is seared hard, then cooked through more gently, or vice versa.

Next, we start focusing on the smoke that comes off the fire. By the end of the chapter, the grill turns into a smoker with various kinds of coal beds.

Together, I hope these rustic preparations expose you to a full range of grilling possibilities. Many of these meals are warm-weather appropriate, but plenty are geared toward the cooler months too, when the warmth and scent of the grill are very welcome.

1

HARD-GRILLED JUMBO SQUID WITH TWO FENNELS

SERVES 4

This is a straightforward, high-heat grill: What you are chasing here is a deep, cara-melized grill mark on your squid. Squid is tender until the instant it turns rubbery, so move fast and only work over the highest heat to bring out its sweet savoriness.

Use your hands and eyes to gauge the temperature of the coals and the grate, making sure to take advantage of both as they peak temperature-wise. The coals should be white hot: a thin layer of ash coating angry red. If you hold your hand 6 inches above the grate (see page 204), it should only be bearable for 2 or 3 seconds. At this point, lay down the squid and watch them sizzle.

Grilling squid is easy: When their flesh tightens, whitens through, and shrinks, turn them. When the reverse side does the same, remove them from the heat. Since squid morphs and curls quickly, signaling perfect doneness, watch for these changes to prevent overcooking.

Served alongside are pickled and raw fennel, providing crunch, acidity, and a seafood-loving anise flavor. Serve this with crusty bread and a salad. For a heartier meal, the Sardinian Couscous (page 44) would be a terrific pairing.

½ small fennel bulb, halved

½ pound Fennel alla Grecque, at room temperature (recipe follows)

1½ pounds large squid, whole or cleaned by your fishmonger

Coarse sea salt and freshly cracked black peppercorns

2 tablespoons olive oil, plus more for the grill

2 tablespoons roughly chopped dill fronds

2 tablespoons roughly chopped fennel fronds

4 oil-cured Calabrian chiles or 1 tablespoon Serrano Chile Oil (page 294)

Flaky sea salt

PREPARE THE FENNEL

Peel away the fennel bulb's tough outer layer and discard. With a sharp knife or mandoline, finely slice or shave the fennel halves crosswise into thin slivers. Place the slivers in a medium bowl filled with ice water and refrigerate for 10 minutes to crisp.

Drain the Fennel alla Grecque from its preserving liquid and cut it into bite-size pieces.

Just before grilling the squid, remove the raw fennel from its ice bath and dry it thoroughly. Set the fennel aside, scattered over paper towels.

CLEAN THE SQUID, IF NECESSARY

If you have whole squid, snip off the end of the body at the opposite end of the tentacles and pull out the hard quill. Then, with the dull side of a chef's knife, "squeegee" out the ink sack and other organs from within the squid's tube. At my table, I like to serve these creatures whole, asking guests to watch out for the inedible beaks between the tentacles. But if you prefer, pull the tentacles away from the body and cut them off. Find the spot where the tentacles come together and push down. A hard beak will pop out. Cut it off. In this instance, the tentacles will obviously need to be grilled separately.

(recipe continues)

GRILL THE SQUID

Pat the squid very dry with paper towels and lay them on a platter. Generously season the squid all over with coarse salt, pepper, and the 2 tablespoons olive oil.

Light a full chimney starter of charcoal. Once the coals are very hot, glow red, and lightly ash over, pour them out into a pile. Rake the coals into an even bed, wide enough to fit all the squid comfortably. Set the grill grate in place and, when you can hold your hand 6 inches above it for only 2 seconds, indicating high heat, scrape it clean.

With a kitchen towel cinched between tongs, wipe the grate with olive oil. When the grate is raging hot, grill the squid. If necessary, where the flesh curls, press the squid gently down onto the grate. Timing will vary depending on the size of your squid, so watch it carefully. When the flesh whitens, shrinks, and firms up, turn the squid and char the other side for 1 minute, or until the flesh firms up all the way around. Transfer the grilled squid to a serving platter.

DRESS AND SERVE THE SQUID

Scatter both the chopped Fennel alla Grecque and the fresh fennel slivers over the hot squid. Garnish with the dill, fennel fronds, and chiles. Season with flaky sea salt and serve immediately.

FENNEL ALLA GRECQUE

MAKES 1 POUND

Anything done alla Grecque, a popular pickling approach among the French grand-mother set, involves cooking an ingredient until it turns tender, then covering it in an aromatic, lemony brine. Sometimes wine is used, but in this recipe the fennel's blanching liquid is repurposed to temper the acidity, resulting in a milder brine.

---

1 tablespoon kosher salt

1 pound fennel bulbs, cut into 1-inch-thick wedges

1 tablespoon coriander seeds, toasted and lightly crushed

1 tablespoon fennel seeds, toasted and lightly crushed

1 teaspoon hot pepper flakes

¾ cup champagne vinegar

¼ cup lemon juice (from 2 lemons)

½ cup olive oil

Pour 1 quart water and the salt into a large saucepan and bring to a boil over high heat. Reduce to a gentle simmer and add the fennel to the pot. Simmer the fennel for 6 minutes, or until the wedges are just tender and easily pierced in their thickest parts. With a slotted spoon, transfer the fennel to a deep, medium nonreactive container with a lid. Turn off the heat and set the pot of water aside.

Once the fennel cools slightly, pour 1½ cups of the reserved cooking water over it. Add the coriander and fennel seeds, hot pepper flakes, vinegar, and lemon juice. Gently stir to combine and let the fennel cool to room temperature.

Pour in the olive oil, secure the lid, and refrigerate for 12 hours. The fennel keeps for 2 weeks in the refrigerator.

HOW TO PLAN THIS MEAL:

1 day before: Make Fennel alla Grecque.

30 minutes before: Set up grill.

10 minutes before: Grill squid and assemble platter.

2

PORK CHOPS SCOTTADITO WITH COAL-ROASTED SWEET POTATOES

SERVES 4

The inspiration for this meal comes from the late Italian cookbook doyenne Marcella Hazan. For me, and countless others, she remains a constant source of inspiration. This simple pork chop scottadito—which translates to "burnt little fingers"—came to be after I read a recipe of hers for lamb chops prepared this way. Flattened and then rubbed in pungent aromatics, scottadito chops are cooked just long enough for their fat to crisp deliciously along the bones. Just try not to burn your fingers picking them up.

This is a straightforward, single-heat grill method. The grill shouldn't be a fearsome inferno, but you really do want it quite hot. Since these chops are on the thin side, you don't have much time and a nice, crisped edge is what I think Marcella would have insisted upon.

¼ cup roughly chopped fresh sage leaves

1 teaspoon finely grated lemon zest (from about 1 lemon)

1 garlic clove, roughly chopped

5 tablespoons olive oil, plus more for the grill

1 tablespoon red wine vinegar

1 tablespoon coarse sea salt

½ teaspoon coarsely ground green peppercorns

4 bone-in pork rib chops (2½ pounds total)

1½ teaspoons lime juice (from 1 lime)

PREPARE THE RUB

Finely chop the sage, lemon zest, and garlic together. Transfer the mixture to a small bowl and pour in ¼ cup of the olive oil, the vinegar, salt, and green peppercorns. Stir to combine.

POUND AND SEASON THE CHOPS

Lay a large square of plastic wrap on your work surface and set one of the pork chops on it. Cover the chop with another square of plastic. Use a meat mallet or a small, sturdy pan to gently but firmly pound the chop, working from the bone out, until the meat is a uniform ¾ inch thick. Repeat with the other chops.

Rub the chops with the sage rub, saturating every inch in oil and seasonings. Lay the chops on a cooling rack set over a rimmed baking sheet and refrigerate, uncovered, for 3 to 24 hours. The longer the meat rests, the more flavor it picks up from the rub.

GRILL AND SERVE THE CHOPS

Remove the pork chops from the refrigerator and re-pound them to a ¾-inch thickness if necessary. Let the chops stand at room temperature for 30 minutes before grilling.

Meanwhile, set up the grill using a full chimney starter of coals. Once the coals are very hot, glow red, and lightly ash over, pour them out and rake them into an even bed across the grill. If serving these chops with the Coal-Roasted Sweet Potatoes, rake down the preexisting coal bed and ashes before adding the fresh coals. (See the accompanying "How to plan this meal" box and the potato recipe.)

Set the grate in place and, once hot, scrape it clean. Then, with a kitchen towel cinched between tongs, wipe olive oil all over the grate until it glistens. Once the coals start to ash more deeply along their corners, the coal bed should

emit an even, medium-high heat, and you should be able to hold your palm 6 inches above the grate for no more than 3 or 4 seconds. Lay the pork chops on the grate.

Grill the pork for 6 minutes, rotating the chops 45 degrees every 2 minutes, or until they turn an even, rich golden brown, and both the meat and the fat along the bone caramelize. Flip the chops and grill the other side for 2 minutes, rotating them 90 degrees halfway through, or until the meat is cooked to medium and retains a touch of blush at its center. Grill actively and trust your instincts; if need be, lift the chops from the grill to slow down the cooking of the meat and just singe the bones and their fat on the grate.

Transfer the chops to a warm platter and drizzle them with the remaining 1 tablespoon olive oil and the lime juice. Serve the chops with Coal-Roasted Sweet Potatoes with Crème Fraîche, Pomegranate, Olives, and Herbs (recipe follows).

HOW TO PLAN THIS MEAL:

3–24 hours before: Pound and rub chops.

90 minutes before: Set up grill.

70 minutes before: Coal-roast sweet potatoes.

50 minutes before: Light a second chimney of charcoal and temper chops.

25 minutes before: Remove sweet potatoes from coals. Pour in new coals and grill pork chops. Grill and plate pork and sweet potatoes.

COAL-ROASTED SWEET POTATOES
WITH CRÈME FRAÎCHE, POMEGRANTE, OLIVES, AND HERBS

SERVES 4

Here we roast sweet potatoes directly on the coals until their flesh turns fluffy, infused with smoke. The skins become very charred, which I love, but you can peel them partially or even fully after cooking if you prefer a milder character. Once cracked open, we nestle them into a crème fraîche smear. Castelvetrano olives, pomegranate seeds, and plenty of herbs take the plate in sweet, tart, salty, herbal directions. It's a simple but impressive introduction to one of my favorite cooking techniques.

---

4 medium white sweet potatoes (about 2 pounds)

Kosher salt and freshly cracked black peppercorns

½ cup Crème Fraîche (page 310)

2 tablespoons olive oil

1 tablespoon lime juice (from about 1 lime)

½ cup pomegranate seeds

½ cup whole Castelvetrano olives, cracked, pitted, and roughly chopped

¼ cup fresh cilantro or flat-leaf parsley leaves, roughly torn

¼ cup wild arugula, radish tops, or other peppery green

COAL-ROAST THE POTATOES

Set up the grill using a full chimney starter of coals. Once the coals are very hot, glow red, and lightly ash over, pour them out and rake them into an even, flat bed.

As the coals heat, tear off eight 12-inch sheets of aluminum foil and place 1 sweet potato on each of 4 sheets. Season the potatoes with salt and cinch the foil around them. Double wrap each parcel with a second sheet of foil.

Using tongs, nestle the sweet potatoes into the coals. Move more coals around the potatoes so they are totally surrounded, laying a few hot coals on top to loosely cover them in a single, even layer.

Coal-roast the potatoes for 45 minutes, or until they turn very tender and a skewer or paring knife easily pierces their centers. Turn the potatoes once

halfway through and cover them up again. If necessary, you can continue roasting the potatoes while you add fresh coals and reset the grill to cook the pork chops.

Lift the potatoes out of the coal bed and transfer them to a cutting board. Carefully unwrap them and let cool until just cool enough to handle. The skin will be very charred; if it's too much for your liking, peel the potatoes partially or fully.

ASSEMBLE THE DISH

Season the crème fraîche with salt and pepper and spread it across a platter. With your hands, crack the sweet potatoes in half. Place the halves, flesh sides up, over the crème fraîche and season the exposed flesh with the olive oil, lime juice, and salt and pepper. Sprinkle the pomegranate seeds and chopped olives on top and garnish the platter with herbs and greens. Serve hot.

3

GRILLED FATTY TUNA WITH CITRUS PESTO AND COAL-ROASTED FIGS

SERVES 4

Tuna belly is expensive, beautiful stuff. Prized at sushi counters, it practically dissolves on the tongue.

Though cooking such a fine cut over a live fire may seem reckless, the objective is simple: Get a quick, light browning to flavor and just firm up the tuna's surface, keeping the inside a lush red. As an evolution of the hard-charging technique used for the squid, this recipe calls for setting up a cool zone beside the coal bed to provide the fish with a safe haven if flare-ups occur due to the tuna's fat.

To round out this meal, serve it with the Cucumber, Mint, and Olive Salad (page 121) and some steamed short-grain white rice.

---

4 4-ounce slabs of fatty tuna belly, about ¾ inch thick

Fine sea salt and freshly cracked black peppercorns

Olive oil, for greasing the grill

16 ripe Mission figs

1 cup **Citrus Pesto** (recipe follows)

12 fresh basil leaves, roughly torn

GRILL THE TUNA

Light a full chimney starter of coals. Once the coals glow red and lightly ash over, pour them out. Rake the coals into a high, flat bed, just wide enough to fit all of the tuna comfortably; it should come within 3 to 4 inches of the grate.

Once the coal bed is raked, set the grate in place. Pat the tuna very dry with paper towels until the meat feels tacky on both sides. Season the fish generously with salt and pepper. When the grate is very hot, scrape it clean. You should be able to hold your hand 6 inches above the grate for just 2 seconds, indicating high heat. With a kitchen towel cinched between tongs, wipe olive oil over the grate until it glistens.

Lay the tuna over the coal bed. Sear for 1 minute, then, using a spatula, rotate each piece 90 degrees and sear for another 30 seconds, or until lightly browned and crisped along their edges. If flare-ups occur, move the tuna to a cooler spot on the grill until the flames subside. Then continue grilling the tuna over high heat.

Flip the tuna and lightly sear the other side for 45 seconds, or until it just turns opaque with gentle grill marks. When done, the tuna should be lightly colored on one side, golden on the other, and very rare within. Transfer the tuna to a cutting board and let it rest.

COAL-ROAST THE FIGS

While the tuna rests, use your tongs to lift up the grill grate. Rake the coals about so you shake off some collected ash, exposing their hot embers.

Carefully nestle the figs directly onto these medium-hot coals and, using tongs, place a few more hot coals around and over the figs to loosely cover the fruit. Coal-roast the figs for 2 minutes, or until they smell sweet and their exteriors ash over. Unearth the fruit and rotate them. Re-cover the figs and continue roasting them for 2 to 3 minutes more, or until they plump and their skins harden all the way around. Gently brush or shake off excess ash.

Slice the tuna and serve with cracked-open figs, pesto, and basil.

CITRUS PESTO

MAKES ABOUT 2 CUPS

Tiny bits of broccoli—just the very tips of the florets—lend this pulpy, floral, sweet citrusy pesto a bit of body and a surprising amount of savory, vegetal depth.

1 lemon

1 lime

1 medium orange

1 small grapefruit

Fine sea salt

1 cup loosely packed fresh basil leaves

2 tablespoons finely shaved broccoli floret tops

¼ cup olive oil

½ teaspoon agave syrup or honey

Freshly cracked black peppercorns

SUPREME THE CITRUS

Finely grate the lemon, lime, orange, and grapefruit zest and set aside. Slice off the tops and bottoms of each fruit. Stand the fruit up straight and, with a sharp paring knife, cut away the peel and pith, following the contours of the fruit. Discard the peel and pith.

Working over a medium bowl, hold a piece of fruit in one hand. Cut toward the center of the fruit along each side of the membrane walls to release the supremes, or whole citrus segments, into the bowl. Squeeze the cut membranes over the bowl to capture all the juices.

With a spoon, gently break the supremes into ½-inch pieces. Season lightly with salt.

ASSEMBLE THE PESTO

Place the basil leaves in a large mortar. With a pestle, pound the leaves to break them down. Add the reserved zests and a pinch of salt and continue pounding until a coarse paste forms. You can also do this in a small food processor.

Transfer the basil paste to a medium bowl and stir in the shaved broccoli tops. Add the citrus segments, reserving their juice in the small bowl.

Stir the olive oil and agave into the basil-citrus mixture. Season with salt, pepper, and splashes of the reserved citrus juice. Set the pesto aside, at room temperature, for 30 minutes before serving. Leftover pesto, tightly covered in the refrigerator, keeps for up to 2 days, but it is best fresh.

HOW TO PLAN THIS MEAL:

90 minutes before: Make pesto.

40 minutes before: Set up grill.

10 minutes before: Grill tuna and figs. Arrange platter.

4

GRILLED SKIRT STEAK
WITH CRISP MARJORAM AND GREEN TOMATOES

SERVES 3 TO 4

To get at a skirt steak's sweet spot, you have to grill it just over the medium-rare mark so its center remains blush but its texture takes on a bit more structure. You also want to develop a good char along its outside without overcooking the interior. My strategy is pretty basic: Because charring both sides would overcook this thin cut, just do a good job on one side and call it a day.

Fried marjoram lends the beef a lovely floral boost. Otherwise, the meal is homey and pretty quick to pull off. Vinegar "rinsed" green tomatoes give a little soft crunch and refreshing tartness. If you like, serve with Remina's Piadini (page 29) or swap the tomatoes out for Caramelized Parsnips (page 136) in the winter. Salted crème fraîche (page 310) makes for a great sauce.

To make this recipe in even less time, skip the dry-brining step and just season these steaks generously right before cooking. This is a weird suggestion coming from me, I know, but I've made this streamlined version before and the result, while less robustly flavored, makes for a fine steak dinner.

---

1 1½-pound skirt steak, preferably with thin fat cap

2 teaspoons coarse sea salt

2 teaspoons freshly ground black peppercorns

Olive oil, as needed

20 fresh marjoram sprigs, thick stem ends discarded

Fine sea salt

DRY-BRINE THE STEAK

Lay the steak on a clean work surface and rub both sides with the coarse salt and pepper. Transfer the meat to a cooling rack set over a rimmed baking sheet and refrigerate, uncovered, for 12 to 24 hours.

FRY THE MARJORAM

Pour enough olive oil into a medium saucepan to cover the bottom by 1 inch and set over medium-high heat.

Once the oil is shimmering-hot, add a marjoram sprig. If it sizzles instantly, then add half of the marjoram to the oil. Fry the herbs, at a steady sizzle, until they turn bright green and crisp, about 40 seconds. Using tongs, transfer the sprigs to a paper towel–lined plate. Sprinkle with fine sea salt. Repeat with the remaining marjoram.

GRILL THE STEAK AND SERVE

Let the steak sit at room temperature for 30 minutes before grilling. Pat it very dry with paper towels.

Light a full chimney starter of charcoal. Once the coals are very hot, glow red, and lightly ash over, pour them out into a pile. Rake the coals into an even bed, wide enough to comfortably accommodate the steak. Keep the remaining grill area free of coals.

Once the coal bed is in place, set the grate 1 or 2 inches above the coals, if you can. If you can't, either don't worry about it, or rake up your coal bed to increase its height. You should only be able to hold your hand 6 inches above the grate for 2 to 3 seconds, indicating high heat.

(recipe continues)

Once the grate is hot, scrape it clean. Then, using a kitchen towel cinched between tongs, wipe olive oil all over the grate until it glistens. Lay the steak on the grate. Grill the steak for 1 minute and rotate it 45 degrees. Continue grilling the meat over high heat, rotating it 45 degrees every minute, for 3 minutes total, or until the steak is evenly and thoroughly browned.

Flip the steak and grill the other side just 1 minute more, rotating it 90 degrees halfway through. When it is just over medium rare, transfer the steak to a cooling rack set over a cutting board. Let the meat rest for at least 5 minutes, loosely tented with foil.

Serve the steak on a serving platter and scatter the fried marjoram over the top. Serve with Vinegar-Rinsed Tomatoes alongside (recipe follows).

VINEGAR-RINSED TOMATOES

MAKES 3 CUPS

Green tomatoes' tart flesh takes kindly to this speedy, pickle-like treatment. These are rinsed, as opposed to submerged, so the tomatoes maintain much of their own flavor while drinking up a measured amount of the tart-sweet vinaigrette.

½ pound unripe green tomatoes or tomatillos

1 pound Green Zebra or other heirloom green tomatoes

2 tablespoons champagne vinegar

1 teaspoon fine sea salt

1 teaspoon sugar

Slice the unripe tomatoes into ¼-inch-thick rounds and cut the Green Zebra tomatoes into 1-inch wedges. Place all the tomatoes in a shallow bowl and toss them with the vinegar, salt, and sugar. Taste and adjust the seasoning as necessary.

Let the tomatoes marinate for 5 minutes, or until the vinegar seeps into the slices. Using a slotted spoon, transfer the tomatoes to the steak platter, leaving the extra vinegar behind in the bowl.

HOW TO PLAN THIS MEAL:

1 day before: Dry-brine steak.

50 minutes before: Fry marjoram. Temper steak. Set up grill.

15 minutes before: Make tomato salad. Grill steak.

5

"BISTECCA FIORENTINA" WITH OLIVE OIL–MARINATED BLUE CHEESE

SERVES 4

Bistecca Fiorentina is the classic Tuscan steak that Italian carnivores go mad for. Typically served with just a lemon wedge and some standard sides like roasted potatoes, white beans, and spinach, the preparation is tremendously satisfying. But it *can* be improved upon. This recipe is how I think that makeover should look.

Made with a porterhouse, which has a T-bone at its center joining a lean fillet to a New York strip, this bistecca first gets a flavor boost from a simple salt and pepper dry brine.

I get the grill blazing hot and set the grate as close to the fire as possible. If your grate doesn't lower, I recommend lighting up more charcoal than usual and building up a higher bed below. Increasing the temperature of the grate increases the char on your steak, and a delicious crust is essential. As with the previous steak, this method calls for cooking one side longer than the other, to maximize browning without overcooking and to give a bit of textural contrast to your bites. Keeping a coal-free zone on the grill is also useful here in case flare-ups occur.

Off the grill, I gild the lily with a flourish of olive oil–marinated blue cheese. Pickled okra refreshes and seals this new and improved deal. Borrowed from Italy and tweaked in New York, this makeover is all the more lavish when you brush the steaks with whipped lardo; the cured pork fat adds a deliciousness you can't quite put a finger on. When feasting on a beautiful steak, I like to focus my attention almost purely on the meat, but if you'd like to add sides to the meal, the Grilled Zucchini with Fried Shallot Bread Crumbs (page 226), Roasted Tomatoes (page 90), and Bruschetta (page 298) would be terrific here as well.

---

2 22-ounce porterhouse steaks, about 1 inch thick

4 teaspoons coarse sea salt

2 teaspoons freshly cracked black peppercorns

Olive oil, for greasing the grill

2 tablespoons whipped lardo, room temperature

½ cup baby arugula

DRY-BRINE THE STEAK

Pat the steaks very dry with paper towels. Rub the coarse salt and pepper into the meat, coating both sides. Set the steaks side by side on a cooling rack set over a rimmed baking sheet. Transfer the steaks to the refrigerator and let them rest, uncovered, for 24 hours. The meat should feel dry to the touch, almost leathery on the surface.

SET UP THE GRILL

Remove the steaks from the refrigerator 1 hour before grilling. Meanwhile, light the coals using a chimney starter. Once

they are very hot, glow red, and lightly ash over, pour the coals into a pile occupying two-thirds of the grill. Rake the coals into a tall, even bed, just large enough to cook both steaks directly over. Keep the rest of the grill coal-free.

Immediately set the grate in place, about 2 inches from the top of the coal bed, if possible. If your grate is not adjustable, you may have to do some wrangling to get the grill extra hot. Here are the options: Either fire up some more coals to raise the height of your coal bed or rake the existing coals into an even more compact, high pile, if possible. The final option is to just deal with the grate at the standard 4-inch height above the coals for a regular high-heat sear—the steaks will still be deliciously browned, but perhaps not as crusty.

GRILL THE STEAKS

Once the grate is hot, scrape it clean. When the grate is *very* hot, meaning you can hold your palm 6 inches over the grate for only 1 or 2 seconds at most, use a kitchen towel cinched between tongs to wipe olive oil over the grate until it glistens. Immediately lay the steaks on the grate, cooking them over very high heat. Sear the meat for 2 minutes, or until lightly charred. Continue grilling the steaks over this heat, rotating them 90 degrees every 2 minutes, for 8 minutes total, or until they are thoroughly and evenly charred and the fat is extra crisp. If flare-ups occur in the process, transfer the steaks to the cool zone of the grill until flames subside.

Flip the steaks and continue grilling them over high heat for another 4 minutes total, rotating them 90 degrees every minute. At this point, the steaks should be deeply charred on one side, caramelized on the other, and cooked to medium rare, about 125°F, in the center. When they are done, move the steaks to the coal-free portion of the grill. Using tongs, roll them, one at a time, along their edges over high heat for 1 or 2 minutes more, or until their sides crisp and brown. Transfer the steaks to a cutting board. Immediately brush the meat with lardo. Loosely tent with foil and let the steaks rest for 10 minutes before serving.

SLICE AND SERVE THE STEAK

Serve the steaks whole, or slice: With the tip of a sharp knife, cut around the bones to free the meat from the T-bone. Slice the steaks across the grain into ½-inch pieces. Fan the meat out on a warm serving platter and scatter arugula over the top. Spoon the Olive Oil–Marinated Blue Cheese and its flavored oil over the top. Scatter the Pickled Okra around the meat or serve it alongside (recipes follow).

PICKLED OKRA

MAKES 1 QUART

Since okra has a slightly murky yet sweet flavor, the mild vinegars and sugar used in this pickling liquid play to its character.

¾ pound okra

1 cup champagne vinegar

1 cup rice wine vinegar

¼ cup palm, raw, or brown sugar

1 tablespoon kosher salt

1 fresh bay leaf, bruised

3 tablespoons coriander seeds, toasted

1 tablespoon yellow mustard seeds, toasted

½ teaspoon hot pepper flakes

1 2-inch strip of lemon peel, bruised

Place the okra in a clean glass quart jar.

Pour the champagne vinegar, rice wine vinegar, sugar, salt, bay leaf, coriander and mustard seeds, hot pepper flakes, lemon peel, and ½ cup water into a small saucepan and set it over medium-high heat. Bring the brine to a boil, then immediately remove the pot from the heat and carefully pour the hot brine over the okra.

Let the okra cool to room temperature. Cover the jar and refrigerate for 24 hours for the brine to penetrate the okra. Okra pickles keep, refrigerated, for up to 1 month.

OLIVE OIL-MARINATED BLUE CHEESE

MAKES ABOUT 1 CUP

I started making this about ten years ago, and it has been a hit ever since. Marinating this cheese transforms it, softening its bite and lending it roundness.

If possible, use a Tuscan or Umbrian oil to dress the cheese: Its green, spicy flavor pairs perfectly with the Valdeón, a Spanish blue I like a bit better than standard Gorgonzola for its extra-spicy bite and crumbly texture. That said, Gorgonzola picante or Stilton are fine substitutes.

¼ pound Valdeón or other blue cheese, broken into ½-inch pieces

¼ teaspoon freshly cracked black peppercorns

¼ cup red wine vinegar

½ cup olive oil

Place the cheese in a small container that will allow the crumbled cheese to fit snugly in a single layer. Season the cheese with pepper and vinegar and toss to combine.

Spread the cheese into one layer and pour the olive oil over the top. Cover with plastic wrap and refrigerate for at least 12 hours, until the oil picks up the blue cheese's essence and the cheese softens.

Let the cheese stand at room temperature for at least 1 hour before serving.

HOW TO PLAN THIS MEAL:

1 day before: Pickle okra. Marinate blue cheese. Dry-brine steaks.

1 hour before: Temper marinated cheese, steaks, and pickles. Set up grill.

30 minutes before: Grill steaks. Assemble platter.

6

SPICE-RUBBED MACKEREL WITH GRILLED ZUCCHINI AND FRIED SHALLOT BREAD CRUMBS

SERVES 4

Coating mackerel fillets in a spice rub that combines eight aromatic ingredients is my roundabout nod to Sicily, where, thanks to the Moors, spices are employed with a confident hand. Mackerel is one of the few fish rich enough to hold its own against such a coating. Once grilled, its oily flesh benefits from the rub's perfume, while the spices themselves crisp up around the fillet's edges, lending them extra texture.

Like the preceding steak, these fillets grill mostly on one side to concentrate heat on their skin, and the coal-bed setup calls again for a cool zone to escape flare-ups. To flip your fish when ready, work gingerly and use a spatula, as tongs will mangle the fillets.

2 teaspoons coriander seeds, toasted

1 teaspoon cumin seeds, toasted

1 teaspoon fennel seeds, toasted

¼ teaspoon pink peppercorns, toasted

2 teaspoons kosher salt

1 teaspoon dried oregano, finely crumbled

1 teaspoon dried thyme, finely crumbled

Finely grated zest of 1 lemon

½ teaspoon ground cinnamon

4 skin-on mackerel fillets (about 1½ pounds total)

2 tablespoons olive oil, plus more for the grill

½ lemon, cut into wedges

MAKE THE SPICE RUB

In a spice grinder, blend the coriander, cumin, and fennel seeds, and the pink peppercorns until a coarse powder forms. Transfer the ground spices to a small bowl and stir in the salt, oregano, thyme, lemon zest, and cinnamon.

SCORE AND SEASON THE MACKEREL

Lay the mackerel fillets, skin side up, on a clean work surface. Pat them very dry all over with paper towels. With a sharp paring knife, lightly score the skins, on the diagonal, at 1-inch intervals. Take care not to cut too far into the flesh; aim to just cut the skin if possible.

Evenly rub the spices all over the fish, coating both sides. Lay the seasoned mackerel fillets on a cooling rack set over a rimmed baking sheet and refrigerate, uncovered, for 30 minutes.

GRILL AND SERVE THE MACKEREL

Meanwhile, set up the grill using a full chimney starter of coals. Once the coals are very hot, glow red, and lightly ash over, pour them out and rake them into a flat, even bed that occupies two-thirds of the grill. Across the remaining third of the grill, the coal bed should thin and slope out. Set the grate in place over the coals. You are looking for a medium to medium-high heat in the hottest zone; you should only be able to hold your hand 6 inches above the grate for 4 to 5 seconds.

Once the grate is hot, scrape it clean. Using a kitchen towel cinched between tongs, wipe olive oil all over the grate until it glistens.

Right before grilling, remove the fish from the refrigerator and gently rub both sides of the fillets with 2 tablespoons olive oil, taking care to keep the spices in place. Lay the fillets, skin side down, on the grate over the hottest zone.

(recipe continues)

Grill the fillets for 2 minutes, or until their skins begin to color. Using a spatula, carefully rotate the fish 45 degrees and continue grilling for about 2 minutes more, or until the skin evenly crisps up and the fish is more than halfway cooked through. If flare-ups occur, transfer the fillets to the cooler portion of the grill until the flames subside. Or if your skin is crisped and taking on a lot of color while the flesh is still undercooked, move the fillets to the cooler zones of the grill.

With a spatula, carefully loosen the skin from the grate and flip the fish. Grill the flesh side of the fillets just long enough to turn it opaque, about 15 seconds. Once the fillets flake when pressed, they're done. Transfer the mackerel to a warm platter, skin side facing up.

Serve the grilled fish warm with lemon wedges and the Grilled Zucchini with Fried Shallot Bread Crumbs alongside (recipe follows).

GRILLED ZUCCHINI
WITH FRIED SHALLOT BREAD CRUMBS

SERVES 4

This side dish takes advantage of the grill's quick charring power while making good use of summer's most prolific vegetable, zucchini. Simply grilled on just one side, the rounds turn sweet and supple without becoming formless. A fried shallot–bread crumb topping provides an irresistible, aromatic crunch.

Only some of the oil that deep-fries the shallots will get repurposed to crisp these bread crumbs. The rest of this infused oil should be enjoyed elsewhere, like drizzled on toast or over a salad or onto a soup or . . .

---

2 large shallots, halved lengthwise and thinly sliced

Olive oil, as needed

Kosher salt and freshly cracked black peppercorns

2 cups ½-inch pieces of ciabatta or sourdough bread, torn from inside the loaf

2 pounds zucchini, sliced into ½-inch-thick rounds

½ cup mixed leafy greens, such as baby spinach, shiso, sesame leaves, and arugula

FRY THE SHALLOTS

Place the shallots in a medium high-walled sauté pan and pour in enough olive oil to float the shallots.

Gently warm the oil over medium heat until small bubbles form along the shallots' edges. Reduce the heat to medium-low and slowly fry the shallots at a gentle but persistent sizzle—around 235°F if you're using a thermometer—for 15 to 20 minutes, or until the shallots turn a rich golden brown. While the shallots fry, occasionally and carefully stir them. Using a slotted spoon, transfer the shallots to a paper towel–lined plate. Season with salt.

Once the oil cools to room temperature, carefully pour it through a cheesecloth-lined sieve into a medium bowl. Reserve the oil, discard the caught sediment, and wipe the pan clean.

FRY THE BREAD CRUMBS

Pour ½ cup of the strained shallot oil into the cleaned pan. (Refrigerate the rest of the oil for another use; it's delicious.) Heat the oil over medium heat and, once it shimmers, add the

bread crumbs. Sauté the crumbs, stirring and flipping often, for 5 minutes, or until they turn golden and crisp. With a slotted spoon, transfer the crumbs to a second paper towel–lined plate. Season with salt.

Toss the cooled bread crumbs and shallots together in a small bowl. Break up any large bread crumbs, so all pieces are roughly the size of BBs. If not using the crumbs immediately, transfer them to an airtight container, where they will keep for up to 3 days at room temperature.

GRILL THE ZUCCHINI AND SERVE

Set up the grill as detailed in the mackerel recipe (see page 225).

In a medium bowl, toss the zucchini rounds with 2 tablespoons olive oil and a few generous pinches of salt and pepper. Grill the zucchini rounds on one side over medium-high heat for 3 minutes, or until charred and warmed through.

Without flipping, transfer the zucchini rounds to a medium serving platter, arranging them so their charred side faces up. Scatter the shallot bread crumbs and greens on top.

HOW TO PLAN THIS MEAL:

90 minutes before: Fry shallots. Fry bread crumbs.

1 hour before: Score and season mackerel. Set up grill.

20 minutes before: Grill zucchini and mackerel. Assemble platters.

7

KAFFIR LIME OCTOPUS
WITH PERFECT CHICKPEAS AND BLISTERED PEPPERS

SERVES 4 TO 6

I run kitchens inspired by Italy, but today's culinary landscape is broad and border-less. That's where this kaffir lime rub, which points to Southeast Asia, comes in. Smeared over poached octopus that is then grilled crisp, it lends unexpected citrusy, floral flavor to a Mediterranean mainstay.

In terms of technique, this recipe is all about searing that beautiful, green rub firmly into the octopus. When making the paste, make sure it is extra, extra thick so it fully adheres to the octopus on the grill. Since what you are cooking is a bulbous creature with spindly legs, you have to move the octopus around on the grill: press its tentacles flat onto the grate; turn its body to char along the curved surfaces; rock it over the grates as needed. You have to keep touching the food, watching, smelling, listening to it change as you caramelize and crisp its nooks and crannies.

Off the grill, this dish skews back into the Italian zone, served with simple blis-tered peppers and chickpeas.

---

2 2-pound octopi, heads and beaks removed by your fishmonger

Kosher salt

1½ teaspoons coriander seeds, toasted and coarsely smashed

1½ teaspoon fennel seeds, toasted and coarsely smashed

¼ teaspoon hot pepper flakes or 1 small oil-cured red chile, stemmed

1 garlic clove, roughly chopped

6 tablespoons olive oil, plus more for the grill

⅓ cup fresh oregano leaves

½ cup kaffir lime leaves, stringy centers removed

1 cup roughly sliced fresh flat-leaf parsley

3 tablespoons orange juice

1 teaspoon honey

1 handful greens, for garnish

BUNDLE THE OCTOPUS

Lay two 12-inch squares of cheesecloth on a clean work surface. Place an octopus in the center of each, tentacles facing down. Pull the cloth up and around the octopus so it forms a tight ball and firmly tie up the parcel with butcher's twine.

Place the octopi in a large, deep pot and add enough water to cover them by 1 inch. Season the water with enough salt to make it taste lightly salty. (The octopus simmers for a few hours, so the salinity will concentrate somewhat as the water reduces.)

SIMMER

Bring the water to a simmer over medium heat. Reduce the heat to low and very gently simmer the octopus for 2 to 3 hours, or until its meat is tender, but still has a bit of pleasant chew. To check, pierce the thickest part of a tentacle with a cake tester or a paring knife; it should feel as though you are piercing a hard-boiled egg. Cooking times may vary widely depending on your octopus, so start checking on the doneness after about 90 minutes of simmering. When done, remove the pot from the heat and let the octopi cool in the cooking liquid.

Once the octopi are cool enough to handle, remove them from the liquid. Discard the cheesecloth, drain the octopi, and thoroughly pat them dry with paper towels. Halve both octopi through their middles, yielding 4 halves with 4 tentacles each.

Transfer the octopi to a cooling rack set over a rimmed baking sheet and refrigerate for 1 hour.

MAKE THE RUB

In a food processor or blender, place the coriander and fennel seeds, hot pepper flakes, garlic, and 6 tablespoons olive

oil. Pulse to combine. Add the oregano, kaffir lime leaves, parsley, orange juice, and honey. Continue processing until completely smooth. Season the rub with salt; it should taste well seasoned but not salty.

Set the octopi halves on a clean work surface. Pat them with paper towels again, if necessary, to make sure the flesh is completely dry. With your hands (or a stiff pastry brush), smear a nice thick coat of the kaffir lime rub all over each half, paying special attention to coating the tentacles and all their suckers.

Place the octopi back on the cooling rack and refrigerate the halves, uncovered, for at least 3 hours and up to 12 hours.

GRILL AND SERVE

Temper the rubbed octopus for 30 minutes before grilling. Set up the grill by lighting a full chimney starter of charcoal. Once the coals are very hot, glow red, and lightly ash over, pour them out into a pile, raking them into an even bed across the grill.

Immediately set the grate in place and, when hot, scrape it clean. Then, with a kitchen towel cinched between tongs, wipe olive oil over the grate until it glistens. Once the coal bed burns down to medium-high heat, or when you can hold your hand 6 inches above the grate for only 3 or 4 seconds, lay 2 octopus halves on the grate with the suckers facing down.

Sear the octopus for 8 minutes, or until the rub browns and crisps all over the flesh. Use the tongs to roll, press, and prod the octopus to thoroughly char the tentacles all over. Unfurl the tentacles so they flatten onto the grate. Once the rub sets on one spot, twist and turn the tentacles as needed to crisp them elsewhere. Work toward even crisping and browning, but do not scorch the meat. Pay special attention to the suckers, as they will crisp faster than the smooth sides. Once the tentacles of both halves are all crisped, flip them up to focus on the body portions.

Sear the bodies for another 3 to 5 minutes, or until they are thoroughly crisped. While the octopus bodies are searing, place the other 2 octopus halves on the grill, suckers face down over medium-high heat, and repeat the searing process. As each octopus half finishes cooking, place it on a warmed serving platter.

Serve the octopi with the Perfect Braised Chickpeas, greens, and Blistered Shishito Peppers (recipes follow).

PERFECT BRAISED CHICKPEAS

SERVES 4 TO 6

When the *New York Times* reviewed the Alimentari, these chickpeas were the star of the very first sentence. Their secret begins with great ingredients. While dried beans can technically last forever, they cook up creamier when fresher. South Asian or Mediterranean markets, where the customers buy lots of chickpeas, are always a good bet. Once cooked, the chickpeas are dressed up in a vinaigrette and finely diced raw winter vegetables. That's it. Bet you'll get rave reviews too.

2 cups dried chickpeas

2 lemons

12 fresh thyme sprigs

2 fresh bay leaves

4 garlic cloves

Kosher salt and freshly cracked black peppercorns

3 tablespoons champagne vinegar

2 tablespoons finely diced celery

2 tablespoons finely diced carrot

2 tablespoons finely diced fennel

2 tablespoons finely diced red onion

⅓ cup olive oil, plus more for drizzling

SOAK AND BRAISE

Pour the chickpeas into a deep container and cover with 6 cups water. Refrigerate for 12 to 24 hours.

Drain the chickpeas and transfer to a medium Dutch oven. Add fresh water to cover them by 2 inches. Set the pot over medium-high heat and bring to a boil. Boil the chickpeas for 2 minutes, skimming the scum.

Use a vegetable peeler to remove peel from 1 lemon. Press down on the thyme, bay, and lemon peel with the broad side of a chef's knife to release their oils. Toss the herbs, peel, and garlic into the pot.

Reduce the heat, so the liquid gently simmers, and cook the chickpeas for 1½ hours, or until the beans are still whole but tender and creamy within. Add water as needed to keep them covered by at least 1 inch. Once the chickpeas are tender, add salt and pepper to season the liquid and chickpeas. Let the beans cool to room temperature in the liquid; this is best done by setting the whole pot in a sinkful of ice water.

The chickpeas can be held in their liquid, refrigerated, for 2 days.

MAKE THE DRESSING

Finely grate the zest of the second lemon (it should yield 1 teaspoon) and then juice it into a medium bowl. Whisk in the vinegar, lemon zest, celery, carrot, fennel, and red onion. Season with salt and pepper and let marinate for 5 minutes. Whisk in the olive oil and reseason.

REHEAT AND SEASON

Drain the chickpeas, reserving the cooking liquid. Gently rewarm them in a large saucepan over medium heat with about a cup of the cooking liquid. Once the beans are heated through, use a slotted spoon to transfer them to a large bowl. Dress the chickpeas to taste with the dressing.

Serve the seasoned chickpeas warm or at room temperature and drizzle with extra olive oil just before serving.

BLISTERED SHISHITO PEPPERS

SERVES 4 TO 6

These bite-size peppers are delightful on their own, but when hit hard with searing heat and sprinkled with coarse salt, they take on an addictive quality. Simple to prepare, these peppers are a tapas spread staple, and a perfect match for grilled octopus.

1½ pounds shishito peppers

1½ tablespoons olive oil

Coarse sea salt

SPECIAL EQUIPMENT

12-inch wooden skewers

Soak the skewers in water for 20 minutes, then pat dry.

Thread the peppers lengthwise onto the skewers, spacing them out so they just touch. Lay the skewers on a medium platter and brush the peppers with the olive oil.

While the grill is still hot from cooking the octopus, grill the peppers over medium-high heat for 2 minutes on each side, or until they puff up and blister. Remove the skewers from the grill and sprinkle with salt. Serve immediately.

HOW TO PLAN THIS MEAL:

2 days before: Soak chickpeas.

1 day before: Cook chickpeas.

7 hours–1 day before: Cook octopus.

4–12 hours before: Make kaffir lime rub. Rub and dry octopus.

90 minutes before: Make chickpea vinaigrette. Rewarm and dress chickpeas.

1 hour before: Set up grill. Skewer peppers.

30 minutes before: Grill octopus and peppers. Assemble platters.

8

GRILLED DUCK BREAST WITH CHARRED GREENS, GRAPES, AND CELERY

SERVES 4 TO 6

Mellow duck, crisped skin, a garlicky, pine nut emulsion, juicy grapes, and the textures of burnt greens and crisp celery: This is a dish that hits almost every pleasure center in my brain.

These duck breasts (and the following sausage coil) serve as a bridge in this chapter, leading us away from the straightforward grilling of cuts mainly just in need of a char, toward more complex methods, like whole or bone-in grilled meats that need to be cooked over a few different heat levels.

This recipe calls for cooking the breasts fat side down over indirect heat. That gradually melts much of the fat away, so the skin crisps, gently cooking the meat in the process. Once properly rendered, flip the breasts and position their meat sides directly over the hot coal bed to give them a beautiful sear.

4 duck breasts (2 pounds total)

1 tablespoon coarse sea salt, plus more to taste

1 teaspoon freshly cracked black peppercorns, plus more to taste

2 teaspoons finely smashed juniper berries

½ teaspoon finely grated lime zest (from 1 lime)

Olive oil, for greasing the grill

SCORE, RUB, AND DRY-BRINE THE DUCK

Lay the duck breasts, skin sides up, on a work surface. Pat them very dry with paper towels. With a sharp knife, score the skin on the diagonal at ¼-inch intervals, making sure not to cut into the meat.

In a small bowl, combine 1 tablespoon coarse salt, 1 teaspoon pepper, the juniper berries, and lime zest.

Rub the scored skins well with the juniper-salt rub and arrange the breasts, skin side up, on a cooling rack set over a rimmed baking sheet. Refrigerate the duck, uncovered, for 12 to 24 hours; the skin should feel a bit leathery when ready.

SET UP THE GRILL

Set the duck breasts out at room temperature 30 minutes before grilling. Meanwhile, light a full chimney starter of charcoal. Once the coals are very hot, glow red, and lightly ash over, pour them out into an even bed occupying half the grill. Keep the rest of the grill coal-free.

Place a large disposable aluminum drip pan right next to the coal bed, in the empty portion of the grill. Set the grate in place. Once it is hot, scrape the grate clean. Then, with a kitchen towel cinched between tongs, wipe olive oil all over the hot grate until it glistens.

GRILL THE DUCK AND SERVE

Place your hand 6 inches above the grate right where the coals meet the drip pan. You should feel an even, medium heat and be able to hold your hand at that height for 5 seconds before having to pull it away. Lay the duck breasts, skin side down, right along that line, so that the skin is taking as much heat as possible without being directly over the coals and its fat falls into the drip pan.

Render the duck breasts, rotating them 90 degrees every 2 minutes. Cook the fatty skin in this fashion for 10 to

15 minutes, or until it crisps and less than 1/8 inch of fat remains between the skin and the meat. If necessary, move the breasts around the grate, always keeping them over indirect heat, to ensure that all the fat melts uniformly.

When the skins are crisped, use the towel to re-oil the grate directly over the coals. Season the meat sides with salt and pepper and flip the breasts, setting the meat sides directly over the coals. Sear them for 1 to 2 minutes, rotating them 90 degrees every 30 seconds, or until the duck is cooked to medium doneness and the meat sides have browned nicely.

Transfer the breasts to a cutting board and let them rest, skin sides up, for 5 minutes. Slice the breasts crosswise into thick pieces. Serve the duck on plates smeared with the Garlic and Pine Nut Emulsion and scatter the Charred Greens with Green Grapes and Celery on top (recipes follow).

CHARRED GREENS WITH GREEN GRAPES AND CELERY

SERVES 4 TO 6 AS A GARNISH FOR THE DUCK

I love duck best in the fall, so I'm quick to work another autumnal favorite, grapes, into this meal. Though tart green grapes are specified, any variety would work here. I like concords, for example.

This side is really more of a savory-sweet-tart garnish that cuts through the gamy meat. To make it more robust, bulk up the recipe with extra greens and serve this tangle over a smear of the Garlic and Pine Nut Emulsion (recipe follows).

¼ pound large-leaf spinach, dandelion greens, or other medium-bodied green, stems on

3 tablespoons olive oil

Fine sea salt and freshly cracked white peppercorns

2 cups green grapes, halved lengthwise and seeded

2 tablespoons lemon juice (from 1 lemon)

2 celery stalks, sliced crosswise into ½-inch pieces

1 teaspoon finely grated lemon zest (from 1 lemon)

CHAR THE GREENS

Toss the greens in a bowl with 1 table-spoon of the olive oil. Gather a few spinach leaves together, gripping them by their stem ends. Using the grill setup described in the preceding duck recipe, lay the tips of the leaves on the grate, in the hottest part of the grill.

Slowly drag the leaves back and forth across the grate so the leaves start to wilt and lightly char on both sides. Set the charred leaves on a baking sheet and char the remaining spinach in this same fashion. Season with salt.

ASSEMBLE THE SALAD

In a large bowl, toss the grapes with the remaining 2 tablespoons olive oil, the lemon juice, and salt and pepper to taste. Set the grapes aside and let them marinate for 10 minutes. Toss the celery, lemon zest, and charred leaves into the bowl with the grapes until evenly combined. Serve immediately.

GARLIC AND PINE NUT EMULSION

MAKES 1½ CUPS

Smoked salt is the chef-y ingredient du jour, and normally I am skeptical of such things. But in this creamy sauce of milk-soaked pine nuts blended with garlic, the seasoning lends a hit of depth and aroma. Of course, if you'd rather not make a trip to the fancy food store for it, sea salt is fine.

¾ cup pine nuts

1 cup whole milk

1 garlic clove, finely grated

½ teaspoon finely grated lemon zest (from ½ lemon)

Flaky smoked or plain sea salt and freshly cracked white peppercorns

SOAK AND SIMMER THE PINE NUTS

Place the pine nuts in a small bowl or lidded container and pour the milk over them, covering the nuts by ½ inch. Cover the bowl and refrigerate for 12 to 24 hours, or until the nuts are swollen and soft.

Pour the pine nuts and their soaking liquid into a small saucepan and add the garlic. Bring the milk to a gentle simmer over low heat and cook for 3 minutes, or until the flavors meld and the garlic's bite mellows. Remove from the heat and let the mixture cool to room temperature.

MAKE THE EMULSION

Pour the pine nut mixture into a blender and add the lemon zest. Blend on low speed for 30 seconds, or until the pine nuts are evenly and finely chopped. Increase the speed to high and process the sauce for 60 seconds, or until it is creamy and completely smooth. Season with salt and white pepper to taste.

HOW TO PLAN THIS MEAL:

1 day before: Rub duck and soak pine nuts.

90 minutes before: Make garlic and pine nut emulsion.

1 hour before: Temper duck and set up grill.

30 minutes before: Grill duck and greens. Prepare charred greens salad. Arrange platter.

9

GRILLED SAUSAGE COILS WITH CHARRED ESCAROLE AND SPICY BROWN BUTTER–HAZELNUT VINAIGRETTE

SERVES 6 TO 8 (MAKES TWO 2-POUND SAUSAGE COILS)

This is one of the most straightforward meals in this book, but it's a favorite: juicy, porky sausages perfumed with fennel and chiles, browned on a smoky grill with some greens and a super-nutty vinaigrette.

It also makes me a little nostalgic for when I was just eighteen, enrolled at the Culinary Institute of America (technically I am still enjoying my leave of absence). One weekend, I stopped into a restaurant where I used to work in New Jersey and asked my old chef if I could play around in his kitchen. At the time we were making sausages up at school and I was having a hard time with the lessons.

It was there, without textbooks and teachers, where I finally understood how sausage making works. I learned how important it is to keep your meat cold throughout the process so its fat emulsifies later on. After a few exploding links, I learned the importance of stuffing the right amount of farce (the French name for the meat mixture) into the casing, so that it's smooth and taut but not stretched. (An overstuffed sausage bursts during cooking, and an understuffed sausage will deform.)

And I learned that nothing improves a sausage link more than the sear and smoke of the grill. Most backyard cooks are happy to throw a sausage on the grill and just forget it until it's done. But I've found that active grilling of sausages, over multiple heat zones, gives you rich browning and a gently cooked interior that keeps the farce's fat emulsified, yielding the juiciest bite.

Incidentally, that first batch of sausages I made all those years ago was oversalted. But making my first quasi-successful batch without a recipe got me over a hurdle. I hope this sausage coil does the same for you—but with better results your first time around.

---

4 pounds boneless pork shoulder, cut into 2-inch cubes

5 garlic cloves, crushed

2½ Thai bird chiles or other small hot, fresh chiles, stemmed and sliced thin

2 tablespoons fresh oregano leaves

1 tablespoon fennel seeds, toasted

1½ teaspoons fennel pollen (optional)

1 tablespoon Aleppo pepper (optional)

3 tablespoons kosher salt

7 feet of pork sausage casings

Olive oil, for greasing the grill

SPECIAL EQUIPMENT

Meat grinder with sausage stuffing attachments; four 12-inch skewers, soaked

DRY-BRINE THE PORK SHOULDER

In a large bowl, combine the cubed pork, garlic, chiles, oregano, fennel seeds, fennel pollen, Aleppo pepper, if using, and kosher salt. Thoroughly rub the seasonings into the pork until the pork feels slightly frayed. (Don't forget to wash your hands after handling the chiles.)

Cover the bowl tightly with plastic wrap and refrigerate for 24 hours. Refrigerate a medium-grind plate and all the other required attachments, as well as the mixing bowl and paddle for a stand mixer, for at least 2 hours.

SOAK THE CASINGS

An hour or two before stuffing, rinse the sausage casings under cold running water until no salt remains. Place the rinsed casings in a bowl, cover with cold water, and refrigerate until ready to use.

GRIND AND WHIP THE PORK

Secure the chilled medium-grind plate onto the grinder. Place ice water in a large bowl and set a second large bowl inside it. Place the stacked bowls under the grinder to catch the farce.

Remove the pork from the refrigerator. Pass the meat and all its seasonings through the grinder's feed tube, collecting the farce in the chilled bowls below. Next, take half the ground farce and pass it through the feed tube again, regrinding it. Fold all the meat together with a spatula to thoroughly combine the two grinds.

Transfer the farce to the chilled bowl of your stand mixer. Secure the bowl and the chilled paddle into place. Whip the farce at medium speed while slowly drizzling in $1/2$ cup very cold water. Beat the farce for 4 minutes, or until the pork feels tacky and starts to cling to the bowl's walls. Remove the bowl from the mixer and cover the farce with plastic wrap. Refrigerate the meat while you set up the sausage stuffer. (If you just want to make sausage patties, you can form them now and you're done.)

STUFF THE SAUSAGES

Set up the meat grinder for sausage stuffing. Wet its nozzle, from which the farce will extrude, and tightly cinch the casing around the nozzle's tip, pulling the casing toward the machine and bunching it along the nozzle, leaving a 3-inch casing overhang off the tip.

Fill the feeder with farce and turn the machine on low. With one hand (or with a partner), use a plunger to slowly push the farce through the feeder and, with your other hand, keep a gentle hold on the nozzle. Monitor the stuffing process so the farce slowly and evenly fills the casing, until it feels taut and few, if any, air pockets appear.

Refill the feeder as needed and continue stuffing until half the farce is encased. Turn off the machine and loosen 2 inches of empty casing from the nozzle. Cut the empty casing and lay the sausage flat on a work surface.

Repeat the sausage-stuffing process with the remaining farce.

PRICK AND TIE THE SAUSAGES

Prick the sausage links at $1/2$-inch intervals with a sausage pricker or a thin needle, paying special attention to any area where air pockets have formed. If the casings are not evenly filled, gently press down on them to evenly distribute the farce and release air pockets. Then tie the loose ends up in tight double knots at the link's endpoints.

SKEWER AND DRY COILS

Line a baking sheet with parchment paper. On a clean work surface, spin both of the long sausage links into approximately 9-inch-wide coils. Run two 12-inch metal or soaked wooden skewers through each of the coils, forming a plus-sign. Place the coils on the baking sheet and refrigerate, uncovered, for at least 6 hours, or until the casings feel dry and taut and the farce within the casing feels relaxed. The sausages can be coiled and skewered up to 2 days in advance.

GRILL AND SERVE THE SAUSAGES

Remove the sausages from the refrigerator 30 minutes before grilling. Meanwhile, set up the grill, lighting a full chimney starter of coals. Once the coals are very hot, glow red, and lightly ash over, pour them out into the grill

and rake them into a sloping bed, with half of the coals piled high in a third of the grill and the remaining half of the coals gradually sloping down across the grill. You want to create multiple heat zones emitting high, medium, and low heat (see page 204 to determine how hot each zone is with your hand). Immediately set the grate in place. Once it is hot, scrape the grate clean. Then, using a kitchen towel cinched between tongs, wipe olive oil all over the grate until it glistens.

Lay 1 coil onto the grill so a quarter of the sausage coil cooks over high heat and the rest cooks over medium-high to medium heat. Grill the sausage in this position for 1 to 2 minutes, or until the casing lightly browns and crisps. Rotate the hottest portion of the sausage away from the high-heat zone and toward the medium-heat zone. Continue rotating and grilling the coil every 1 to 2 minutes, partially over high heat and partially over medium heat, for 6 minutes more,

or until the underside of the sausage coil is evenly golden . Flip the coil and grill the reverse side in the same manner.

Once both sides are evenly browned, flip the sausage and set it over medium-low heat for 2 minutes to ease it through the last stage of cooking. Flip the coil once more and cook it for 2 to 4 minutes more, or until the casing looks puffy and golden all the way around and the meat, when prodded, bounces back. Transfer the coil to a cutting board and let it rest for 7 minutes.

Repeat the grilling process with the second coil. (If you want to serve both coils hot at the same time, place the rested sausage in a warm oven or over a cool zone on the grill.)

Serve the sausage coils with Charred Escarole with Spicy Brown Butter–Hazelnut Vinaigrette (recipe follows) and some chewy rolls.

CHARRED ESCAROLE WITH SPICY BROWN BUTTER–HAZELNUT VINAIGRETTE

SERVES 4 TO 6, WITH LEFTOVER DRESSING

Escarole heads lose their hot, mustardy bite when cooked. Once the heat sets in and the greens caramelize, their bodies go from leafy to meaty.

---

4 tablespoons (½ stick) butter

1 cup hazelnuts

¾ teaspoon finely grated lime zest (from 1 lime)

1 garlic clove, finely grated

½ teaspoon piment d'Espelette or hot paprika

1 or 2 red Thai bird chiles, stemmed, seeded, and finely grated

1 tablespoon palm, raw, or light brown sugar, or more to taste

¼ cup fresh cilantro leaves, roughly torn

1 tablespoon lime juice (from 1 lime), or more to taste

1 tablespoon colatura or high-quality fish sauce, such as Red Boat, or to taste

2 tablespoons hazelnut oil (or substitute olive oil)

Fine sea salt

4 heads baby escarole, halved lengthwise

2 tablespoons olive oil

MAKE THE VINAIGRETTE

Heat the butter in a large heavy sauté pan over medium-high heat. Once it foams, add the hazelnuts and fry them, shaking the pan, for 4 minutes, or until they turn light golden. Remove the pan from the heat and transfer the nuts to a work surface, leaving the browned butter in the pan.

Lightly crush the toasted hazelnuts and transfer to a medium bowl. Add the lime zest, garlic, piment d'Espelette, chiles, sugar, and cilantro. Stir in the lime juice, 1 tablespoon colatura, the hazelnut oil, and reserved brown butter. Season the dressing with salt or more colatura and extra lime juice or sugar as needed. This vinaigrette can be made up to a few hours in advance and held at room temperature. Gently rewarm it to melt the butter and rewhisk just before serving if necessary.

GRILL THE ESCAROLE

Set up the grill as instructed in the preceding sausage coil recipe. Brush the cut sides of the escarole heads with the olive oil and season with salt.

Lay the escarole, cut sides down, on the oiled grate over high heat. Cook for 2 minutes, rotating the heads 45 degrees halfway through. Once they are well charred on their cut sides, flip the heads and grill the curved sides for 30 seconds, or until warmed through.

Transfer the grilled escarole, cut sides up, to a warm serving platter. Drizzle some of the hazelnut vinaigrette on top and serve with the remaining vinaigrette alongside for drizzling.

HOW TO PLAN THIS MEAL:

2 days before: Dry-brine pork shoulder.

1 day before: Prepare for sausage stuffing. Grind and stuff sausages. Coil, skewer, and dry links.

90 minutes before: Make vinaigrette.

80 minutes before: Prepare grill and temper sausage.

40 minutes before: Grill escarole and sausage.

10

GRILLED QUAIL WITH BROCCOLINI AND COAL-ROASTED GARLIC

SERVES 4

Like chicken soup, but way more varied and refined, this meal is a stunner: whole grilled quail on crostini with broccolini and coal-roasted garlic cloves for smearing. A glug of reduced chicken broth, spiked with vinegar and plenty of black pepper, ties everything up. Instead of breaking this down into component recipes, the whole meal is presented together, as I encourage you to make this one in full.

At its heart this is a rustic dish that takes full advantage of a glowing coal bed. Flip-flop the quail over the grate, until their meat feels bouncy-tender and their lime rub picks up some caramelization. Then, use the heat that remains to promptly grill most of the meal's other elements, all of which cook in rapid succession; you can even rewarm the broth right on the grill if you have space. Throughout it all, the garlic heads soften and cook underneath, in the smoldering coals.

A note about the quail: Buy them "semi-boneless," which means that their backs and rib bones have been removed. They should look slightly deflated and lie flat; that's what you want for good contact with your grill grate.

---

4 to 6 limes

2 serrano chiles, stemmed, seeded, and finely chopped

2 teaspoons kosher salt, plus more as needed

Olive oil, as needed

8 semi-boneless quail (about 2 pounds total)

6 cups Chicken Broth (page 288)

1 pound broccolini, ends trimmed

Freshly cracked black peppercorns

2 heads of garlic, whole and unpeeled

4 1-inch slices sourdough country bread

1 lemon, sliced into ¼-inch rounds

1 teaspoon red wine vinegar

RUB THE QUAIL

Finely grate the zest from enough limes to yield 2 tablespoons. Reserve 2 of the zested limes for finishing the dish, and save the remaining ones for another purpose.

Place the lime zest, chiles, and 2 teaspoons kosher salt in a mortar or on a cutting board. Smash with a pestle or the back of your knife until pulpy. Stir in 1 tablespoon olive oil.

Thoroughly pat the quail dry with paper towels and lay them on a work surface. Massage the lime-chile rub all over the skins. Lay the rubbed quail on a cooling rack set over a rimmed baking sheet. Transfer to the refrigerator and dry-brine the quail, uncovered, for at least 3 hours; preferably 24.

REDUCE THE BROTH AND BLANCH THE BROCCOLINI

Meanwhile, pour the chicken broth into a medium saucepan and bring it to a simmer over high heat. Reduce the heat to medium and simmer the broth for 20 minutes, or until reduced by half. Turn off the heat and set the pot aside.

Bring a medium pot of generously salted water to a boil over high heat. Set up an ice water bath nearby. Blanch the broccolini for 1 minute. Drain the broccolini and place it in the ice bath to cool completely. Remove the spears from the bath and thoroughly pat them dry.

Place the broccolini in a medium bowl and toss it with 2 tablespoons olive oil and a pinch of salt and pepper.

(recipe continues)

SEASON AND ROAST THE GARLIC

Tear off 2 pieces of aluminum foil and place a garlic head on each sheet. Drizzle each head with ½ tablespoon olive oil and season with salt and pepper. Cinch the foil around the garlic heads and double-wrap each parcel with a second sheet of foil.

If you are short on time or are cooking on a gas grill, simply roast the garlic in a 400°F oven for 40 minutes and skip to the next section to prepare the grill for the quail. If you plan to coal-roast the garlic, which is the best-tasting option but doubles the time, set up the grill in this way: Light a half chimney starter's worth of coal. Once the coals are very hot, glow red, and lightly ash over, pour the charcoal into the grill. Rake a gently sloping coal bed out across the grill.

Using tongs, nestle the garlic parcels along the outer edges of the thinning coal pile. Place a few of the coals over the parcels, loosely covering them in a single layer. Gently coal-roast the garlic for 40 minutes in this medium-low heat, or until the cloves turn sticky, sweet, and very tender. As the coals cool, you may need to relocate the garlic parcels higher up on the sloping bed so they roast at a more or less constant temperature. Remove the garlic parcels and set them aside.

SET UP THE GRILL FOR THE QUAIL AND BROCCOLINI

Remove the quail from the refrigerator 30 minutes before cooking.

Meanwhile, after the coal-roasted garlic parcels have cooked for 10 to 15 minutes, fully fill the chimney starter with charcoal, light the paper below, and, since your grill is occupied, set the starter on a safe, fireproof surface (like slate or cement).

Once the fresh coals are very hot, glow red, and lightly ash over, lift the garlic out of the grill and set it aside. Now, rake the old coals in the grill to level the bed, and pour the fresh coals on top.

Rake two-thirds of the coals into a taller, flat coal bed that occupies about half the grill, giving you enough room to comfortably cook all the quail. Rake the remaining coals so they slope away from the flat bed's peak, spreading and thinning out across the rest of the grill's base. Check the garlic parcels for doneness; if the cloves are not yet fully soft and sticky, nestle the parcels back into the thinnest part of the coal bed to finish coal roasting.

Set the grill grate in place. Once it's hot, scrape it clean. Then, with a kitchen towel cinched between tongs, wipe olive oil all over the grate until it glistens.

Hold your hand 6 inches above the grate over the hotter side of the grill; when you need to pull your hand away in 4 seconds, indicating a medium-high heat, the grill is ready. Lay the quail, breast sides down, on the grate, pressing the birds' legs and wings flat onto the grate. Grill the quails for 6 minutes, rotating the birds 45 degrees every 2 minutes, or until they evenly brown. While grilling, don't be afraid to lightly press or rock the birds over the grate to make sure all their surfaces are in contact with the hot metal.

Flip the quail and continue grilling them for 2 to 4 minutes, rotating them 45 degrees every minute, or until their legs wiggle easily at their joints and the meat is cooked to medium. The meat should feel tender but bouncy and remain a touch blush at its center. Transfer the grilled quail to a warm platter.

Lay the broccolini over the grill's medium-high heat zone. Blister the spears, turning them every minute for 3 minutes, or until they char all the way around. Transfer the broccolini to the platter with the quail.

GRILL THE LEMON AND BREAD

Brush the bread slices on both sides generously with olive oil and season with salt. Grill both sides over medium-high heat for 1 to 2 minutes, or until golden and charred in spots. Transfer the crostini to a cutting board and halve the slices crosswise.

As the bread grills, lay the lemon slices over medium-low heat and grill them on just one side for 2 to 3 minutes, or until they caramelize. Set the crostini and lemon rounds aside.

ASSEMBLE THE DISH

Use tongs to pull the garlic parcels out of the coals. Carefully unwrap the packets and let the heads cool slightly. Snip off their papery tops with kitchen shears, exposing the roasted cloves within, and set the garlic on small serving plates.

Meanwhile, rewarm the reduced chicken broth until it just simmers. Remove the broth from the heat and season it with the red wine vinegar and extra pepper to taste.

Halve the 2 reserved limes. Set 2 crostini halves in 4 wide, warmed bowls. Place a grilled quail over each crostino and drape the broccolini over the birds. Pour some broth into the bowls, creating a shallow pool around the crostini. Garnish each serving with a few grilled lemon rounds, a drizzle of raw, good olive oil, and a squeeze of fresh lime juice. Serve the bowls immediately with the coal-roasted garlic alongside for guests to smear on the crostini.

HOW TO PLAN THIS MEAL:

4–24 hours before: Rub quail and let rest.

70 minutes before: Reduce broth. Blanch and season broccolini. Roast garlic, either in coals or in the oven.

40 minutes before: Temper quail and set up grill.

20 minutes before: Grill quail, broccolini, crostini, and lemon rounds. Heat and season broth. Plate garlic. Assemble bowls.

11

GRILLED POUSSINS WITH SMASHED YUCCA AND CAPER-ONION SALSA

SERVES 2 TO 4

Poussins are young chickens, and I find their meat more elegant, flavorful, and supple than that of their larger relatives. Plus, there's a satisfaction in giving guests every cut of the bird for them to savor in one sitting. These poussins are perfumed with Provençal herbs and served with a salty, pungent caper and onion salsa; mellow, simple smashed yucca root tempers the bold flavors. Serve the meal with a simple vegetable, like Grilled Corn (page 269), for a bit of fresh contrast.

These birds are flattened out, which maximizes their contact with the grill grates, and cooked over a coal bed with three distinct heat zones to help ensure even doneness and great caramelization.

2 poussins or Cornish game hens (about 2½ pounds total)

2 teaspoons coarse sea salt

½ teaspoon freshly cracked black peppercorns

3 tablespoons herbes de Provence

1 teaspoon finely grated lemon zest (from 1 lemon)

Olive oil, for greasing the grill

½ bunch of watercress

Flaky sea salt

FLATTEN AND RUB THE BIRDS

Lay the birds breast up on a work surface. With the palm of your hand, press down on the breastbone until it cracks. Next, hold the bird down firmly with one hand and with your free hand, pull the leg straight out from the body until the drumstick and thigh joints pop, loosening it from the body. Repeat with the other leg. Flip the bird and press down on its backbone, cracking and flattening it. The bird should now be about 1 inch high. Repeat with the other bird.

In a small bowl, mix the coarse sea salt, pepper, herbes de Provence, and lemon zest together.

Pat the birds all over with paper towels until very dry. Rub the herb-salt mixture onto the poussins and set them on a cooling rack set over a rimmed baking sheet. Transfer the poussins to the refrigerator to dry-brine for 12 to 24 hours; their skin should feel tacky when done.

SET UP THE GRILL

Let the birds stand at room temperature for 30 minutes before grilling.

Meanwhile, light a chimney starter full of charcoal. Once the coals are very hot, glow red, and lightly ash over, pour them into the grill. Rake half the coals into a high, flat bed occupying a third of the grill, or an area just large enough to accommodate both birds comfortably. Rake the other half of the coals into a second, lower plateau, a few inches shorter than the first pile. This second plateau should occupy one-third of the grill and then slope out and down across the remaining third of the grill. This setup creates high, medium, and low heat zones. (See page 204 to determine how hot each zone is with your hand.)

Set the grate in place. Once it is very hot, scrape the grate clean. Then, with a kitchen towel cinched between tongs, wipe olive oil all over the grate until it glistens.

(recipe continues)

Lay the birds, breast sides down, on the grate over high heat. Grill them for 1 minute, or until their skins just begin to brown. Next, move the birds to the medium-heat zone and rotate them 90 degrees. Grill the poussins over medium heat for 16 to 20 minutes, rotating them 90 degrees every 2 minutes, or until their exteriors brown nicely and the breast meat starts to feel firm when prodded at its thickest point. If the skin darkens too quickly before the meat is properly cooked, move the birds to medium-low heat to prevent scorching.

Flip the poussins and grill their reverse sides over medium heat, rotating them 90 degrees every 2 minutes, for 10 to 15 minutes more, or until their skins crisp and legs wiggle easily at their joints. Transfer the birds to a cutting board and let them rest for 5 to 10 minutes.

BUTCHER AND SERVE

Using a chef's knife, halve the birds lengthwise through their breastbones.

Scoop the Mashed Yucca (recipe follows) onto a large, warmed serving platter. Arrange the birds over the mash. Scatter the watercress over the birds and sprinkle on some flaky salt. Spoon some Caper-Onion Salsa (recipe follows) on the platter and serve the rest alongside.

MASHED YUCCA

SERVES 4

Yucca, also known as cassava or tapioca root, is popular in South America and Asia. But inexplicably, the delicious root is generally underappreciated here. It's sweet and creamy and, unlike potato, doesn't need butter to make it taste its best when mashed.

The knobby-looking brown plant, once peeled and simmered, turns soft and tender. Let it rest in its cooking liquid until its dense flesh softens a bit more and its intense sweetness mellows. Then mash, season, serve, and surprise.

---

2 pounds yucca

Kosher salt and freshly cracked black peppercorns

Olive oil, as needed

¼ cup sliced fresh flat-leaf parsley

BOIL THE YUCCA

Fill a large bowl with water. Peel the yucca with a vegetable peeler and immediately submerge each piece in the water, to prevent oxidation and to rinse off some of the starch. Cut each piece of yucca into 1-inch chunks and return the chunks to the water.

Drain the yucca and place it in a large saucepan. Pour in enough water to cover the yucca by 1 inch, and season it well with salt. Set the pot over medium-high heat, bring the water to a boil, then reduce the heat to a gentle simmer. Cook the yucca, uncovered, for 35 minutes, or until it is easily pierced with a knife.

Remove the pan from the heat and let the yucca cool in its cooking water for no more than 30 minutes. The yucca should soften completely but not disintegrate.

SEASON THE MASH

With a slotted spoon, transfer the yucca to a medium bowl, reserving the pot of cooking water.

Season the yucca with salt, pepper, and a generous amount of olive oil. Using a potato masher or the back of a spoon, coarsely mash the yucca, adding splashes of cooking liquid or olive oil to create a creamy mash. The mash can be made up to 2 hours ahead of time. To rewarm, reheat it over moderate heat, stirring constantly and adding a few splashes of water as needed.

Just before serving, fold the parsley into the mash and reseason it with salt, pepper, and oil if necessary. Serve warm or at room temperature.

CAPER-ONION SALSA

MAKES 2 CUPS

A pungent, salty salsa that cuts through the yucca's sweetness, this is also an ideal foil for the smoky, grilled poussin.

½ cup olive oil

1½ cups diced red onion

¾ cup water-brined capers, rinsed and dried

1 red Fresno chile, stemmed and thinly sliced into rounds

1 serrano chile, stemmed and thinly sliced into rounds

3 tablespoons fresh lemon juice (from about 1½ lemons)

Fine sea salt and freshly cracked black pepper

In a medium heavy sauté pan, heat 1 tablespoon of olive oil over medium-high heat and add the onion. Sauté for 8 minutes, stirring occasionally or until the onion softens and browns in spots. Stir in the capers and sauté for 4 minutes, or until lightly colored and aromatic. Add the sliced chiles and sauté for 1 minute more, or until the peppers soften.

Transfer the vegetables to a medium bowl and stir in the lemon juice and remaining olive oil. Season to taste with salt and pepper. The salsa keeps at room temperature for several hours and up to 3 days in the refrigerator. Before serving, let the chilled salsa come up to room temperature.

HOW TO PLAN THIS MEAL:

1 day before: Dry-brine poussins.

90 minutes before: Make yucca and caper-onion salsa.

75 minutes before: Temper poussins and set up grill.

45 minutes before: Grill poussins.

10 minutes before: Reheat yucca, if desired. Arrange platter.

12

GRILLED HERB-MUSTARD RABBIT LEGS WITH CHARRED ENDIVE, FAVA BEANS, PEAS, AND FARMER'S CHEESE

SERVES 4

In this recipe, rabbit's underappreciated flavor—subtle, tender, sweet, and just the tiniest bit gamy—gets a sharp herbal lift from the mustard-herb rub. To make sure the rub doesn't fall off on the grill, dry the rabbit well before grilling and brush it with olive oil. Start cooking the legs over high heat, which sets the rub, and then hop them over to a moderate heat zone to gently cook them through. Handling lean cuts in this fashion helps get you a tender bite.

A charming spring salad that combines farmer's cheese, seared endive, blanched favas, and snap peas pairs and contrasts beautifully. For a little more substance, Mashed Yucca (page 253) or the warm black-eyed pea salad (page 48) would be nice as well.

---

1 fresh bay leaf

6 fresh flat-leaf parsley sprigs

6 fresh thyme sprigs

½ cup kosher salt

2 quarts water

¼ cup plus 1 teaspoon honey

½ lemon, sliced into rounds

1 tablespoon black peppercorns, toasted and cracked, plus more to season

4 meaty, skinless rabbit hind legs (2 pounds total)

¼ cup Dijon mustard

2 tablespoons herbes de Provence

Coarse sea salt

1 tablespoon olive oil, plus more for the grill

BRINE THE RABBIT LEGS

With the broad side of a chef's knife, press down on the bay leaf and parsley and thyme sprigs to release their essential oils. Toss the herbs into a deep, nonreactive container and pour in the kosher salt, water, ¼ cup honey, the lemon rounds, and 1 tablespoon peppercorns. Stir until the salt dissolves. Submerge the rabbit legs in the brine and refrigerate for 12 hours.

RUB THE RABBIT LEGS

Remove the legs from the brine and pat them very dry with paper towels.

In a small bowl, mix the mustard, remaining 1 teaspoon honey, and herbes de Provence together. Spread the mustard rub all over the rabbit legs, coating both sides evenly.

Lay the legs, meaty sides up, on a cooling rack set over a rimmed baking sheet. Refrigerate the legs, uncovered, for 12 to 24 hours, or until the rub hardens and feels tacky.

GRILL AND SERVE

Remove the rabbit from the refrigerator and let stand at room temperature for 30 minutes. Meanwhile, prepare the grill.

Light a full chimney starter of coals. Once the coals are very hot, glow red, and lightly ash over, pour them into the grill. Rake the coals into a sloping bed, with half the coals piled in one-third of the grill, forming a raised, flat bed. The remaining half of the coals should gradually slope down across the other two-thirds of the grill. This setup creates multiple zones emitting high, medium, and low heat. (See page 204 to determine how hot each zone is with your hand.) Immediately set the grate in place and, once it's hot, scrape it clean. Then, with a kitchen towel cinched between tongs, wipe olive oil all over the grate until it glistens.

Just before grilling, lightly sprinkle the legs with coarse salt and black pepper, just to wake up the surface of the flesh.

(recipe continues)

Drizzle the legs with 1 tablespoon olive oil and immediately lay them, meaty side down, onto the grill over the high-heat zone.

Sear the legs for 1 to 2 minutes, or until the rub sets and darkens. Move the legs to medium heat and continue cooking them, without flipping, for 8 to 10 minutes more. Rotate the legs 45 degrees every 1 to 2 minutes so the rub browns evenly on the grill.

Flip the legs and continue grilling them over medium heat. Grill the bony sides for 5 to 7 minutes, turning them 45 degrees every 1 to 2 minutes, or until the drumsticks wiggle easily at their joints, the meat is white throughout, and the crust richly caramelizes. Before removing the legs from the grill, roll them over high heat, wherever necessary, to ensure the rub crisps all the way around.

Transfer the legs to a platter and let them rest for 10 minutes. Serve the rabbit alongside or layered into Charred Endives with Fava Beans, Snap Peas, and Farmer's Cheese (recipe follows).

CHARRED ENDIVE WITH FAVA BEANS, SNAP PEAS, AND FARMER'S CHEESE

SERVES 4

This textured spring salad layers creamy, crunchy, and vegetal bites. The vegetables are plated over the cheese, which serves as the dish's sauce, something lush to run your fork through.

Kosher salt

1 cup young shelled fava beans or shelled edamame

2 cups sugar snap peas, ends trimmed

2 Belgian endive, halved lengthwise

¼ cup olive oil

Freshly cracked black peppercorns

1 tablespoon fresh lemon juice (from ½ lemon)

2 tablespoons chardonnay vinegar

2 tablespoons finely snipped fresh chives

2 tablespoons finely chopped fresh dill

1 cup farmer's cheese or Fresh Ricotta (page 312)

BLANCH THE BEANS AND PEAS

Bring a medium pot filled with well-salted water to a boil over high heat. Set up an ice water bath nearby.

Blanch the favas for 1½ minutes, or until they turn bright green and tender. Using a slotted spoon, immediately transfer the beans to the ice water bath to cool. Keep the water over high heat.

Next, blanch the snap peas for 1 minute, or until they turn bright green and still have snap. Transfer the snap peas to the ice water bath and let them cool. Drain the peas and beans and dry thoroughly. If necessary, peel the favas.

CHAR THE ENDIVE

Set up the grill as directed for the rabbit legs on page 255. Brush the endive's cut sides with 1 tablespoon of olive oil and season with a pinch of salt and pepper.

Lay the endive, cut sides down, on the grill over high heat. Sear the halves for 30 seconds, or until charred in spots and crunchy within. Transfer the charred endive to a cutting board and halve them lengthwise on a 45-degree angle.

SEASON THE SALAD

Just before serving, combine the endive, beans, and peas in a large bowl. Toss with the lemon juice, vinegar, remaining olive oil, chives, dill, and salt and pepper to taste.

To serve, spread the cheese across a large platter. Top with the grilled rabbit legs, if serving them together. Arrange the dressed vegetables over and around the meat. Spoon a little of the salad dressing over the salad and meat.

HOW TO PLAN THIS MEAL:

24–36 hours before: Brine rabbit legs. Make ricotta, if using.

12–24 hours before: Dry rabbit and apply mustard rub.

90 minutes before: Blanch beans and peas.

1 hour before: Temper rabbit and set up grill.

30 minutes before: Grill rabbit and endive. Assemble rabbit and salad platters.

13

BANANA LEAF–WRAPPED STRIPED BASS WITH SUMMER FIXINGS

SERVES 4

One of the most memorable meals of my life happened when I was cooking at Sunset Beach, a jet-set beachfront restaurant on Long Island. It was a hot summer's day and my sous chef, Lou Gibbs, was off the clock, fishing. He caught a twenty-five-pound striped bass, came ashore, and hauled his catch straight to our kitchen: It was cause for throwing ourselves a party.

A few feet from Sunset's entrance, we dug a hole in the sand and built a fire. We wrapped Lou's bass in foil and laid it over the flames. After a few beers we unearthed the fish and peeked at its meat. Supple, sticky, and tender, the fillets wanted only a few splashes of grassy olive oil and a sprinkle of salt. Pickles and good bread, nicked from our kitchen, rounded out the meal. Manicured guests were noshing behind us, but our meal, eaten by the water with our fingers and plenty of mediocre beer, was the best thing going.

This recipe for Banana Leaf–Wrapped Striped Bass, served with a few jars of savory preserved vegetables, is inspired by that impromptu feast. But there are a few differences. First is wrapping with banana leaves (which I generally find in Asian markets in the freezer section) instead of foil. Roll the bass in at least three layers. That way, if one or two leaves burn away, perfuming the fish with their tea-like scent in the process, another layer will remain to protect the fish. Then there is the coal bed. In this aboveground take, the bass roasts *in between* two large mounds of hot coals, which cook the fish evenly from the sides.

Note that this meal is scaled for four but the pickle accompaniments serve more; the preserves keep for weeks. Plus, this fish recipe easily scales up—just throw another wrapped fish between the coal beds once you pull one out. Or, build a longer trough and lay multiple fish down nose to tail. And remember to have plenty of extra beer on hand.

---

1 3- to 4-pound whole striped bass, scaled and gutted

12 fresh thyme sprigs

12 fresh oregano sprigs

Kosher salt

1 lemon, sliced into thin rounds

5 banana leaves, each about 12 × 36 inches

STUFF AND SEASON THE BASS

Rinse the striped bass under cold running water and lay it on a work surface. Thoroughly pat the fish dry inside and out.

Press on the thyme and oregano sprigs with the broad side of a chef's knife to release their essential oils. Evenly season the fish, inside and out, with salt. Stuff the cavity with lemon slices and pressed herbs. Set the fish on a baking sheet.

WRAP THE BASS

Lay 4 banana leaves vertically on the work surface, shingling them so each leaf overlaps the previous one by 6 inches. Lay the last leaf horizontally across the bottom of the shingled bed, about 6 inches from the bottom. Set the fish in the center of this horizontal leaf.

Fold the ends of the horizontal banana leaf over the fish's head and tail. Lift the bottom of the shingled bed of banana leaves up and over the bass, encasing its

body. Roll the fish up into the leaves like a cigar, creating a tightly rolled packet.

Fold the ends of the banana leaf bed under the fish, sealing the packet. Return the rolled fish to the baking sheet, seam side down. Refrigerate the wrapped fish while setting up the grill.

COAL-ROAST AND SERVE THE BASS

Set up the grill, lighting a full chimney starter of coals. Once the coals are very hot, glow red, and lightly ash over, pour them into the grill and rake them into an even bed. Let the coals burn until they glow orange and emit an even, medium heat, 10 to 15 minutes.

Rake an 8-inch-wide channel through the coals, leaving a single layer of coals on the grill floor. While raking, mound the remaining coals up evenly on either side of the channel. Carefully lay the wrapped fish, seam side down, in the channel over the thin bed of coals. Rake the mounded coals around the wrapped fish, then cover it with a single loose, even layer of coals. Coal-roast the fish for 15 minutes.

Brush the coals away from the fish. Using 2 pairs of tongs, grip the fish and carefully roll it over, so its wrapping remains in place and the seam side now faces up. Rake the hot coals back around and over the fish, as before.

Continue roasting the bass for another 12 to 18 minutes, or until a skewer or paring knife easily slides through the thickest portion of the fish. Rake away the coals and lift the wrapped fish onto a large platter or baking sheet. Let it rest inside the banana leaf packet for 5 minutes.

To serve, cut away and discard the charred leaves. Let guests serve themselves, along with the Oil-Cured Tomatoes (recipe follows), Seared Oil-Cured Baby Artichokes (page 84), or, better yet, the Hand-Chopped Artichoke Pâté and Pickled Pole Beans (recipes follow).

OIL-CURED TOMATOES

MAKES ABOUT 1 QUART, INCLUDING OIL

Peeled and preserved, these whole, tart-sweet cherry tomatoes keep their vibrancy in a well-seasoned olive oil bath. The grassy oil tempers the tomatoes' edge and lengthens their savory aftertaste. Incidentally, the oil is also killer when spooned over forkfuls of coal-roasted fish.

Kosher salt

1½ pounds ripe cherry tomatoes

1 fresh bay leaf

1 2-inch strip of lemon peel

1 cup olive oil, or as needed

1 teaspoon fine sea salt

1 tablespoon coriander seeds, toasted

1½ teaspoons hot pepper flakes, toasted

BLANCH AND PEEL THE TOMATOES

Bring a medium pot of water to a boil, and salt it so it tastes like the sea. Set up an ice water bath nearby. Meanwhile, use a sharp paring knife to cut a small, shallow X into the bottom of each tomato.

Add half the tomatoes to the boiling water and blanch them for 45 seconds, or until their skins begin to split. Using a slotted spoon, transfer the tomatoes to the ice water bath. Blanch and shock the remaining tomatoes.

Once they are chilled, remove the tomatoes from the ice water and dry them thoroughly on paper towels. With a paring knife, peel away the skins and discard. Transfer the tomatoes to a medium lidded nonreactive container.

SEASON AND PRESERVE THE TOMATOES

Press down on the bay leaf and lemon peel with the broad side of a chef's knife to release their essential oils. In a small bowl, combine 1 cup olive oil with the sea salt, coriander, hot pepper flakes, bay leaf, and lemon peel.

Pour the seasoned oil over the tomatoes so they are totally submerged. If necessary, add more oil. Cover the tomatoes and refrigerate for at least 12 hours, or until the oil and tomatoes' flavors meld. Before serving, let the tomatoes stand at room temperature for 1 hour, or until the oil liquefies. The tomatoes keep in the refrigerator for up to 2 weeks.

HAND-CHOPPED ARTICHOKE PÂTÉ

MAKES ABOUT 1½ CUPS

Artichokes, with their deep, nutty flavor and meaty bite, are one of the sexiest, most savory vegetables. Here, they turn into a coarsely chopped spread that eats like a pâté, but is lighter, brighter, and better suited for summer feasts. For this vegetarian pâté you can use store-bought preserved artichokes, as long as they are preserved in good olive oil, or use my recipe (page 84). (If using homemade, skip the searing step in that recipe.)

Hand chopping the hearts creates varied bites, which is more interesting than a uniform puree.

---

2 cups oil-preserved artichokes, at room temperature (store-bought or homemade, page 84)

½ cup tightly packed fresh mint leaves, finely sliced

¼ cup finely snipped fresh chives

2 teaspoons finely chopped peel from Preserved Lemons (page 302)

1 teaspoon finely grated lemon zest (from 1 lemon)

Fine sea salt and freshly ground black peppercorns

Lift the artichokes out of their oil and transfer to a cutting board; reserve the oil. Chop the artichokes into irregular bits and place them in a medium bowl.

Stir in the mint, chives, preserved lemon, and lemon zest. Season with salt and pepper to taste. Stir in just enough of the reserved oil to make the chunky mixture loose and spreadable.

Cover and refrigerate the artichoke pâté for at least 12 hours, or until the flavors meld. Remove from the refrigerator at least 1 hour before serving. Refrigerated, the pâté keeps for 1 week.

PICKLED POLE BEANS

MAKES ABOUT 5 CUPS, INCLUDING LIQUID

These refreshing, snappy beans provide texture and acidity. But the brine is mild and the rest time is short, so these end up tasting fresher than your average pickled pole bean.

Kosher salt

1 pound long beans, green beans, or haricot verts, ends snipped

1 cup champagne vinegar

1 cup rice wine vinegar

¼ cup honey

2 tablespoons coriander seeds, toasted

1 garlic clove, lightly smashed

1 strip of lemon peel, removed with a vegetable peeler

2 fresh bay leaves

Bring a medium pot of well-salted water to a boil over high heat. Meanwhile, set up an ice water bath nearby. Once the water boils aggressively, blanch the beans for 30 seconds, or until their color brightens. Drain and transfer beans to the ice water bath. Once cool, remove the beans from their bath and dry them thoroughly. Next, transfer them to a medium nonreactive container.

Wipe the pot clean and pour in ½ cup water, the champagne and rice wine vinegars, honey, coriander, garlic, and 1 tablespoon kosher salt. Press on the lemon peel and bay leaves to release their essential oils and toss them into the brine. Set the pot over high heat and bring the brine just up to a boil.

Pour the brine over the beans so they are completely submerged. Let the beans cool to room temperature. Cover and refrigerate for at least 12 hours, or until the beans take on the brine's flavor. Refrigerated, the pickles keep for 2 weeks.

HOW TO PLAN THIS MEAL:

1 week–1 day before: Make preserved tomatoes, artichoke pâté, and pickled pole beans.

2 hours before: Temper tomatoes and artichoke pâté.

90 minutes before: Stuff and wrap bass.

80 minutes before: Set up grill.

40 minutes before: Coal-roast bass.

14

VEAL MEATBALLS WITH GINGERED BUTTERMILK AND CORN TWO WAYS

SERVES 4

Who isn't delighted at Japanese yakitori restaurants, where all sorts of tiny skewered morsels hang over a sizzling coal bed? Smoke billows upward, imbuing the bites with an alluring, meaty perfume while creating a gentle sear. The cooks stand over the smoke, turning the skewers around and around with their callused fingers.

It's a fascinating technique that uses the heat and smoke of the grill but without the searing char you get from the grate. The constant turning browns the food evenly and keeps it uniformly tender. At home we simulate the grill by bunching up aluminum foil and suspending skewers between makeshift tubes.

One of my favorite yakitori items is *tsukune*, or miso-seasoned ground chicken molded around a skewer. In this recipe, ground veal is called for instead—the meat is richer and milkier. That delicacy is enhanced, counterintuitively, by precooking part of the veal. The cooked veal keeps some of the raw meat from binding to itself, similar to the effect of bread crumbs, but without diluting the flavor.

Alongside, there is sweet corn in an aromatic, ginger-infused buttermilk sauce. If you want to add to the meal, the Blistered Shishito Peppers (page 235) are a terrific pairing, easily adapted to the makeshift yakitori grill. Chanterelle and Pea Conserva (page 148) or the Herbed Melon and Cucumber Salad (page 153) would also be wonderful. A side of steamed short-grain rice would complete the table.

---

2 pounds ground veal

2 tablespoons red miso

1 teaspoon kosher salt

2 teaspoons finely grated lemon zest

1 teaspoon hot pepper flakes

2 teaspoons dried oregano

1 teaspoon cracked black pepper

½ cup minced shallots

2 ears of corn, kernels cut off

1 cup arugula

Fresh horseradish, peeled, to taste

SPECIAL EQUIPMENT

Sixteen 8- to 10-inch wooden skewers, preferably square, soaked in water for 1 hour

COOK AND SEASON THE VEAL

Chill the paddle attachment and work bowl of a stand mixer.

Set a large heavy sauté pan over medium heat. Once it is hot, put ⅔ pound of the ground veal in the dry pan. Sauté the meat, breaking it into small pieces with a wooden spoon, for 4 minutes, or until the meat turns opaque and just cooks through; you're not looking for any browning. Transfer the veal and its juices to a large mixing bowl and let cool completely.

Turn the cooled veal out onto a cutting board. Finely chop the cooked meat and transfer it to the stand mixer bowl. By hand, fold in the remaining raw ground veal, miso, salt, lemon zest, hot pepper flakes, oregano, black pepper, and shallots until evenly distributed.

ASSEMBLE AND SKEWER THE MEATBALLS

Using the paddle attachment, whip the mixture at medium speed for 1 minute, or until it looks tacky and fat streaks the bowl's sides. Line a rimmed baking sheet with parchment paper.

Roll 2 ounces, or ¼ cup, of the veal mixture between wet, clean palms, shaping it into an approximate 2-inch ball. Set the meatball on the lined baking sheet and continue rolling the rest of the meatballs.

(recipe continues)

Hold 2 wooden skewers parallel, ½ inch apart. Thread 1 meatball onto the two skewers, piercing it in 2 points equidistant from the ball's center. Thread a second meatball onto the skewer, stacking it ½ inch above the other. Set the skewered veal balls back on the baking sheet and skewer the remaining meatballs in this fashion.

Loosely cover the skewers with plastic wrap while setting up the grill. If you're prepping ahead, you can refrigerate the skewered meatballs for up to 12 hours.

GRILL AND SERVE THE MEATBALLS

Remove the skewers from the refrigerator 30 minutes before grilling. Meanwhile, light a full chimney starter of charcoal. Once the coals are very hot, glow red, and lightly ash over, pour them out into a pile in the grill. Rake the coals into an even bed. Immediately set the grate in place. Once it's hot, scrape the grate clean.

As the grill heats up, scrunch heavy foil into two 1½-inch-wide cylinders, 20 to 24 inches long. When the coals emit a medium heat—you should be able to hold your hand 6 inches above the grate for only 5 seconds—set the foil on the grate, 6 inches apart. Lay the skewers on the tubes so the meatballs dangle, suspended, above the grate. Turn the skewers about a quarter-turn every minute for 10 minutes, or until the veal turns golden all the way around and gently cooks through.

Transfer the skewers to a warm platter and scatter the raw corn kernels and arugula leaves on top. Finely grate horseradish over the platter and serve with the Ginger-Buttermilk Sauce and Grilled Corn alongside (recipes follow).

GINGER-BUTTERMILK SAUCE

Cool, sweet, and sharp, thanks to the ginger, this accompaniment can be served either on the platter or alongside the skewers in a bowl. Use the thickest, richest buttermilk you can find.

1½ cups buttermilk, chilled

1½ teaspoons agave syrup or honey

1½ teaspoons finely grated fresh ginger

½ teaspoon fine sea salt

In a medium bowl, whisk the buttermilk, agave, ginger, and salt until smooth. Let the sauce stand for 10 minutes, or until the flavors meld.

The sauce can be made 2 hours ahead and held, covered, in the refrigerator. Before serving, let the sauce temper at room temperature for about 10 minutes.

GRILLED CORN

SERVES 4

This corn cooks directly on the hot grate. When the kernels blacken and blister, they become less cloying and way more interesting.

2 large ears corn, shucked

1 teaspoon fine sea salt

2 teaspoons olive oil

1 lime, halved

Rub the corn with salt and olive oil. Using the grill setup as described for the veal meatballs, lay the cobs on the grate over medium-high heat. Grill the cobs for 4 minutes, rotating them every minute, or until they char and blacken in spots all the way around.

Transfer the cobs to a cutting board. Using a sharp knife, halve them crosswise. Squeeze lime juice all over the ears and serve immediately.

HOW TO PLAN THIS MEAL:

2–12 hours before: Make veal meatballs. Make ginger-buttermilk sauce.

45 minutes before: Temper meatballs and set up grill.

15 minutes before: Temper sauce. Grill corn and meatballs. Assemble platters.

GRILL-SMOKED COD WITH MUSSELS, CLAMS, AND BURST TOMATOES

SERVES 4 TO 6

This is a wonderful feast, somewhere between a stew and a warm seafood salad.

When you cook with live coals, you can turn your grill into a smoker simply by closing the lid. If you are cooking with gas, you can create a similar effect: Soak a handful of wood chips in water for an hour. Then drain the chips and place them in a disposable roasting pan, sealing it with a couple layers of foil. Poke half a dozen holes in the foil and set the pan directly over a medium-high flame, under the grate, off to one side. Close the lid and let the smoke fill the grill.

I recommend you make the Kombu Vinegar (page 295) and salt cod (page 307). Kombu vinegar has a mineral, lingering depth and the salt cod's bite is extra meaty.

1½ pounds salt cod, in 1 or 2 large pieces (page 307)

1 pound mussels, debearded

1 pound littleneck clams

6 tablespoons olive oil, plus more

1 pint cherry tomatoes (¾ pound)

½ pound ripe beefsteak tomatoes

2 tablespoons Kombu Vinegar (page 295) or rice wine vinegar

1 to 2 tablespoons colatura or high-quality fish sauce, such as Red Boat

2 tablespoons lime juice (from about 2 limes)

2 scallions, trimmed and thinly sliced

¼ cup fresh flat-leaf parsley leaves, finely chopped

Fine sea salt and freshly cracked black peppercorns

½ teaspoon agave syrup or honey

Small handful fennel fronds, for garnish

SPECIAL EQUIPMENT

Grill basket or wooden skewers, soaked in water for 1 hour

SOAK THE SHELLFISH AND DRY THE COD

Soak the salt cod as instructed on page 307. (This is a 2- to 3-day process.) Remove the cod from the water and thoroughly pat it dry. Place the cod on a cooling rack set over a rimmed baking sheet and let rest, uncovered, in the fridge for up to 24 hours.

About 4 hours before cooking, soak the mussels and clams, in separate bowls, as instructed on page 69.

SET UP THE GRILL

Light a chimney full of charcoal. Once the coals are very hot, glow red, and lightly ash over, pour them out into a pile. Rake the coals into a uniform bed. Set the grate in place and, once it is hot, scrape it clean. Then, with a kitchen towel cinched between tongs, wipe olive oil all over the grate.

STEAM THE CLAMS AND MUSSELS

While the coals burn down to medium heat, about 15 minutes, set a large Dutch oven on the stovetop over medium-high heat and swirl in 2 tablespoons olive oil. Drain and add the cleaned mussels to the pot and stir to coat the shells in the oil. Add a few splashes of water and cover the pot. Steam the mussels for 3 minutes, or until their shells just open. With a slotted spoon, transfer the mussels to a large bowl, leaving their juices in the pot.

Drain and add the clams to the mussel juices, cover, and steam for 4 minutes, or until their shells pop open. Transfer the clams to the bowl with the mussels. If there are stubborn clams, remove the opened ones and let the closed ones steam for a couple more minutes; discard them if they don't open after that. Remove ¼ cup drippings from the pot and pour it over the shellfish to keep them moist. Reserve the remaining shellfish juices for another use.

GRILL THE CHERRY TOMATOES AND COD

Arrange the cherry tomatoes in a grilling basket, spreading them out in a single layer. (Or slide them onto soaked wooden skewers, spacing them

¼ inch apart.) Once the coal bed emits an even, medium heat, where you can hold your hand 6 inches over the grate for just about 5 seconds, set the basket on the grate and grill the tomatoes for 6 minutes, flipping halfway through (if using skewers, turn them every minute), or until tomatoes blister and their skins split. Transfer all but 6 of the tomatoes to a small bowl. Reserve the 6 tomatoes in another small bowl.

At this point, the heat should be on the cool side of medium; you should be able to hold your hand 6 inches above the grate for 6 seconds. If it's hotter than that, lift the grate and scatter some of the coals to dissipate the heat. Re-oil the grate.

Lay the cod, skin side down, on the grate. Close the grill lid and smoke the cod for 10 minutes, or until the flesh flakes easily when pressed and turns opaque throughout.

Lift the lid and, using a large spatula, transfer the cod to a work surface. Once cool enough to handle, flake the cod into 2-inch pieces, removing any bones. Discard the skin and bones. Place the smoked cod on a medium platter and set it aside.

MAKE THE TOMATO VINAIGRETTE

Set a box grater in a wide bowl. Halve the beefsteak tomatoes and rub the cut sides on the widest holes, collecting about ¾ cup of pulp. Grate the 6 reserved cherry tomatoes into the bowl. Discard the tomato skins.

Whisk the vinegar, colatura, remaining ¼ cup olive oil, and lime juice into the grated tomato pulp. Stir the scallions and parsley into the dressing and season with salt and pepper (it may not need salt, because of the colatura). Add some sweetness with the agave syrup.

ASSEMBLE AND SERVE

Pool some of the vinaigrette on a platter. Spread the clams, mussels, grilled cherry tomatoes, and cod on top. Spoon over some more of the vinaigrette and garnish with fennel fronds. Serve the salad warm or at room temperature with country bread alongside. Better still, serve with the Bruschetta (page 298) and maybe some Aioli (page 297).

HOW TO PLAN THIS MEAL:

1 week before: Make DIY salt cod and kombu vinegar, if using.

2–3 days before: Soak DIY salt cod.

1 hour before: Set up grill. Steam shellfish. Grill cherry tomatoes.

30 minutes before: Smoke cod. Make vinaigrette.

15 minutes before: Assemble.

16

GRILLED LOBSTER WITH SPICED FRIED RICE

SERVES 4

Grilling lobster has a reputation for being tricky, which is why most people opt to boil their lobsters and give them just a quick kiss on the grill. But cooking them all the way through over the coals gives them a more intense, sweeter, smokier flavor. And it isn't all that hard if you control the shape of your coal bed—a practice we've been honing throughout this chapter.

Instead of a sloping coal bed with multiple heat zones, as called for in some of the preceding recipes, this setup involves raking hot coals into two adjoining piles. One is bigger, hotter, and more intense than the other; that is where the head and claws will cook. The smaller pile, whose peak should be just below the lobsters' tails, is less intense to gently cook the tail through. This arrangement ensures that all the lobster parts cook in unison. A little time with the lid down gives the lobsters a whiff of smokiness.

---

4 1½-pound live lobsters

1 teaspoon finely grated lemon zest (from 1 lemon)

1 teaspoon fennel seeds, toasted and roughly smashed

2 teaspoons coarse sea salt

4 teaspoons olive oil, plus more for the grill

BUTCHER THE LOBSTERS

Freeze the live lobsters on a rimmed baking sheet for 20 minutes; this numbs them and slows their movement.

Lay 1 lobster on its back on a cutting board so its legs point up. Place the tip of a chef's knife at the point where the body and tail meet, with the blade of the knife positioned toward the head. Pierce the body, then swiftly cut down through the head. Be careful not to cut all the way through its shell; the goal is to stop just short of splitting the lobster in two. Now your lobster is dead, though its legs may continue to move for a bit.

Place the tip of your knife where the initial incision began and bring the blade down, splitting the tail, again being careful to stop short of cutting through the shell. The split lobsters should hold together in one piece.

Next, crack the claws by hitting their fattest portion with the back of a chef's knife until the meat is exposed. Crack the knuckles (the thick joint between the claws and the body) in this same fashion.

To clean the lobster, locate the long vein, which runs down the length of its body, and carefully remove it while taking care not to displace the green tomalley and any roe in the body cavity. Next, locate the head sac, an inedible, fluid-filled sac right behind the eyes in the head cavity. Remove and discard it.

Set the lobster, cut side up, on a large rimmed baking sheet. Repeat with the remaining lobsters.

RUB THE LOBSTERS

In a small bowl or mortar, lightly smash the lemon zest, fennel seeds, and salt together until combined.

(recipe continues)

Gently rub the salt mixture into the exposed lobster meat in the tails, body, and claws. Drizzle the meat of each lobster with 1 teaspoon of the olive oil. Refrigerate the lobsters while setting up the grill.

GRILL AND SERVE

Light a full chimney starter of coals. Once the coals are very hot, glow red, and lightly ash over, pour them into the grill and rake them into a pile large enough to comfortably fit all 4 lobsters. Rake two-thirds of the coals into a taller, concentrated pile near the front of the grill and the remaining coals into a lower mound toward the back. The two beds should adjoin and occupy the same amount of grill area, but they will have different heights.

Immediately set the grate in place. Once it is hot, scrape it clean. Then, with a kitchen towel cinched between tongs, wipe olive oil all over the grate until it glistens. When the coals glow red and the ash coating deepens slightly, feel for medium-high heat: Hold your hand 6 inches above the grate along the line where the 2 coal mounds meet; you should be able to tolerate the heat for just 3 to 4 seconds. Arrange the lobsters, cut sides down, on the grate, taking care to center their claws and heads over the tall pile and their tails over the small pile. Cover the grill and cook the lobsters, without moving them, for about 8 minutes, or until their shells turn bright red and their meat is opaque and bouncy.

Using a large spatula, loosen the lobsters from the grill and carefully flip them, keeping their tomalley and roe intact. Transfer the lobsters to a large serving platter and serve them hot with the Spiced Fried Rice (recipe follows).

SPICED FRIED RICE

SERVES 4 TO 6

Brown rice is healthier than white, but that's not why I love it. It's also nuttier, chewier, and more charismatic. After simmering with spices, the grains can be used immediately or held for later. If they get a chance to rest, in fact, their flavor and texture are all the better. Just before serving, we crisp the rice with slivered peppers, bits of citrus, and thinly sliced scallions

---

2 teaspoons coriander seeds, toasted

1 teaspoon fennel seeds, toasted

½ teaspoon celery seeds, toasted

¼ teaspoon Aleppo pepper or other fragrant, mildly hot chile powder, toasted

2 teaspoons kosher salt, plus more to season

Olive oil, as needed

1 medium red onion, finely diced

2 cups short-grain brown rice

2 plum tomatoes, cut into ½-inch pieces

1 lemon

1 orange

8 shishito peppers, stemmed and thinly sliced into rounds

¼ cup thinly sliced scallions

Small handful snipped chives

MAKE THE SPICE MIX

Place the coriander, fennel, and celery seeds in a mortar. Coarsely smash the seeds with a pestle, then stir in the Aleppo pepper and 2 teaspoons salt. (You can also do this in a spice grinder.)

COOK THE RICE

Heat a medium Dutch oven over medium heat until hot. Stir in 2 tablespoons olive oil and the red onion. Gently sauté, stirring regularly, for 10 minutes, or until the onion softens and begins to turn golden.

Stir in the rice and spice mix. Sauté the grains at a steady sizzle for 1 minute, or until they glisten and the spices' scent blooms. Stir in the tomatoes and 4 cups water. Bring the liquid to a simmer and cover the pot. Reduce the heat to low and gently simmer the rice for 40 minutes, or until the grains completely tenderize and absorb the liquid.

Remove the pot from the heat, uncover, and fluff the rice with a fork. Season to taste with more salt. Let the rice cool to room temperature, then refrigerate 2 to 24 hours ahead of time.

SUPREME THE CITRUS

Finely grate the lemon and orange zests and set 1 teaspoon of each zest aside. Slice off the tops and bottoms and stand the fruit straight up. With a sharp paring knife, cut away the peel and pith from the citrus and discard. Working over a medium bowl, supreme both fruits by cutting along the membrane's walls to release the segments into the bowl below. Use a spoon to gently break up the segments into small pieces. If the supremes are to rest for more than 1 hour, squeeze the membranes' juices over the top to keep them moist. Supremes will hold for up to 3 hours in the refrigerator.

FRY THE RICE

Remove the rice from the refrigerator. Set a large heavy skillet over high heat. Once hot, swirl in 1 tablespoon olive oil and add the shishito peppers. Sauté for 3 minutes, or until fragrant and lightly browned. Transfer the peppers to a medium serving platter and set them aside.

Set the pan back over high heat and swirl in enough olive oil to generously coat the pan. Add the rice and spread the grains out evenly. Cook the rice, without stirring, for 4 minutes, or until it crisps and browns. Stir and fry the rice for 4 minutes more, or until hot and crispy. (If necessary, crisp the rice in batches so as not to overcrowd the pan; re-oil the pan as needed.)

Turn off the heat and stir in the scallions, chives, reserved fried peppers, citrus zest, and as many of the broken citrus supremes as you like. If using supremes held in juice, lift up the fruit and leave the juices behind in the bowl. Season with salt to taste. Serve hot or at room temperature.

HOW TO PLAN THIS MEAL:

4–24 hours before: Cook rice.

90 minutes before: Cut and season lobsters.

1 hour before: Supreme citrus. Set up grill.

30 minutes before: Fry rice. Grill lobsters.

17

BEER-BRINED SUCKLING PIG WITH PLUM AND BASIL SALAD

SERVES 12

If ever a meal could draw a crowd, it's a suckling pig roast. My version of it is brined in beer, rubbed in mustard, and smoked on the grill. Work with your butcher to get the right pig. I recommend a 15-pound pig, which means it is still very young and tender. When talking with your butcher, specify that the pig's inner cavity must be cleaned, gutted, and trimmed of excess fat. You also want to have it butterflied: its breastbone split lengthwise and its legs released so the pig can lie flat on its back. Typically, butchers can handle all this, but it's important to place the order in advance and iron out the details.

The cooking process for this pig is done over an indirect grill; most of the coals should not be directly under the pig, to prevent scorching during the long cooking time. Instead, most of the coals are pushed toward the edges of the grill, providing a controlled, radiant heat that allows the skin to slowly render and crisp as the meat cooks. This requires a large grill, at least 30 inches wide and 20 inches across. Ideally your grill grate is adjustable, too, so it can rest 8 inches above the coal bed. Those extra few inches of height will help, but aren't necessary; you'll just have to be a little more vigilant without them. You'll also need a sizable tub or cooler in which to brine the pig. Since it will be too big for your refrigerator, you will need to keep the pig chilled on ice throughout the brining process. This is a busier brining step for sure, but the way this hoppy beer brine complements the pork justifies the hustle.

When it comes to serving this meal, you can just set the whole pig out—an awesome sight—for guests to pull at the succulent meat and crunchy cracklings themselves, then stuff it into split ciabatta rolls and slather with whole-grain mustard. Or you can carve it up and arrange the cuts on a few large platters with fixings on the side.

---

12 12-ounce cans lager beer

¾ cup agave syrup or light honey

2½ cups kosher salt, plus more

1 head of garlic, cloves separated and peeled

6 jalapeños, stemmed and sliced

¼ cup freshly cracked black peppercorns, toasted, plus more

1 gallon water

6 fresh bay leaves

Zest of 2 lemons, removed with a vegetable peeler

25 cilantro stems, leaves removed

1 15-pound suckling pig, butterflied

10 pounds ice, plus more as needed

2 cups Whole-Grain Mustard (page 296)

Olive oil, for greasing the grate

12 to 24 individual ciabatta rolls

SPECIAL EQUIPMENT

Large grill (at least 30 × 20 inches); a large cooler for brining (a 48-quart cooler, 26 inches long, 14 inches across, and 14.5 inches deep, works well); at least 2 pairs of heavy-duty tongs; 4 large spatulas

(recipe continues)

BRINE AND DRY THE PIG

In a large, deep cooler, whisk together the beer, agave, kosher salt, garlic, jalapeños, peppercorns, and water until the salt dissolves. With the broad side of a chef's knife, press down on the bay leaves, lemon peel, and cilantro stems to release their essential oils, then stir them into the brine.

Submerge the pig in the brine and add 10 pounds of ice on top. Close the cooler and let the pig brine in a cool, dark place for 48 hours. Monitor the temperature every 8 hours to ensure that the brine's temperature never rises above 39°F. If it does, add 5 pounds of ice to chill it and ¼ cup salt to maintain its salinity. Continue monitoring, adding ice and salt as needed.

The night before cooking, remove the pig from the brine and lay it out on a large work surface. Thoroughly pat the pig dry on all sides and hoist it onto a large cooling rack set over a large rimmed sheet pan, skin side down. (You may need 2 set up side by side for it to fit.)

Brush the dried cavity with 1 cup mustard, coating it evenly. Transfer the pig to the refrigerator and let it dry, uncovered, for 12 to 24 hours.

SET UP THE GRILL

Let the pig stand at room temperature for 90 minutes before cooking. Lightly season the cavity with extra kosher salt and pepper.

Light a full chimney starter of coals and set up a large workstation of several cutting boards lined up end to end near the grill.

Once the coals are very hot, glow red, and lightly ash over, pour them out into a pile. Rake the coals into 2 equal-size mounds running the length of the grill; they should press up against the grill's sides and slope toward the center. Create an 8-inch channel between the 2 piles.

Set the grate in place, preferably 8 inches above the coals. Once the grate is hot, scrape it clean. Then, with a kitchen towel cinched between tongs, wipe olive oil all over the grate until it glistens.

GRILL THE PIG

Allow the coals to burn down until they are coated with a thin layer of ash and emit a steady, medium heat. Hold your palm 10 inches above the coal piles; if you can tolerate the heat for 5 seconds, you're ready.

Set the pig on the grate, skin side down, with the pig's center suspended over the gap between the coal piles. Cover the grill, making sure the vent is open.

After 10 minutes, uncover the grill and check the pig's underside. If the skin is already darkening, remove the pig from the grill and set it aside. Push the coal mounds farther against the grill walls, or toward the areas of the grill where the pig will not be suspended directly over. Return the grate and pig to the grill and re-cover it.

After 15 minutes of grilling, light another chimney's worth of coals on a safe, brush-free area (over cleared concrete is great). By the time these coals are ready, in another 25 minutes, the coals in the grill should have cooled to a low heat. At this point, the pig's skin should be a light golden. You'll have to move the pig to the workstation you set up nearby while you refresh the coals underneath. Moving the pig is cumbersome, and you have to be careful about the fat puddled in the cavity. This mostly will get reabsorbed into the meat later on, but when moving the pig, work very carefully, using 2 sets of sturdy tongs (or heat-resistant gloves), and preferably an assistant, to keep the fat from swooshing about. Whenever you move the pig on and off the grill keep this in mind; if lots of fat puddles up, tip it off into a drip pan.

Pour the new coals into the grill and rake the 2 piles back into place as you had them before. If you noticed the skin darkening more in certain parts, rake fewer coals in that direction. The coal beds should emit a medium heat. Check with your palm as directed above; if the coals are hotter than a medium heat, let them burn down for a few minutes. Carefully lay the pig back on the grate, again centering it over the channel, and re-cover the grill.

(recipe continues)

After 15 to 20 minutes, light another full chimney of coals, and then check on the pig in another 25 to 30 minutes: the coals should be emitting a low heat. Repeat the coal-refreshing process as above.

Re-cover the grill and continue smoking the pig for 20 to 35 minutes more, checking on it every 15 minutes to ensure the skin is browning gently.

When done (after 1½ to 2 hours total), the meat should be cooked through and very tender, the legs should wiggle easily at their joints, and the skin should be a deep, caramelized brown. With a helper and 4 large spatulas, loosen the skin from the grate and transfer the pig to your workstation. Let the pig rest for at least 20 minutes before serving.

SERVE WHOLE, OR SECTION THE PIG

If you like, serve the pig whole with split ciabatta rolls, the remaining 1 cup mustard, and Plum and Basil Salad (recipe follows). Allow guests to pull hunks of meat and skin from the pig with tongs.

Alternatively, carve and serve the meat in generous cuts. As you cut, remember that the meat will be very tender, so light incisions are enough to separate pieces.

First remove the hind legs: Hold one trotter down. With a sharp, heavy knife, trace along the curve where the leg meets the belly, until you reach the hip joint. Pop the joint out of its socket. It should come off freely with a light twist and backward bend. Then turn the blade toward the tail and slice along the spine until the leg is removed. Repeat with the other hind leg. From this point, the meat and skin can be pulled off the legs with tongs, or you can serve the legs whole.

Remove the forelegs: Hold one fore trotter and press the knife into the flesh between the shoulder meat and rib cage. Slice until you reach the shoulder socket. Remove the knife and cut into the seam where the shoulder meets the neck until you reach the socket. Bend the joint backward and pull the leg free. Repeat with the remaining leg. Again, the meat and skin can be pulled off the legs with tongs, or you can serve the legs whole.

Butcher the body: Cut along either side of the spine, searching for the joints where the ribs meet the spine; this is soft tissue you can cut through. This frees the ribs and belly.

Slice the belly away from the ribs and cut the belly into 2-inch chunks. Then slice between the ribs, separating them into 2-rib sections. With hands or tongs, pull any remaining meat from the back, neck, and head of the pig (look for meat in the jowl—a buried treasure!).

PLUM AND BASIL SALAD

SERVES 12

This salad, lightly pickled and seasoned with sweet basil, can be stuffed into crusty smoked pork sandwiches, scattered over a platter of the pulled pork meat, or eaten on the side. Peaches, any other stone fruit, and even watermelon rinds work here in place of plums.

1 pound daikon radish, peeled and shaved thin on a mandoline

6 pounds ripe red plums, pitted and sliced into 1-inch wedges

2 teaspoons freshly cracked black peppercorns, plus more to season

2 tablespoons red wine vinegar

Fine sea salt

1 teaspoon finely grated lemon zest (from 1 lemon)

2 tablespoons fresh lemon juice (from 1 lemon)

¼ cup olive oil

4 cups fresh basil leaves, roughly torn

Crisp the daikon slices in a large bowl filled with ice water. Chill for at least 10 minutes and up to 1 hour. A few minutes before serving, remove them from the ice bath and thoroughly dry the rounds.

In a very large bowl, toss the plums with the pepper, vinegar, and salt to taste. Let the fruit macerate at room temperature for 10 minutes. Gently fold in the lemon zest, juice, and the olive oil, and marinate 2 minutes more. Lift the plums from the bowl, leaving their drippings behind, and lay the fruit across a large serving platter, mounding it in the center.

In a medium bowl, toss the basil leaves and radish together. Pour in enough of the reserved plum drippings to lightly dress. Season with salt and pepper to taste.

Scatter the radish slices and basil leaves all around the plums. Drizzle the remaining plum drippings over the salad or the pulled pork.

HOW TO PLAN THIS MEAL:

3 days before: Brine pig and make mustard, if desired.

1 day before: Remove pig from brine and dry.

3 hours before: Temper pig.

2½ hours before: Set up grill.

2 hours before: Grill pig.

40 minutes before: Make plum salad. Rest and carve pig, if necessary. Assemble platters.

FOUNDATIONS AND FINISHES

Broths, condiments, a few preserves, and other secret weapons
to make your food more delicious from beginning to end

DASHI

MAKES ABOUT 1 GALLON

This broth is a Japanese staple that I use all the time, even in Italian braises. Its lightly smoky, mineral flavor is the perfect foil for nearly any dish. And it takes just minutes to assemble, lends great depth of flavor, and has countless applications. Its two ingredients, kombu seaweed and smoked, dried bonito flakes, are available at Asian markets and increasingly in grocery stores.

1¼ pieces of 12-inch-long kombu (about 1¼ ounces)

5 cups bonito flakes (about 1¼ ounces)

Pour 1 gallon water into a deep stockpot. Add the kombu and let it soak for 20 minutes, or until it turns pliable.

Set the stockpot over medium-high heat and bring the liquid to just under a boil. Immediately reduce the heat and very gently simmer the kombu, with only lazy bubbles coming to the surface, for 5 minutes, or until the kombu softens and turns leathery. Do not simmer too long or the kombu will turn bitter.

Turn off the heat and remove and discard the kombu. Stir the bonito flakes into the pot. Cover and let the flakes soak for 10 minutes, or until the bonito clumps and the dashi takes on a smoky perfume.

Pour the dashi through a cheesecloth-lined strainer into a deep, heatproof container. Press on the flakes to extract all their liquid. Set the strained dashi aside and discard the strainer contents. Use the dashi right away or let it cool to room temperature; this is best done by placing the pot in a sinkful of ice water. Transfer to containers, cover, and refrigerate. Dashi keeps for 1 week in the refrigerator and up to 3 months in the freezer.

BURNT-ONION DASHI

MAKES ABOUT 1 GALLON

More than anything else, this is my go-to broth. I often prefer it to meat and vegetable broths because it has a subtle, mineral quality that complements but never overpowers.

Inspired by Michel Bras's *aïgo boulido*, essentially garlic water, here I use a versatile, quick broth, dashi, and give it some depth and edge with hard-seared onions. These humble ingredients work together to make a liquid that has universal appeal.

¼ cup olive oil

2 large red onions, quartered

2 large leeks, halved lengthwise, cleaned, and thoroughly dried

4 large shallots, halved

1 large head of garlic, cloves separated and smashed

1 gallon Dashi (recipe precedes)

BROWN THE ONIONS AND ADD THE DASHI

Set a heavy stockpot over medium heat. Swirl in the olive oil. Once it is hot, add the onions, leeks, shallots, and garlic. Sear all the onions, flipping them occasionally, for 15 minutes, or until they deeply brown and just begin to look burnt on all sides.

Carefully pour the dashi into the pot; it will sputter and steam immediately. Increase the heat to medium-high and bring the liquid up to a boil. Reduce the heat to medium and gently simmer the broth for 20 minutes, or until the dashi takes on the onions' flavor. Turn off the heat and let the dashi cool. Cover and refrigerate for at least 12 hours.

STRAIN AND USE THE DASHI

Skim the fat off the top of the dashi and discard. Set a large strainer lined with cheesecloth over a deep container. Pour the dashi through the strainer and press on the onions to extract as much flavor as possible. Discard the pressed onions.

Use the burnt-onion dashi right away or cover and refrigerate it for up to 2 days. The broth keeps for up to 3 months in the freezer.

CHICKEN BROTH

MAKES 3 QUARTS

Even if you have a beloved chicken broth recipe in your family, I encourage you to try this one. No offense to Granny, but this one is probably better—golden and meaty with big chickeny flavor and a mix of aromatics that both soothe and invigorate. The rich, clean flavor of this broth is a result of cooking in two stages: The first, quick simmer releases any blood or impurities; the second, prolonged simmer extracts flavor and body from the bird. A final, off-heat steep of herbs keeps their flavor bright.

Another advantage of this broth is that the gentle cooking results in chicken that is fine for serving in salad, stews, or on its own with mayo on white bread.

Incidentally, I only very lightly season my broths so they remain versatile. That way, if the broth reduces for a while as is required in braises, the salt doesn't concentrate and overpower the dish.

---

2 tablespoons olive oil

1 red onion, halved equatorially

1 4- to 5-pound skin-on chicken, rinsed

2 tablespoons tomato paste

1 head of garlic, halved crosswise

1 large carrot, halved lengthwise

1 tablespoon black peppercorns

2 fresh bay leaves

15 fresh thyme sprigs

Kosher salt

CHAR THE ONION

Slick a medium heavy sauté pan with the olive oil and set over high heat. Once the oil is shimmering-hot, lay the onion halves, cut sides down, in the pan. Sear for 8 minutes, or until blackened and softened. Remove from the heat.

SIMMER THE CHICKEN AND STRAIN

Place the chicken in a stockpot and add cold water to cover by 1 inch. Bring to a simmer over medium-high heat, then adjust the heat to gently simmer the chicken for 5 minutes. Set up an ice water bath in a large bowl by the stove.

Using tongs, carefully lift the chicken out of the pot and place it in the ice water. Discard the hot cooking liquid.

RESIMMER THE CHICKEN AND BUILD THE BROTH

Wipe the stockpot clean and return the chicken to the pot. Add water to cover the bird by 2 inches. Set the pot back over medium heat and bring the water to a gentle, lazy simmer. Reduce heat to maintain a lazy bubble.

Meanwhile, place the tomato paste in a small bowl. Stir in some of the simmering broth until the paste dissolves, then pour the liquid into the pot.

Add the charred onion, the garlic, carrot, and peppercorns to the broth. Very gently simmer for 1½ hours, or until the broth is aromatic, richly flavored, and light brown. Do not let it boil, and do not skim off any fat as the broth simmers.

Carefully, use tongs to again remove the poached chicken from the broth; reserve it for another use. If necessary, reduce the broth to 3 quarts, until the flavor is lightly concentrated.

Bruise the bay leaves and thyme. Turn off the heat and stir the bay leaves and thyme into the broth. Cover and allow the herbs to steep for 20 minutes, or until aromatic. Season the broth very lightly with salt, bearing in mind that if reduced later, the salt will concentrate.

STRAIN AND SERVE

Set a cheesecloth-lined strainer over a deep container. Pour the broth through the strainer and press on the solids to extract as much flavor as possible. Use immediately or allow the broth to cool; this is best done by placing the pot in a sinkful of ice water. Transfer to containers, then refrigerate. The broth holds for 3 days in the refrigerator and 3 months in the freezer. Skim the congealed fat just before using.

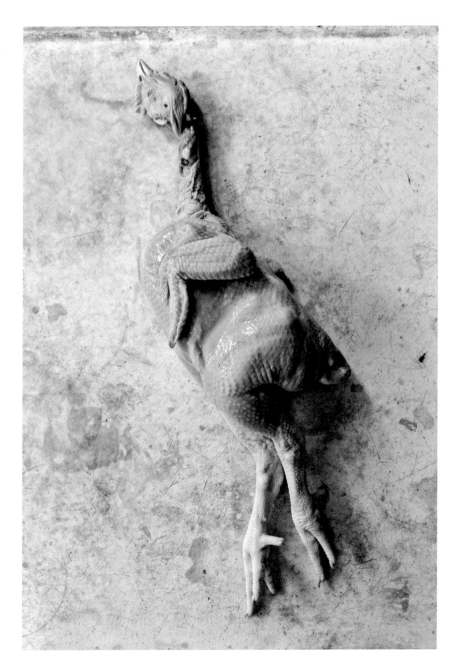

PARMESAN-PECORINO BROTH

MAKES 1 QUART

I am partial to the savory depth a cheese-rind broth imparts to a whole host of dishes—use it as the base of a soup, or braise any vegetable in it. Plus, what better use is there for those cheese butts knocking around in the refrigerator?

This quick-cooking broth heralds the virtues of smart, scrappy cooking, Italian-style. I like to use a mix of salty pecorino and nutty-sweet Parmesan rinds. But use whatever rinds are on hand. Or ask someone at a cheese counter if they have any rinds they're trying to find a home for; chances are they will.

1½ cups 1-inch pieces of Parmesan rinds

1½ cups 1-inch pieces of pecorino rinds

Kosher salt

10 fresh thyme sprigs

MAKE THE BROTH

Fill a heavy saucepan with 5 cups water and add all the cheese rinds. Bring the liquid to a gentle simmer over medium-high heat. Lower the heat to medium-low and gently simmer the broth for 25 minutes, or until the rinds soften and infuse the water.

Remove the pan from the heat and season the broth lightly with salt, remembering that if you plan on reducing the broth later, the salt will intensify. Bruise the thyme sprigs and add them to the pan. Cover and let the herbs steep for 25 minutes, or until aromatic.

STRAIN AND USE

Line a fine-mesh sieve with cheesecloth. Pour the broth through the sieve into a deep container. Press on the rinds and herbs to extract all their flavor, then discard them. Use the broth right away, or let it cool to room temperature, cover, and store in the refrigerator for up to 1 week. The broth also holds in the freezer for up to 1 month.

ROASTED LAMB BROTH

MAKES 2 QUARTS

Roasting lamb bones brings out their depth. If you can get bones with a bit of meat attached, all the better.

2 tablespoons olive oil

1 red onion, peeled and halved equatorially

1 large carrot, halved lengthwise

5 pounds lamb bones, preferably not scraped clean

1 head of garlic, halved crosswise

2 large celery stalks

1 tablespoon black peppercorns

2 tablespoons tomato paste

2 fresh bay leaves

10 to 15 fresh thyme sprigs

Kosher salt

BLACKEN THE VEGETABLES AND ROAST THE BONES

Preheat the oven to 325°F. Slick a medium heavy sauté pan with the olive oil and set over high heat until shimmering-hot. Lay in the onion and carrot halves, cut sides down. Without flipping, sear the carrot for 5 minutes, or until blackened, and the onion for 8 minutes, or until blackened.

Rinse the lamb bones and pat dry. Place the bones in a large roasting pan onto the oven's center rack. Roast the bones, turning them every 10 minutes, for 30 to 45 minutes, or until golden and aromatic. Remove the bones from the oven and transfer them to a large, deep stockpot.

BUILD THE BROTH

Add enough cold water to the pot to cover the bones by at least 2 inches and bring to a simmer over medium-high heat. During the first 10 minutes of simmering, skim off any scum that rises. Reduce the heat to medium-low so the broth comes to a lazy-bubbling simmer and add the blackened vegetables, garlic, celery, and peppercorns.

Place the tomato paste in a medium bowl. Whisk a ladleful of the broth into the tomato paste until it dissolves. Pour the liquid into the stockpot.

Gently simmer the lamb broth for 3 hours. Turn off the heat, bruise the bay leaves and thyme, and add them to the pot. Cover the pot and let the broth stand for 20 minutes, or until aromatic. Season very lightly with salt.

STRAIN THE BROTH

Place a large, cheesecloth-lined sieve over a deep, heatproof container. Remove the bones from the pot and pour the broth through the sieve. Press on the vegetables to extract as much liquid as possible. Discard the bones and strainer contents. Let the broth cool to room temperature; this is best done by placing the pot in a sinkful of ice water.

Transfer the broth to containers and cover and refrigerate for 12 hours, or until its fat congeals on its surface. The broth holds for 4 days in the refrigerator and up to 1 month in the freezer.

Before using, skim off any congealed fat from the surface and discard. Carefully ladle out the broth, being careful to leave the sediment in place at the bottom of the container.

COD BROTH

MAKES 2 QUARTS

Whenever I make fish broth, cod bones are my first choice to go into the pot. They have more flavor and collagen than any other fish carcass, which enriches this stock and provides it with great body.

You'll notice that in many of my broths, thyme goes in only once its last bubble has burst. The longer an herb simmers, the more muddled its essence becomes. Allowing herbs to just steep keeps their flavors clean.

3 tablespoons olive oil

2 medium red onions, peeled and halved equatorially

1 medium fennel bulb, halved and outer layers removed

10 garlic cloves

Zest of ½ lemon, removed with a vegetable peeler

1 tablespoon tomato paste

1 tablespoon black peppercorns, toasted and roughly crushed

3½ to 4 pounds clean cod bones, preferably collars (about 6 collars)

12 fresh thyme sprigs

Kosher salt

BUILD THE BROTH

Set a large heavy skillet over medium-high heat until hot, then swirl in 2 tablespoons of the oil. Lay in the onion halves, cut sides down, and sear, without flipping, for 8 minutes, or until the cut sides blacken and soften. Set the onions aside on a platter. Add the fennel halves, cut sides down, to the pan and scatter in the garlic cloves. Still over medium-high heat, sear the garlic for about 1½ minutes on each side, or until both sides brown. Sear the fennel, without flipping, for 6 minutes, or until it deeply caramelizes. Set all vegetables aside.

Set a stockpot over medium heat. Swirl in the remaining tablespoon of olive oil. Press the lemon strips with the broad side of a chef's knife to release their oils. Once the oil is shimmering-hot, stir in the tomato paste, lemon peel, and peppercorns. Sauté until aromatic, about 2 minutes. Stir the seared vegetables and the cod bones into the pot.

Pour in 3 quarts water and raise the heat to high. When the water comes to a simmer, reduce the heat to medium-low and gently simmer the broth for 10 minutes. Skim off any scum that rises to the surface.

Continue to simmer, uncovered, for 45 minutes, or until it turns amber in color and has a pronounced fish flavor. Turn off the heat, bruise the thyme, and add to the pot. Season with just enough salt to brighten the broth's flavor, making sure to tread lightly so it remains versatile—that is, not so much salt that it will get too salty if you reduce it down later.

STRAIN THE BROTH

Pour the broth through a cheesecloth-lined sieve set over a deep container. Press on the solids to extract all liquid and flavor from the strained ingredients. Use immediately or let cool; this is best done by placing the pot in a sinkful of ice water. Transfer to containers. This broth holds for 3 days refrigerated, or for 3 months in the freezer.

TOMATO WATER

MAKES ABOUT 6 CUPS

If you aren't going to simmer a broth for long, then you have to use one with tons of flavor that's ready to be consumed immediately. This tomato water—a striking, raw, bright liquid flavored with lemongrass and sweet basil—fits the bill.

Made like a gazpacho with an extra aromatic kick that is then strained, what results is a clean, lean liquid with a startlingly pronounced flavor.

4 pounds Brandywine, beefsteak, or other very ripe, juicy tomatoes, preferably with stems attached

1 English cucumber, halved lengthwise

2 celery stalks

1 1-inch piece of lemongrass

2 fresh bay leaves

1 cup fresh basil leaves

2 teaspoons kosher salt

GRATE AND SEASON THE VEGETABLES

Remove the stems from the tomatoes and set them aside. Halve the tomatoes equatorially. Set a box grater over a wide, large bowl. On the large holes of the grater, rub the cut sides of the tomatoes until nothing but their skins remain. Set the skins aside. Grate the cut sides of the cucumber halves until nothing but their skins remain. Set the skins aside. Grate the celery. Finely slice the tomato and cucumber skins and stir them into the bowl with the pulp.

With a mortar and pestle or in a medium bowl, roughly smash the lemongrass, bay leaves, basil, 3 or 4 of the reserved tomato stems, and salt together. Once the salt dissolves, stop pounding. Stir the mixture into the vegetable pulp. Cover and refrigerate for 24 hours.

STRAIN THE WATER

Set a fine-mesh strainer lined with a double layer of damp cheesecloth over a deep container. Pour the tomato pulp into the strainer. Let it drain through, agitating it with a ladle occasionally to help it pass, and finally press down on the solids to extract as much flavor as possible. Discard the solids.

Use the strained tomato water immediately or cover and refrigerate for up to 2 days.

SERRANO CHILE OIL

MAKES ½ CUP

Time is how this oil transforms into something floral and striking. Since nothing is cooked, the fruity, raw qualities of both the olive oil and chile remain intact.

3 serrano chiles

¼ teaspoon fine sea salt

½ cup olive oil

On the small holes of a box grater or with a Microplane, grate the chiles. Transfer the pulp to a clean jar and stir in the salt. Let rest for 10 minutes, or until the salt dissolves.

Pour in the olive oil and secure the jar's lid. Let the oil infuse for at least 30 minutes, but it is best after 3 days. The infused oil stays fresh, refrigerated, for 1 month. Bring to room temperature before using.

TOASTED CAPER OIL

MAKES ABOUT 1 CUP

For this condiment, we slow-toast capers to dry and crisp them, then blend them into oil. Delicious on just about anything, this caper oil provides a salty, sharp contrast that is totally irresistible. If you like it very mellow, soak the capers longer to remove more salt before toasting them.

½ cup salt-packed capers

1 cup olive oil

Freshly ground black pepper

PREP THE CAPERS

Place the capers in a small sieve and rinse off the salt under cool running water. Transfer the capers to a medium bowl and cover them with 1 inch of cold water. Soak the capers for 15 minutes, or until they plump and are not too salty. Drain the capers and toss them dry.

Preheat the oven to 250°F. Line a rimmed baking sheet with parchment paper and scatter the capers evenly across the pan. Roast the capers, rotating the tray every 15 minutes, for 60 to 80 minutes, or until they crisp and their perfume deepens. Remove from the oven and let the capers cool 5 minutes.

MAKE THE OIL

Pour the oil into a blender or food processor. With the machine running at high speed, slowly pour in the roasted capers. Stop blending once all the capers are incorporated and the oil resembles a thin puree.

Transfer the caper oil to a small container. Season with pepper to taste. Use immediately or store, covered, in the refrigerator for up to 1 month.

TARRAGON VINEGAR

MAKES 2 CUPS

Capture all the essence of this gentle, lifting, licorice-like herb in your vinegar bottle.

12 fresh tarragon sprigs

2 cups rice wine vinegar

Rinse the tarragon under slightly warm water. Press the sprigs with the broad side of a chef's knife to release their essential oils. Place the herbs in a medium nonreactive bowl and pour the vinegar over them. Cover with plastic wrap and let stand at room temperature for 3 hours, or until the vinegar takes on the flavor of tarragon.

Strain the vinegar and store it in an airtight container. Refrigerated, this keeps indefinitely.

KOMBU VINEGAR

MAKES 2 CUPS

Another way I like to use dashi is to temper a vinegar with kombu's mineral charm. When I want a bit of acid and extra depth, this is what I use.

1 cup Dashi (page 286)

1 cup rice wine vinegar

Combine the dashi and rice vinegar in a covered container. Refrigerated, this keeps indefinitely but the flavor of the dashi begins to diminish after a few days.

WHOLE-GRAIN MUSTARD

MAKES 2½ CUPS

Use this spicy whole-grain mustard immediately or, better yet, make it three days ahead of time so the mustard seeds' bite mellows and the spread gels. As for mustard powder, Colman's is my brand of choice.

1 tablespoon mustard powder

1 cup yellow mustard seeds, toasted

½ cup brown mustard seeds, toasted

1 cup champagne vinegar

1½ teaspoons fine sea salt

Place the mustard powder in a small bowl and stir in 2 tablespoons water. Set the bowl aside for 5 minutes, or until the powder is completely dissolved.

Place the yellow and brown mustard seeds in a blender or food processor and pour in the champagne vinegar. Process until the seeds crack and the mustard thickens, about 20 seconds. Scrape down the sides and add the salt and mustard paste. Pulse to combine. Then, with the blade running, pour in about ½ cup water, or enough so the mustard is spreadable.

Scrape the mustard into a medium jar and cover. Refrigerate for 3 days, or until the flavors meld. Mustard keeps indefinitely, refrigerated.

AIOLI

MAKES ABOUT 1 CUP

Making a great aioli requires constant whisking and focus for about 10 minutes. It's not hard work, but it is essential that you add the oil drop by drop, at least in the beginning, and power through the whisking without pause. This gets the sauce emulsified, lush, and spreadable. (Here's a little tip: Chilling the oil in the refrigerator for an hour beforehand helps the aioli emulsify.)

You can make this with a food processor or a bowl and whisk (or, most traditionally, a mortar and pestle). I strongly prefer making my aioli by hand, as it doesn't overwork the olive oil and change the flavor—have you noticed how some extra-virgin olive oil vinaigrettes or aiolis taste bitter? That's because some of these oils break down when over-agitated by powerful blender motors.

1 plump garlic clove or 2 pieces of spring garlic

Kosher salt

1 large egg yolk, at room temperature

1 tablespoon lemon juice (from ½ lemon), or to taste

1 tablespoon Dijon mustard

1 cup olive oil

1 teaspoon piment d'Espelette or hot paprika (optional)

PREPARE THE GARLIC AND MAKE THE PASTE

If using regular garlic, simply smash the clove open with the broad side of a chef's knife. If using spring garlic, separate the white and light green portions from the stalk. Discard the tough green portion. Thinly slice the garlic crosswise.

Place the prepared garlic and a generous pinch of salt in a mortar or on a cutting board. Smash the contents to a fine, smooth paste with a pestle or the blunt side of your chef's knife. Scrape the garlic puree into a medium bowl, set on a towel so it doesn't slip.

BUILD THE AIOLI

Add the yolk, half the lemon juice, and the mustard to the garlic paste. Whisk everything together for 30 seconds, or until thick and smooth.

While continuing to constantly and vigorously whisk the yolk mixture, slowly drizzle the olive oil into the bowl, adding just a few drops at a time. Add more oil only once the previous addition has emulsified. Continue drizzling in oil in this slow fashion until half the oil has been added.

Start whisking the second half of the oil into the aioli at a steadier but still very slow stream. What you want to avoid is adding the oil too quickly and/or underbeating it into the aioli. If you do either, the emulsion will split and you will not get a velvety spread.

Once all the oil is incorporated and the aioli is thick, uniform, and voluminous, season it with salt, piment d'Espelette, if using, and the remaining lemon juice to taste. Serve the aioli at room temperature. Covered and refrigerated, it keeps for 1 day.

BRUSCHETTA

MAKES 8 SLICES

There is no great secret to making bruschetta, but there is a correct way to serve it: hot off the grill, with the scent of garlic freshly rubbed into its crumb.

8 ½-inch slices of country bread

2 plump garlic cloves, halved

2 tablespoons olive oil

Lay the bread over a hot grill or under a broiler. Grill or broil it on both sides for 1 to 2 minutes total, or until golden and crunchy.

Remove the toast from the heat and rub with the cut sides of the garlic until aromatic. Drizzle the bread with olive oil and serve immediately.

BREAD CRUMBS

This isn't really a recipe as much as my preferred method for making bread crumbs, which I like to do whenever I have bread lying around. In an airtight container, the crumbs last for weeks and are great to have on hand any time you need a little texture. An oil-fried crumb is richer, while a dry one brings crunch but less flavor.

Country bread, levain, or sourdough, preferably 1 to 2 days old

Olive oil (optional)

Fine sea salt (optional)

Pull rough, 1½-inch croutons from the interior of the bread, leaving the crust. Spread the croutons out in a single layer on a rimmed baking sheet and set them aside. If your bread is fresh, let the croutons dry out at room temperature for 12 to 24 hours before proceeding.

In a food processor or by hand, break the croutons into approximate ⅛-inch pieces, like small BBs.

At this point, the crumbs can be fried in olive oil or dry toasted in an oven.

To fry the crumbs, coat a skillet generously with olive oil. Set the pan over medium heat and when the oil shimmers, add as many crumbs as will fit in one layer. Fry the bread crumbs, tossing throughout the process, until golden on all sides, then remove to a paper towel–lined plate to drain with a slotted or strainer spoon. Season immediately with salt, if desired. Repeat with remaining crumbs.

To dry-toast the crumbs, preheat the oven to 300°F. Spread the crumbs out in a single layer on a rimmed baking sheet. Toast the crumbs until golden all around. Rotate the baking sheet every few minutes to make sure they toast evenly.

ANCHOVY POWDER

MAKES ABOUT ¼ CUP

This sprinkle of crisp anchovy packs a powerful, mysterious umami punch, and the only thing you need to make this magic powder is a good tin of anchovies. You want these to cook slowly, without burning, until they completely dry up. At that point, their flavor is concentrated, they crumble easily, and the powder eats like a fine bread crumb. I'm partial to this as a salad garnish, but use a light hand because it's potent.

If you have a dehydrator, set the temperature to 140°F and dry the fillets for 3 to 4 hours, or until they snap and crumble. Otherwise use your oven at its lowest setting.

---

1 4-ounce tin of high-quality, olive oil–packed anchovy fillets

Preheat the oven to 170°F, or as low as it can go. Blot the anchovies dry on paper towels. Lay the fillets ½ inch apart on a small silicone baking mat or parchment paper–lined rimmed baking sheet.

Roast on the center rack for 2 to 3 hours, rotating every hour, or until the anchovies dehydrate, shrivel, and easily snap. Remove the pan from the oven and set it aside. Crumble the cooled anchovies into ⅛-inch pieces. Stored in an airtight container at room temperature, these keep for up to 3 days.

ANCHOVY PASTE

MAKES ½ CUP

A little bit of this goes a long way. That's always the case with anchovies, but they are a cornerstone of my cooking because they provide so much depth of flavor. When they are used correctly, you almost never know they are there; they just make everything extra delicious.

The truth about the flavor-packed fillets is that quality matters, so spend money on plump, olive oil–packed fillets.

---

4 ounces olive oil–packed anchovies, preferably high-quality

Remove the anchovies from their oil and reserve the oil. Place the anchovies in a mortar and pound with a pestle to form a smooth paste, adding dashes of reserved oil as needed to thin it out. The paste should be evenly combined, spreadable, creamy, and smooth.

Anchovy paste can also be made in a food processor. Just pulse everything until combined, then run the machine, drizzling in more of the reserved oil as needed, until the desired consistency is reached.

Sealed in a small container and refrigerated, the paste keeps for up to 1 month.

GREMOLATA

MAKES ABOUT 1 CUP

Gremolata is a punchy Italian herb sauce that is commonly used to give a spark to rich braised meats. Spooned over oxtails (page 25), it is right at home, but it is just as good when used to embolden fish.

While the classic preparation is made with just parsley, lemon zest, and garlic, in this recipe I add oregano, anchovy, and a few extras for a more complex flavor.

3 tablespoons chopped fresh flat-leaf parsley leaves

3 tablespoons chopped fresh oregano leaves

2 teaspoons sugar

6 tablespoons olive oil

2 oil-packed anchovy fillets, drained and finely chopped

1 tablespoon finely sliced fresh chives

2 teaspoons finely grated lemon zest (from 2 lemons)

¼ cup lemon juice (from 2 lemons)

Fine sea salt and freshly cracked black peppercorns

In a medium bowl, whisk together the parsley, oregano, sugar, olive oil, anchovies, chives and lemon zest and juice. Season with salt and pepper to taste. Gremolata stays fresh, covered, in the refrigerator for 2 days.

PRESERVED LEMONS

MAKES 10 LEMONS (ABOUT 2 QUARTS)

A staple at Upland, where jars of this mellow, complex preserved fruit line the walls, these preserved lemons are salty and citrusy and have an intriguing, aged funk. When the peel is chopped up fine, I can't think of a place it doesn't belong. The trick is separating the peel from the fruit before using. The fruit can be used like lemon juice, but remember it will add saltiness as well. I recommend always having a batch around. Ideally, make these with Meyer lemons, a sweet, aromatic citrus, but regular ones do fine too.

20 lemons (about 5 pounds), rinsed and scrubbed clean

1 cup kosher salt

1 teaspoon black peppercorns

1 teaspoon red pepper flakes

PRESERVE LEMONS

Juice 10 lemons and set the juice aside.

Bring a large pot of water to a boil. Add the remaining 10 lemons to the pot and blanch for 1 minute to kill any bacteria on their surface. Using a slotted spoon, transfer the lemons to a bowl. Discard the blanching water.

When the lemons are cool enough to handle, cut off one end and, starting from that end, slice each fruit into quarters but don't cut all the way through the intact end. The fruit should hold together.

Rub the salt evenly all over the lemons' sides and interior. After each lemon is rubbed, pack it into a sterilized 2-quart glass jar, sprinkling any remaining salt and the peppercorns and red pepper flakes over the lemons. Pour in enough lemon juice to submerge the citrus, but leave some air space. (The salted lemons will release some juice over the next day as well.) Cover the jar securely with a sterilized lid. Refrigerate the lemons for 2 months until their skins soften. When ready, preserved lemons keep for 6 months in the refrigerator.

SEPARATING THE SKIN FROM THE FRUIT

Cut the lemon quarters apart with a paring knife. Then, cut along the peel's curve to release the fruit from its pith. The lemon pulp can be juiced and the peel can be used as is or cut into bits.

QUINCE MOSTARDA

MAKES ABOUT 4 CUPS

Inedible if not cooked, quince is a fruit that requires coaxing. Once stewed, however, it is bewitching and this mostarda is great with cheese or pork.

The longer quince cooks, the sweeter, rosier, and more aromatic it becomes. Due to its high pectin content, its cooking liquid thickens dramatically as the fruit softens. When spices are added to the pot, the sweet stew becomes a mostarda, doing a pungent 180.

Well, let's back up. Traditionally, what truly makes it a mostarda is the addition of mustard, or mustard oil. It gives the condiment a complex, spicy character. But, to be honest, mustard oil can be overwhelming to use outside of a very well-ventilated kitchen, and can sting your eyes and nose. I call for it in this recipe as an option if you have confidence in your ventilation. If you do use it, I recommend looking away from the pot as you add it, to avoid some of the sting.

---

2 pounds quince

½ cup sugar

1 tablespoon kosher salt

2 tablespoons mustard seeds, lightly toasted

1 teaspoon fresh thyme leaves, bruised

2 lemons, quartered, sliced thin, and seeded

½ teaspoon mustard oil (optional)

PREPARE AND SEASON THE QUINCE

Peel, quarter, and core the quince. Slice it crosswise into ¼-inch pieces. Transfer the slices to a large bowl and toss the fruit with the sugar, salt, mustard seeds, thyme, and lemon slices until well combined. Cover and refrigerate for 12 hours, or until the quince loses about 25 percent of its juices, about 1 cup.

STEW THE MOSTARDA

Pour the macerated fruit and all its drippings into a large Dutch oven. You should have a 1-inch layer of fruit in the bottom. Add water to cover the fruit with ½ inch of liquid. Set the pot over medium heat, bring to a simmer, and adjust the heat to maintain a gentle simmer. Cover with a lid, leaving a crack. Stew the quince for 2 hours, stirring occasionally, until the fruit completely softens and its cooking liquid is syrupy.

Throughout the process, check on the mostarda and add splashes of water if the cooking liquid reduces to less than ¼ inch.

If using mustard oil, remove the pot from the heat and stir it in. When adding the oil, look away because the steam can sting your eyes.

Let the mostarda cool to room temperature. Transfer to a container, cover, and refrigerate for 12 hours before using. The mostarda keeps for up to 3 weeks in the refrigerator in an airtight container.

SALT WATER–BRINED TOMATOES

MAKES 1 QUART, INCLUDING BRINE

Clean, sharp, and clear-tasting, these salt water–preserved tomatoes pretty much turn the whole canned-tomato landscape upside down—in the best way possible. Regular canned tomatoes are held in a puree, which often tastes muted and cooked. This recipe preserves the fresh flavor of the raw tomatoes while awakening their depth with a brine.

Occasionally in fine food stores you will find salt water–preserved tomatoes imported from Italy. You should buy those whenever you spot them. They do cost more, but it's a worthy splurge.

Kosher salt, as needed

2 pints cherry tomatoes (about 1½ pounds total)

Fill a medium pot with water, and salt it so that it tastes like the ocean. Set the pot over high heat and bring the water to a boil. Set up an ice water bath nearby. Using a sharp paring knife, cut a small, shallow X in the bottom of each tomato.

Add half the tomatoes to the boiling water and blanch them for 15 seconds, or until their skins begin to split. Using a slotted spoon, transfer them to the ice bath. Blanch and shock the remaining tomatoes.

Remove the tomatoes from the ice bath and dry them thoroughly. With a paring knife, peel away their skins and discard. Transfer the peeled tomatoes to a 1-quart jar.

In a separate bowl, whisk 2 tablespoons kosher salt into 2 cups cold filtered water until the salt dissolves. Pour this brine over the tomatoes until they are covered and the jar is almost full. Secure the lid tightly and refrigerate for at least 24 hours, or until the tomatoes soften and taste seasoned. These tomatoes keep in the refrigerator for 10 to 14 days.

GARLIC CONFIT

MAKES 3 CUPS, INCLUDING OIL

When garlic cloves turn golden, the color of autumn hay, they have made the journey from astringent to sweet and sticky. These garlic confit cloves are savory candy, and their infused oil is delicious anywhere.

2 cups garlic cloves

5 black peppercorns

1 fresh bay leaf, bruised

1 strip of lemon peel, removed with a vegetable peeler and bruised

1½ teaspoons kosher salt

Olive oil, as needed

Preheat the oven to 300°F. In a heavy, lidded, ovenproof saucepan, combine the garlic cloves, peppercorns, bay leaf, lemon peel, and salt. Cover with the oil.

Secure the lid and transfer the pot to the oven. Cook the garlic for 1 hour, or until the cloves are very tender and light golden. Remove from the oven and let cool to room temperature. Use immediately or store the cloves, packed in oil, in a sealed container in the refrigerator. These keep for 2 weeks.

DIY SEMI-CURED SALT COD

MAKES 1½ POUNDS CURED COD

Salt cod is one of the truly great ingredients of the world—vital to Scandinavian and Mediterranean cuisines, among others, and yet it has a little bit of a bad reputation here. Personally, I love its delicate chewiness and deep salinity, but a fully cured salt cod may be a bit of a strong introduction for skeptics.

A full cure takes five to six days before air-drying, and that results in cod that's saltier, stringier, and funkier in flavor. Most of the time when I cure cod I want a mild cure, meaning the fish releases about 25 percent of its moisture over two days. It's flakier, creamier, and has a tense, mouthwatering bite. This is the kind of salt cod called for in this book.

Coarse sea salt, as needed
(up to 8 cups)

2 pounds center-cut cod, skin on

CURE THE COD

Set a medium cooling rack in a medium roasting pan. Cut 2 pieces of cheesecloth large enough to run the length of the rack. Set the 2 pieces of cloth over each other, on a clean work surface, and spread 2 cups salt across its center, making a bed large enough for the cod to lay over. Nestle the cod into the salt bed and tightly pack the remaining salt around the fish, evenly covering it on all sides.

Lift up the cloth and lay the cod on the cooling rack. Transfer the pan to the refrigerator and let the cod rest, uncovered, for 48 hours, or until it is mildly cured and firm to the touch. Check on the cod every 12 hours and discard any runoff juices if necessary.

After 48 hours, unearth the cod from the salt and scrape it clean. Discard the salt. If not using immediately, wrap the fish in fresh cheesecloth, lay it on a clean rack, and refrigerate for up to 3 days. Wrapped in several layers of plastic, the cod can be frozen for up to 1 month.

SOAK THE COD

Before using the cod, rinse it clean. Then soak the cod in a deep dish: Cover it with fresh water and refrigerate for 12 to 48 hours, depending on how salty you like it. Check on the saltiness every 12 hours by cutting off a small taste, and change the soaking water if it needs to release more salt. Once it is soaked to your taste, remove from the water. Soaked salt cod keeps in the refrigerator for 2 days.

OLIVE OIL-CURED SALT COD

MAKES 1½ POUNDS

I love this treatment for salt cod—first reconstituted in water, then poached and finally covered and preserved in olive oil. Once the oil permeates the meat, it takes on a velvety texture and a lingering taste to go with its gentle chew.

If you are not curing your own cod, simply soak the store-bought alternative until it no longer tastes salty before proceeding as instructed. The way you can tell if it's ready is by tasting it, so flake off a piece and try it. If it's not too salty, then you're ready to smother it in oil.

1½ pounds DIY Semi-Cured Salt Cod (page 307) or store-bought salt cod

Olive oil, as needed

2 tablespoons black peppercorns, toasted

1 lemon, thinly sliced

2 fresh bay leaves

SOAK THE COD

(If you have already soaked the cod as in the preceding recipe, skip to the next step.) Place the salt cod in a deep, nonreactive medium container. Cover with water and let it soak, refrigerated, for 36 to 48 hours, or until the flesh feels springy and tastes just a touch salty. Change the soaking water and taste the fish every 12 hours. If using store-bought salt cod, the soaking time may be up to 24 hours longer, though not necessarily—taste to see and replenish the water as necessary.

Remove the cod from the water and pat it dry. Discard the soaking water.

POACH THE COD

Set a small rack in a medium Dutch oven and place the fish, skin side down, on the rack. Add enough water to just cover the fish. Bring to a very gentle simmer over medium heat, then reduce the heat until the bubbling subsides. Gently poach the cod for 9 minutes, or until its flesh flakes when prodded.

Turn off the heat and carefully lift the fish out of the water. Transfer the cod to a cooling rack and pat it dry. Let cool to room temperature.

PACK THE COD IN OIL

Place the cod in a container just larger than the fish. Add enough olive oil to completely cover the fish. Scatter in the peppercorns and lemon rounds. Bruise the bay leaves and add them. Cover the dish and refrigerate for 48 hours, or until the cod tastes buttery. Well sealed, the cod keeps, refrigerated, for 1 week.

CRÈME FRAÎCHE

MAKES 3 CUPS

A staple of every French kitchen, crème fraîche is creamy, beautiful, and tart; a refined, more versatile version of sour cream. Season a little bit of this with some fine sea salt and you have an awesome spread or dip. It's that easy. And that easy to make too.

2 cups heavy cream

1 cup buttermilk (with live cultures)

In a large bowl, gently stir the heavy cream and buttermilk together. Transfer the mixture to a sterilized jar and cover it with cheesecloth. Tightly cinch the cloth around the jar's rim with double-knotted twine.

Let the mixture stand at room temperature for 36 to 48 hours, or until thickened to the consistency of sour cream. Cover and refrigerate the crème fraîche for up to 1 week.

PECORINO BUTTER

MAKES ABOUT ¾ POUND

Flavored with nutty pecorino and black peppercorns, this compound butter ends up spicy, salty, and very easy to eat. It's best to use the fattiest butter base you can find, meaning 83% milk fat or higher. That's the really good stuff.

½ pound (2 sticks) unsalted butter, preferably goat's-milk butter, at room temperature and cut into chunks

1 cup coarsely grated Pecorino Romano

1½ teaspoons black peppercorns, toasted and freshly cracked

In a large bowl, fold the butter, cheese, and pepper together until just combined.

Turn the butter out onto a piece of wax paper. Shape it into a cylinder along the paper's edge. Lift up the length of the paper and tightly wrap it around the butter, rolling it until it forms a tight cylinder. Cinch the ends to seal the tube.

Refrigerate the butter for at least 30 minutes, or until firmed up. The butter can be made up to 3 days in advance, wrapped well in plastic, and frozen for 1 month.

COCHON SPICE BLEND

MAKES ABOUT ¼ CUP

This is a spice mix recipe from my friend Lior Lev Sercarz from La Boîte in Manhattan, and he is a magician of a spice blender. His combinations are some of the most interesting I've ever had, and he deals the best spices in the city.

The uses for this blend are limitless, especially good when it comes to drawing out pork's sweet, subtle appeal.

2 tablespoons coriander seeds, toasted

2 tablespoons fennel seeds, toasted

1 tablespoon cumin seeds, toasted

1 teaspoon caraway seeds, toasted

6 dried bay leaves

2 tablespoons dried oregano

2 teaspoons ground sumac

1 teaspoon chile powder

½ teaspoon fine sea salt

Pulse the coriander seeds, fennel seeds, cumin seeds, caraway seeds, and bay leaves in a spice grinder until finely ground. Transfer the ground spices to a small bowl and stir in the oregano, sumac, chile powder, and salt.

Stored in an airtight container, the spice blend keeps indefinitely at room temperature, although it is best used within 1 year.

FRESH RICOTTA

MAKES 6 CUPS

Making great ricotta is easy—I swear. But the chubby curds and the sweet taste of this milky, fresh cheese may not lead you or anyone else to that conclusion. You will need an instant-read thermometer and animal rennet, which most good cheese stores either carry or will get for you. And of course use the best-quality milk you can find.

Incidentally, when scooping out your ricotta curds, keep the whey—the liquid that separates from the curds—for another use. It makes a great braising liquid.

1 gallon whole milk

7 ounces heavy cream

1¾ teaspoons fine sea salt

1 teaspoon rennet, preferably calf

Combine the milk and cream in a large heavy pot fitted with a thermometer. Set the pot over low heat and gently warm the liquid to 100°F; do not let the milk bubble. Remove the pot from the heat and stir in the salt until dissolved. Stir in the rennet.

Cover the mixture and let it stand at room temperature for at least 30 minutes, preferably 1 hour. The cheese will look like a softly set custard. With a long knife, cut the curd down to the bottom of the pot into 1-inch squares, so that it resembles a checkerboard. Cover the pot and let it stand for 1 hour, or until the curds firm and separate further from the whey.

Meanwhile, line a large strainer with cheesecloth and set it over a large bowl. Using a large slotted or straining spoon, scoop the curds out of the pot, letting the whey drain back into the pot, and transfer the curds to the strainer. Refrigerate the whey for another use or discard.

Refrigerate the bowl and strainer with the ricotta for 1 hour, or until no more whey drips from the curds. (You may let it drain longer, for a drier cheese.) Gently scoop the ricotta into a lidded container and refrigerate until ready to use. The ricotta keeps, tightly covered, for up to 2 days in the refrigerator.

ACKNOWLEDGMENTS

Thanks from Justin:

To my parents, Ron and Paula, who never gave up on me and taught me to dream. To my sisters, Lindsey and Chanel, for being my first guinea pigs. To Mary Neer, my great-grandmother, for giving my palate a sail and pointing me in the right direction. To my grandparents Floyd and Julie Feenie, for always lending a set of ears. To Megumi, again and always, for waiting up and being a wonderful wife and mother to Colin and Oliver. To you two boys, for crowding around the grill and giving me strength. All of you have stood up for me more times than I can remember and I owe you everything.

To Jonathan Waxman, my mentor, friend, and culinary Obi-Wan, and to the entire (and extended) Barbuto family; especially to Jen Davidson, my best friend in this business. To Dan Silverman, for taking me under your wing, getting me organized, and showing me how to do it smart. To Donna Lennard, for giving me a stage to create and sharing a passion for zero corner-cutting and fine olive oils. To Stephen Starr, my partner: Upland has been an incredible journey and I couldn't be more proud. To the whole Upland crew: you are our foundation. This is just the beginning . . .

To all my cooks and colleagues, past and present, front of the house and back of the house: I owe you many beers and endless gratitude. Special shout-outs to Edwin Chu, for always having my back and helping out with the sausage stuffing and other shoot-day shenanigans; Daisy Nichols, a champion in the kitchen and at the computer (thanks for helping with those roast recipes); Roel Alcudia, who stood by me for countless hours in the early years; Anthony Theesfeld, a friend and brother; Lynn McNeely, my center and the one who taught me to keep it pure; Anthony Rose, who showed me to visualize the other side of the pan; Carla and Rory, it was that one summer that started this trip; David Malbequi, for the laughs and rabbits; Joel Hough, for showing me how to transform workspaces; Sam Goinsalvos, for his Alimentari efforts and for cooking more short rib than anyone; Hunter Lewis, for all the support, and late-night, after-work conversations; Mark Pastore and Pat LaFrieda, for the inspiration and education; Bobby Demasco, my fish whisperer; Lisette Magampon, who starts days and (often) puts them to bed; Nevia Noh, one of the toughest, most inspiring and dedicated farmers I know. And last, but not least, to the NYC food scene: the chefs, cooks, bussers, vendors, bon vivants, and weirdos who keep me buzzing.

Thanks from Kitty and Justin:

Kitty Cowles (Justin's agent) for bringing us together and shepherding us through. Francis Lam for taking on our project, flexing his awesome editorial muscle, keeping us psyched, and being an all-around good friend. Ed Anderson for fun shoot days and awesome results; you made the recipes come to life. Mary-Frances Heck, fearless recipe tester, for jumping right in, rolling with it, and doing what it took. Wayne Pate for the beautiful endpaper art. The entire team at Clarkson Potter for working on this book and poring over the long (we'll admit it) recipes. To both our families, friends, colleagues, and mentors, past and present: your guidance, advice and encouragement made this book happen.

To the readers of this book: We are humbled and thrilled to share this work, two years in the making, with you.

INDEX